Field Guide to

Outdoor Gotland

Natural History and Wildlife

Jens-Henrik Kloth and Ulf Lovén

Gotlands Fornsals förlag

Production Gotlands Fornsals förlag

Authors Jens-Henrik Kloth och Ulf Lovén

Editor Stellan Hedgren

Consultants Dan Carlsson, Sara Eliason, Rolf Gydemo,
Stellan Hedgren, Agneta Herlitz, Stig Högström, Erik W. Ohlsson,
Bengt Rosén and Börje Rydenheim.

Translation Kathleen Gow Sjöblom

Front cover Viper's bugloss at Hoburgen. Photographer Stellan Hedgren.

Back cover Sea stacks at Langhammars, Fårö. Photographer Stellan Hedgren.

Title page Wild rabbit. Photographer Stellan Hedgren.

Maps Offprint of topographical and general overview maps.
© The National Land Survey of Sweden, Gävle 2001. Permission: M013125

© Länsmuseet på Gotland/The County Museum of Gotland, 2002
Printed by Godrings Tryckeri AB, Visby 2002

ISBN 91-88036-47-2

Contents

Foreword

Much has been written about the exceptional natural history and wildlife of Gotland, with its forest meadows, rocky ground, plants and birds. This book, however, is the first of its kind, with descriptions of and guides to a large number of Gotlandic areas harbouring natural features of special interest.

The chief responsibility for safeguarding the future preservation of the most valuable features of the Gotlandic habitats is vested in the County Administrative Board, which carried out extensive surveys, mainly in the 1970s, in order to pinpoint the sites harbouring the features of greatest natural value. The results of this survey form the criteria for selection of sites described in this guide.

In response to their own initiative, Jens-Henrik Kloth and Ulf Lovén were assigned the task of writing a book for the general reader, with descriptions of and directions to the gems of the Gotlandic countryside. The selection of sites was made in consultation with the County Administrative Board. Localities harbouring particularly sensitive animal life, and other places, which would be adversely affected by too many visitors, have thus been omitted.

Without mentioning any names, the County Administrative Board would like to thank the numerous experts both on Gotland and the mainland who contributed to this book with their invaluable and knowledgeable advice. All photographs have been kindly donated, the photographers receiving just a mere thank-you as remuneration. As a measure to keep the price of this book at a low level, the Municipality of Gotland and the County Administrative Board have generously contributed to its production.

The County Administrative Board

The first edition of the book (in Swedish) was out of print for some time. The County Museum, Gotlands Fornsal, then took over the rights, enabling the publishing of a second edition. We are now delighted to present an English translation of the second edition.

How to use this book

A good guide book will serve many purposes. *Field Guide to Outdoor Gotland – Natural History and Wildlife* will not only help you to find the most commendable areas of natural interest, but will also describe the natural features of Gotland – geology, habitats, flora and fauna.

Each habitat description ends with a list of recommended places where you can see the habitat in question.

The 100 localities described in the book are presented in geographical order, running from north to south. The 1:250 000 general overview maps clearly indicate where the different localities are situated and how to get there. In most cases you will also find more detailed directions on a map extract drawn to a 1:50 000 scale, which also shows you where to park, the location of the tower hides and nature trails, etc.

At the end of the book you will find an index of the plants and creatures mentioned in the book. The English names are all followed by the Latin names.

We hope you will delight in the natural history and wildlife of Gotland.

Symbols on the detailed maps:

───   *Site boundary*

00   *Site number in the field guide*

P   *Car park*

   Nature trail

   Tower hide

   Viewpoint

   Bathing spot

   Fishing hamlet/harbour

   Camp site

   Picnic site

From coral reefs to cultural landscape

Gotland built by small creatures from the Silurian sea

The natural history of Gotland began just over 400 million years ago, at the beginning of the geological period known as Silurian, when widespread, shallow seas covered large parts of the earth. One of these shallow seas spread out over present day southern Scandinavia and the Baltic. Parts of this area had also been covered by sea throughout most of the Cambrian and Ordovician, periods prior to the Silurian, and enormous deposits of limestone, sandstone etc, already existed at the beginning of the Silurian period in what is known as The Baltic Sea Basin. These beds now lie beneath the Gotlandic Silurian bedrock.

The earth crust is not one solid rock mass, but consists of a number of plates of unequal size, which slowly "float" on the plastic mantle rock beneath the earth crust. Sometimes these plates split and drift apart, sometimes they collide and weld together to larger floes. The location and appearance of the continents have thus undergone constant changes over millions of years, and these changes are still in progress today.

During the Silurian, the continent comprising Scandinavia lay at or close to the Equator. The climate there was tropical – as indeed today – and the sea was thus very warm. The depth was not more than a few tens of metres, and the warm, shallow sea abounded in different types of organisms. Many of these were small and lived in colonies on the sea bed. These small creatures often had shells or calcareous skeletons, and as the colonies grew in size, these skeletons formed connected reefs, similar to the coral reefs that can be found today in the earth's tropical seas. Significant reef-building animal groups in the Silurian sea included stromatoporoids, a now extinct group which was probably related to sponges, as well as various types of corals and bryozoans. Of great significance to the growth of the reefs were the large numbers of the calcite-precipitating algae which coated the reefs.

The limestone which emanates from the reef-building animals can often be found in cliffs and at high altitudes on present-day Gotland. The reefs vary in size from ten to thousands of square metres.

Large numbers of crinoids anchored themselves to the sides of the reefs. Crinoids are a type of echinoderm and are related to starfish and sea urchins. Other animals living on and around the reefs included brachiopods, snails, bryozoans etc, and swimming close to the reefs were ancestors to current day squids and primitive fish.

When the crinoids and other animals died, for example when storm waves wrenched them from the reef wall, they tumbled down beside the reefs. Gradually enormous layers of calcareous skeleton material accumulated, layers which with time would consolidate to rock.

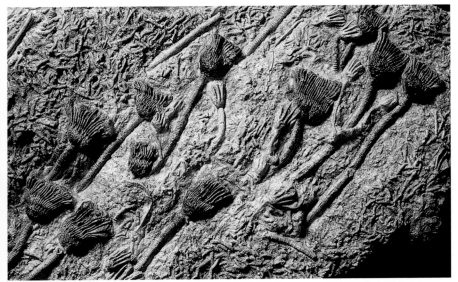

Smaller fragments of the dead animals were transported by waves and currents away from the reefs and out to the sea floor, where they sedimented layer upon layer. With time, the particles were consolidated to what is now called stratified limestone.

Some bacteria and algae secreted or precipitated small calcareous particles from the seawater. These small particles were much smaller than those in the stratified limestone, and they accumulated, along with clay particles and a small amount of sand, at a greater depth on the sea floor beyond the impetus of waves and currents, that would otherwise have carried them away. Lagoons, surrounded by reefs, also offered a calm environment. These soft floors often supported a very rich fauna – trilobites, distant relations to crustaceans, snails, mussels, mussel shrimps, solitary corals and myriads of burrowing worms and other non-skeletal animals which have not been preserved as fossils – all of which lived here on and in the nutritious sea beds. The rock type which developed from this fine-grained material is called marlstone. It is often soft with poor resistence to erosive forces.

The Silurian Sea around present-day Gotland abounded in crinoids, which lived anchored to the sea floor. The body consisted of a long, jointed stem topped by a crown (calyx) with feathery arms extending upwards. These well-preserved specimens had probably been buried in an underwater landslide, and were found at När on the east coast of Gotland.

Forty million years

The Silurian lasted about 40 million years. During this vast time span, both the depth of the Silurian Sea, and its expanse in Scandinavia varied tremendously. On occasions, areas which had long lain underwater, and where reefs and enormous beds had been formed, were raised up above the surface of the sea. Reefs and limestone were then exposed to the disintegrating processes of weathering and erosion. The changing environment of the Silurian has given rise to a rock which varies in composition from one place to another on Gotland.

The reef complex forms three belts parallel to part of the northern coast. The reason for this is that the most favourable depth for the growth of reefs can be found at a certain distance from land. Even today, the Gotlandic landscape is characterized

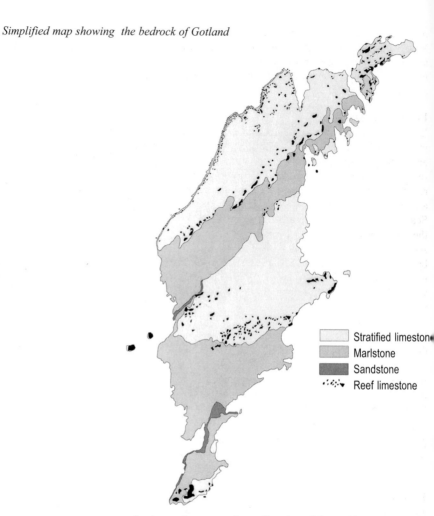

Stratified limestone
Marlstone
Sandstone
Reef limestone

by the southwest-northeast direction of the reef limestone areas. The reef belts were not formed simultaneously, but comprise a number of different reef generations with the oldest in the north west (cliffs) and the youngest in the south east. This partly depends on the fact that the nearshore was gradually silted up with sediment, causing a displacement of the shoreline towards the south east, and thereby also the location of the ideal depth for reef growth.

The rock strata that form Gotland dip slightly towards the south east. This means that the further south you travel, the younger the rock types you find. Another result of this dipping is that the layers on the east coast often slope into the water at a gently declining gradient, resulting in wide and shallow shores. In the north west, on the other hand, the coastline is high and steep.

Retreating sea

Shortly after the Silurian, the Scandinavian bedrock was raised, in connection with the collision between "Northern Europe" and "North America". The sea retreated towards the south east, moving the coastline to Denmark and the Southern Baltic Sea. We know very little about the ensuing history of Scandinavia and the Baltic Sea Basin prior to the Ice Ages, a time span of nearly 400 million years, since post-Silurian deposits are largely absent in this area.

Periods of inland ice

During the 400 million years following the Silurian, Scandinavia moved northwards as a result of tectonic activity, and by the end of the Tertiary (2-3 million years ago), it had more or less reached its present day position. As a result of a general deterioration in the earth's climate the whole of Scandinavia suffered a series of glaciations at this point. The inland ice covering Scandinavia was formed in a period when it was so cold that the Swedish inland winter ice persisted way into the summer. As a result, the annual addition of snow was greater than loss by ablation, and the ever-increasing snow cover was compressed to a one-kilometre thick ice mass. Under pressure, an ice cover, with a depth of more than about 75 metres, will form a thick viscous mass, which will flow towards the snout of the glacier – the ice thus slowly flowed out from the snow-rich inland of Norrland, in a southerly direction, crossing regions such as Gotland and reaching Central Europe where it ablated.

About 12 000 years ago, the latest inland ice started to retreat from Gotland. The island then lay more than 100 metres beneath the surface of the Baltic Ice Lake, and the landscape which lay hidden in the water had more or less the same appearance as today. There were three broad belts of upland country, comprising reef limestone and stratified limestone, which had resisted the impetus of the land ice. In the long, flat valleys between the ridges, soft marlstone is prevalent.

Ice cargo

Abrasion by the land ice produced large quantities of loose material, which was deposited as a coating over Gotland. The two large valleys which ran straight across mid and southern Gotland, as well as many smaller depressions in the ground were filled in to form almost flat ground – today's farmland. The soil deposited on Gotland is rich in calcium and clay particles, and is called clay till or marl. Since clay till is very fertile most of it has been cultivated.

When the inland ice was retreating from the island, gigantic glacial streams plunged through the ice and flowed towards the Gotlandic bedrock. These gushing streams helped to scoop out the deep basins where we now find the Lojsta lakes. The glacial streams also sculpted out several so-called dry valleys. On the mainland, the most distinct landforms created by glacial streams are eskers; these are few and small on Gotland.

Sea cliffs

For long periods following the latest ice age the Baltic Sea was in direct contact with the North Sea. Between these periods, however, land and ablating ice formed barriers, converting the Baltic Sea into a large freshwater lake. Concurrently with these

Erratic boulder of rapakivi granite, transported by the inland ice from Åland to Lilla Karlsö.

9

changes, the water level has periodically risen and fallen. Each period gave the Baltic Sea a new name: Baltic Ice Lake, Yoldia Sea, Ancylus Lake and Littorina Sea.

The vast inland ice had pressed down the land mass, and when the ice ablated, an isostatic rise began, which is still in progress today. About 1000 years after the total retreat of the ice from Gotland, the highest parts of the island broke through the surface of the Baltic Ice Lake. This marked the beginning of a period when the sea waves removed much of the earth cover, and reshaped the bedrock.

When sea waves surged on the clay till deposited by the ice, the fine calcareous and clay particles were swept far out to sea and sedimented to pure clay. Sand, which was coarser and heavier, was not transported as far, but was gradually carried further down the beach as the land successively rose from the sea. In this way the sand eventually covered the clay till, both in many depressions and over large, mainly lowland areas. Around the peaks of the upland areas, as well as in other places which were fully exposed to waves, only stones and blocks remained. They were rounded by abrasion and were banked up by storms. There is a multitude of these so-called shingle beach ridges on Gotland, and the most impressive are the Ancylus and the Littorina Ridges. They are situated on levels where the Ancylus Lake and the Littorina Sea had their respective maximum water levels.

All soil cover was washed away from the steepest slopes, and the sea waves ate themselves into the rock – the steep cliff precipices began to take shape. Much indicates that the underwater ledges – the flat pieces of rock which stretch out to sea at sea level – have been cut into the cliffs by the wave erosion, at

Steeply cliffed coastline north of Blåhäll, Tofta.

a time when cliffs rose from the edge of the present-day under-water ledge. The process is probably still in progress, and this means that the underwater ledges are worn down concurrently with land rise.

The sea cut into the parts of the cliffs, where soft rock dominated, creating overhangs and occasionally complete sea caves. Even sea stacks are to a large extent the result of wave action. Originally, sea stacks were the hard cores of the reef limestone. When the sea waves had worn away the less resistant parts of the reef limestone, all that remained were the sea stacks.

Colonisation by plants and animals

When Gotland started to rise up from the sea about 11 000 years ago, plants, animals and later even people started to colonise the island.

The first vegetation to cover the land was tundra-like with plants such as dwarf Arctic birch, Arctic willow, juniper and mountain avens. The receding ice masses north of Gotland gene-rated a cool climate. Gradually, however, it became warmer, and soon forests of birch and aspen, and later pine began to spread.

Sea stacks are residuals of more resistant rock, left standing following marine erosion of the less resistant surrounding rock.

The Yoldia Sea period began about 10 000 years ago and lasted about one thousand years. Very much is still unclear regarding the extent of the sea at this time and the colonisation of Gotland by different animal species. The Ancylus Lake suc-ceeded the Yoldia Sea. The climate became even warmer, and the fertile clay till was colonised by luxuriant forests of hazel with elements of elm and oak. Pine was then – as now – almost sovereign ruler of the planed inland rock, and of the coastal zones. Gotland was now on the threshold of the post-glacial warm period.

This was followed by the long Littorina Sea period, when the warm period culminated 6000 years ago. Oak-dominating de-ciduous forests with elements of alder, lime, elm and probably even maple and ash covered the most fertile grounds of the island. At about the time when the Littorina Sea reached its highest level, mankind came on the scene.

The climate gradually became cooler, and many deciduous trees began to be superseded by Scots pine in many areas. Soon the Norway spruce appeared and began to compete with the deciduous trees, which meant that the forests took on roughly the same appearance as they have today.

The landscape shaped by human activity

A further significant deterioration of the climate took place about 2 500 years ago, at the beginning of the Iron Age. The harsher climate increased the need of winter fodder for the livestock and thus the forest hay meadow was born. The introduction of forest meadows meant that practically all original deciduous forests were eliminated and subjected to mowing. The coni-ferous forests, lacking herbaceous flora, "heathlands", were used as summer pastures for grazing livestock. The shady landscape of the meadow was prevalent from the first centuries A.D. right up to the end of the 19th century.

In the warm period, some 6000 years ago, the more fertile areas of Gotland were covered with broad-leaved forests. Today these lands have been completely cleared for cultivation. When meadow management ceases, the meadow may once again become a deciduous forest.

The hand of man has changed the Gotlandic landscape in other ways too. Ever since the 17th century, wood distillation for tar production, limestone burning and timber export have demanded vast quantities of pinewood, leading to the disappearance of most of the ancient woodland. During the 19th century, Gotland was deprived of nearly all of its fenlands, which were drained off to provide arable land. One of the consequences was that the once so rich bird life of the wetlands was greatly decimated.

Even today, landscape is affected by the impact of human activity. The old, small-scale and diversified cultural landscape is being substituted by large tracts of uniform landscapes. Large, endless fields with no interruption for ditches or walls, and homogenous coniferous forests of equal age gain ground, at the expense of deciduous forests and meadows.

Fossils on Gotland

No visitor with the slightest interest in nature can avoid encountering fossils. The entire bedrock of the island is largely composed of fossiliferous shells and skeletons of marine organisms. They are often very well preserved despite the 400 million years that have elapsed since the animals were embedded in the sediment on the sea floor. The fauna is extremely rich; over 2 000 fossil species from Gotland have been registered to date, and there are far more just waiting to be discovered. Thus, Gotland assumes a unique position within geology and palaeontology, and scientists from all over the world come to Gotland every year to study the bedrock and its contents.

Fossil collecting

The abundance of fossils on Gotland means that it is not difficult to describe where to concentrate your search. Wherever the bedrock is exposed you will find fossils. The shores beneath the cliffs are probably the best places. Here the sea constantly flushes down new fossils from the exposed layers in the cliff, and here you can also study the structure of the bedrock. You will not need a geological hammer, since the fossils usually fall free from the crumbling soft stones of their own accord. The fossils found in the harder limestone must be enjoyed with eyes only. There would be no point in trying to prise them off – you would just end up with a handful of fragments and a defaced rock. Other excellent fossil locations are the numerous small, abandoned stone quarries.

Some Gotlandic Fossils (see illustrations p. 15)

1. Stromatoporoids ("catskulls", pop.)
Stromatoporoids are massive calcareous skeletons, which grew attached to hard surfaces. Their way of growing, layer upon layer, has provided them with a characteristic contour line pattern on the base, while the dome-shaped top has a completely smooth surface. In some cases, a pattern can be discerned on the surface. "Catskulls" are broadly thought to belong to the sponge category, which is the most primitive of multicellular invertebrates. They were important reef-building organisms on Gotland.

2. Tabulate corals of the *Halysite* genus
The skeletons of the colony-forming tabulate corals are most easily discerned in cross section. They are made up of closely-spaced tubes containing transverse floors. A millimetre-sized individual lived at the top of each tube. The tabulate corals grew on reefs and on the sea floor. A colony required no more than a tiny shell to attach itself to, in order to begin to grow. The genus *Halysites* ("chain coral", pop.) is common throughout Gotland.

3. The Rugose corals of the *Ketophyllum* genus

The rugose corals, like the tabulates, are an extinct group of corals. The rugose corals, contrary to the colony-forming tabulates, lived as separate individuals. Most of them have a cone-shaped skeleton, with a depression at the mouth of the cone. The individual lived in the depression, which always has a distinct radial ribbed pattern. The rugose corals either lived freely on the sea floor, or – as the genus *Ketophyllum* – were anchored to the soft sea floor with a root-like extension.

4. Rugose coral of the *Palaeocyclus* genus

A small, flat coral which lived freely on the sea floor. *Palaeocyclus porpitus*, known as "button corals" are very common along the western cliffed coastline of Gotland.

5. Trilobites of the *Calymene* genus

Trilobites are an extinct group of anthropods. They had a chitinous exoskeleton that was moulted to allow growth. Most trilobite fossils are in fact these moulted shells. A lucky fossil collector may find a complete, often rolled-up specimen, which in most cases will be a *calymene*. Trilobites are characterized by the arrangement of their exoskeleton – two furrows divide the body lengthwise into three lobes – hence the name "trilobite". The animals were predominantly benthic (bottom-dwellers), although some nektonic (free-swimming) species also existed.

6. Gastropod (snails) of the *Oriostoma* genus

There are several groups of molluscs among the fossils on Gotland. Gastropods, which were very common in the seas of 400 million years ago, are equally common today. Their spiral-shaped calcareous shell, or rather the inner impression of them, can be found in abundance in the Gotlandic limestone and marlstone. The genus *Oriostoma* is common in the marl sediments.

7. Bivalves of the *Pterinella* genus

The mollusc group, bivalves (mussels), could also be found in the Silurian Sea, although they are more common today. The body had no head and was surrounded by two bivalves of bilateral symmetry ("mirror images"). Each valve, however, was asymmetrical. Many bivalves lived in burrows, others were bottom-dwellers or were fixed to the sea floor with filaments called byssal threads. Fossilised bivalves are common at certain locations on Gotland, including the southern areas of the island, where the genus *Pterinella* can also be found.

8. Orthoceratites (squids)

Orthoceratites (like most of our present-day squids) are part of the mollusc group of Cephalopoda. The body, with arms surrounding the mouth, was housed at the front of a protective, conical shell. As the animal grew, the sides of the shell were extended forwards and the animal moved forwards in the "cone", and a transverse back wall was formed. The animal remained in contact with "abandoned" chambers by means of a tube

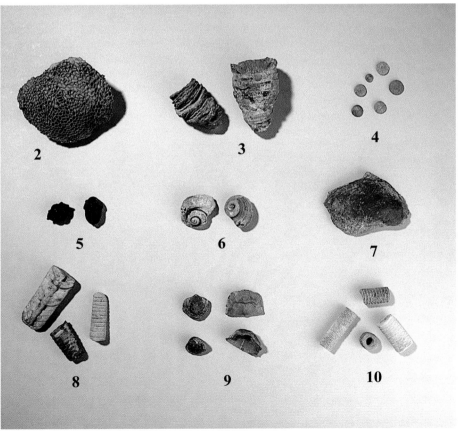

1

2   3   4

5   6   7

8   9   10

The stratified limestone occasionally contains an abundance of crinoidal stems, giving the rock a reddish colour.

known as a siphuncle. Although orthoceratites could altain a length of several metres, only short pieces are commonly found. The shell is recognisable by its conical shape, the inward-curving tranverse walls and the siphon running through the entire length of the animal. Orthoceratites were nektonic predators.

9. Brachiopods (Lampshells) of the *Atrypa* and *Leptaena* genus
The external features of brachiopods are very similar to those of bivalves, but belong to a completely different group. The two valves are completely different, whereas each valve is symmetrical. The animals are attached to the sea floor by a pedicle (”stalk”), which pierces through a small aperture in one of the valves, or alternatively emerges between the two valves. The space between the valves is mainly occupied by a crown of tentacles known as a lophophore, used to extract food particles from the water. Fossils of brachiopods are extremely common in Gotland's stratified limestone and marlstone. The two genera *Atrypa* and *Leptaena* are common throughout the island.

10. Crinoidal stalks (sea lilies)
Crinoids were sessile echinoderms, mainly attached to the sides of reefs. The animal consisted of a cup-shaped body, with a mouth on the upper side, surrounded by a crown of arms. A stalk descending from the underside of the body attached the animal to a hard surface. In some cases, root-like processes at the base of the stalk served as an anchor. Fossils of complete animals are rarely found, since the skeleton disintegrated immediately after death. The fossils most frequently found are of parts of the stalk. Crinoids are rock-forming; limestone predominantly composed of crinoidal remains is known as crinoidal limestone, which can often be found close to reef limestone.

Colony of Halysite *corals.*

Gotlandic habitats

The sea

Following a sequence of phases with alternation between fresh and salt water, the Baltic Sea stabilized its salinity about 2 000 years ago. The salinity of the water of the Baltic Sea gradually decreases towards the north. In the Gulf of Bothnia, salinity is very low. Where the Norrlandic rivers discharge into the less saline water in the Gulf of Bothnia, a southbound current is formed, which escapes through "Öresund", the strait between Sweden and Denmark, and through the Great and Little Belts in Denmark. The outflowing surface currents are replaced by ingoing deeper currents from the North Sea with a higher degree of salinity.

Animals from salt and fresh water

There are no organisms which are directly suitable for life in the brackish water of the Baltic Sea. The fauna and flora mainly consist of salt water species, which can survive in low salinity, but even of plants and animals which normally live in freshwater, but which tolerate a certain degree of salinity. Most marine organisms have entered the Baltic Sea through the strait of Öresund and the Belts. Thus, the number of species gradually declines in a northerly direction. As regards species that can be seen with the naked eye, there are about 1 500 in the Skagerrak, 150 west of Bornholm, but only 80 different faunal species in the water surrounding Gotland.

When animals, which normally live in a saline habitat, find themselves in fresh water, the water endeavours to penetrate the cells of the animal, in order to equalize salinity. If the animal is to survive without being ruptured, great exertion must be employed to keep the water outside its body. Less energy than usual is thus available for growth. For this reason, many of the relatively few salt water animals, which have managed to migrate to the Baltic Sea, become stunted in growth. The common sea mussel, for example, is rarely more than 3 cm in length in the Baltic Sea, whereas decimeter-large specimens can be found off the West Coast of Sweden. Baltic Sea herring is also smaller than North Sea herring.

Plant and animal life varies according to the type of sea bed. Sand beds often lack vegetation, and animals must protect themselves either by burrowing or with protective body colouring. Three of the five bivalve species found along the coasts of Gotland can be found burrowed in the sand. These are the soft shell clam, the Baltic mussel and the cockle *Cardium glaucum*. Bivalves feed on tiny animals and plants, which they filter from surrounding water. The burrowing species have two long siphons that reach out to the surface of the sea bed, where they take in and dispose of water. Of all the fish on the sandy beds, the juvenile flounder is the most common. They can very swiftly cover themselves with sand, which provides an effective camouflage.

The most common bivalves found along the coasts of Gotland are the Baltic mussel (left), the cockle Cardium glaucum *(centre top), the soft shell clam (centre bottom) and the common sea mussel (right).*

The sea surrounding Gotland is the haunt of many different plants, invertebrates, fish and birds.

Species-rich faunal life in seaweed

Algal flora, like faunal life, is poorer when salinity decreases. There are about 500 species of algae off the coast of Norway, 200 in the Strait of Öresund, but around Gotland there are no more than just over a hundred species. On stony and rocky sea beds, the seaweed vegetation is more developed than on soft beds. On the shore platform, the stones are often coated with the long, filamentous strands of *Cladophora glomerata*, often together with the hollow, light green gutweed. When stones and planed rock are brownish black and slippery, this usually means that they are coated with a membrane of blue-green algae. Bladder wrack and serrated wrack are the only larger forms of algae in the Baltic Sea. Along with small, filamentous plants red and brown algae, which often grow on the larger forms of algae, bladder wrack and serrated wrack prevail on the firm beds as far down as the eye can see. Beneath the belt with the large brown algae, which cease to exist at a depth of 5-10 metres, grow the red algae, which can assimilate the weak green and blue light that penetrates the greatest depths of the water.

The branching *thalli* of the bladder wrack provide protection and nourishment to a very species-rich fauna. With access to cyclops, fascinating observations can be made of life in the seaweed in the shallow water. Attached to the seaweed are small common mussels and the *Cardium hauniense* cockles, which filtrate water. One or two species of snails, which are also abundant, keep the seaweed clean by feeding on them. Many different small crustaceans, such as Baltic isopod and beach hoppers, live in tufts of seaweed and provide food for small fish, etc. Some of the small fish swimming among the billowing tufts

18

of seaweed are three-spined and fifteen-spined stickleback, butterfish, viviparous blenny, father lasher and the common pipe-fish.

Beneath the algae belt, the common sea mussel dominates the firm sea floor down to a depth of 30 metres. Mussels within an area of one square metre can weigh a half a kilo, and if the mussels are small, there may be more than 100 000 in the same area. Other species in the Baltic Sea attain no more than a fraction of the weight and number per unit area of common sea mussels. There are several reasons for this tremendous predominance. In the Baltic Sea the competition for space from other species is insignificant, and the common sea mussel is one of the species with the greatest tolerance of low salinity. Sea stars and green shore crabs, which are the common sea mussel's greatest enemy on the west coast of Sweden, do not exist in the Baltic Sea. The flounder and eider, both eaters of common sea mussels, can only devour a fraction of the stock.

Guillemot spend most of their time out at sea, moving ashore only to breed.

Fish

In the Gotlandic coastal waters, typical saltwater fish swim around alongside freshwater fish such as the pike, whitefish and ide, which actually live in a salinity bordering on their tolerance level. A clear majority of fishing catches consists of Baltic sea herring, cod and sprats. Flounder, like turbot, are also among the most frequently caught fish. The marine areas surrounding Gotland have been important salmon fishing waters for a long time. Along the south east coast of Gotland, eel fishing is of long-standing importance. Silver eels, which are caught here, are on their way from the Finnish wetlands and the Gulf of Finland to Öresund. When they reach the east coast of Gotland, they follow it southwards. It is believed, though not certain, that this migration is part of a fantastic life cycle that begins and ends with the eels spawning in the Sargasso Sea off Central America. The eel population has decimated drastically over the last few years, probably because they cannot migrate to the Baltic Sea through the polluted Danish sound.

Hydrogen sulphide is killing the sea floors

Human activity has caused the Baltic Sea to change character dramatically during the 20th century. About 17 million people live around the coasts of the Baltic Sea. Household and industrial wastes constantly discharge nutrients into the Baltic Sea. Top-dressing of fields also leads to significant eutrophication. Increasing nutrient supplies lead to an increase in the populations of plants and animals. At the beginning of the 20th century, the Baltic Sea was a clean and nutrient-poor sea, which had a relatively sparse faunal and floral population. Fertilizers from different emissions, however, have meant that the benthic fauna in many places have more than quadrupled during this century.

When animals and plants die, they fall to the sea floor, where they are decomposed by oxygen-consuming organisms. If there is too much organic material to be decomposed, the oxygen will be totally consumed and replaced by sulphur, leading to

19

The sea stacks on Gotland have been sculpted by the sea into remarkable shapes which fire the imagination.

the formation of hydrogen sulphide which is toxic to all higher life on the sea floor. As a result of human activity, the Baltic Sea floor has become overfertilized, leading to an increase in the amount of plants and animals that are to be decomposed. As a result, death from hydrogen sulphide has affected large parts of the deep-sea floors of the Baltic Sea, not least in areas around Gotland. An important reason why eutrophication has hit the Baltic Sea so hard with anoxic bottom water and the emergence of hydrogen sulphide is that since the deep-sea water is saline and dense, water exchange is very slow. Only when fresh oxygen-rich water has surged in through Öresund and the Belts, which can only happen when there are strong westerly winds and a low pressure over the Baltic Sea, can the sea beds in the deep-sea areas experience a period of recovery.

Discharge into the Baltic Sea has also transported a number of toxic substances. From the mid 1960s high levels of DDT and PCB have been found in fish and birds. Since these toxins have accumulated in the fatty tissue and are secreted very slowly, the animals on the highest levels of the food-chain are the most badly afflicted. Razorbills, guillemots and sea eagles, who mainly feed on fish, have all been afflicted by high toxic level, resulting in thinner egg shells, which are easily smashed beneath brooding parents.

Seals threatened by pollution

The seals of the Baltic Sea were the most important prey of the first hunters to settle on Gotland. About 100 000 grey seals are thought to have existed in the Baltic Sea at the beginning of the 20th century. Since then, the seal population has declined drastically. Today there are about 10 000 grey seals in the entire Baltic Sea Area, while the two other seal species, the harbour seal and the ringed seal have colonies of 200 and 5 000 individuals respectively. Rarely more than 100 individuals of these three species live around the coast of Gotland simultaneously. It has now been established that this decrease depends on high PCB-content in the seals. The toxin leaves many seal cows infertile.

Since the end of the 1960s, the level of DDT and PCB has been regularly measured in Baltic Sea herring and in guillemot eggs from the island Stora Karlsö. As a result of restrictions on the use of toxins, the DDT-content has decreased since the mid 1970s. Even PCB- levels have fortunately decreased somewhat.

Sea cliffs and seastack fields

The huge cliffs which dominate the northwest coast of Gotland are indeed the most dramatic feature Gotland has to offer. The often very steeply cliffed coast stretches from the Tofta shooting range south of Visby right up to Hallshuk in the north. At many points, the cliffs are more than 25 metres high, and at some places the clifftop towers more than 40 metres above the sea. With a few exceptions, there are no cliffs at all along the east and southwest coast of Gotland.

At many places, inland cliffs can be found far from the present day coastline. Inland cliffs have emerged where there has been reef limestone which has been more resistant to inland ice and sea erosion than surrounding limestone rocks. In the walls of the inland cliffs there are often caves and outcrops which have been chiselled out by the waves of the Baltic Ice Lake, Ancylus Lake and Littorina Sea.

The largest cliffs are on the small islands of Stora and Lilla Karlsö, which are the only true bird cliffs of Sweden, with room for thousands of breeding guillemots and razorbills. These auks cannot be found on the main island of Gotland, but ravens often nest on the cliffs, and house martins sometimes nest in dense colonies. The peregrine falcon once had their nests on the Gotlandic limestone precipices.

The cliffs only occasionally plunge straight down into the sea. There is often a narrow, pebbly beach between the foot of the cliff and the shoreline. From the beach it can be observed how the cliff consists of alternate layers of stratified limestone and marlstone, which vary in shape and composition depending on sea conditions at the time the rocks were formed. Projecting parts of the cliffs often consist of reef limestone, which is particularly resilient to sea erosion.

In the bedding planes between the layers of limestone with varying degrees of permeability, cold and highly calcareous water sometimes forces its way out of the cliff and slowly runs down the steep slope. On contact with air, some of the carbon dioxide is lost from the water. As a result, calcium carbonate, which has been diluted in the water, is transformed

from a liquid to a solid substance. Most often the calcium carbonate is deposited on mosses and other plants which thrive in the trickling water, and sometimes the calcium carbonate and plants together form a several decimetre thick rock known as tufa.

The sea stacks – nature's own unsurpassed sculptures – are often found at the foot of gently sloping cliffs. The sea stacks, which consist of hard reef limestone, were originally part of the cliffs. They were left standing when the sea eroded the weaker limestone surrounding the reef limestone. Most sea stack fields lie spread along the east coast of Gotland, and are most densely arrayed along the northeast coast.

First-rate cliffed coasts can be found in localities 12, 15, 18, 37, 43, 63, 64, 80, 81 and 100. The most interesting inland cliffs are described in sites 9, 33, 60, 62, 77, and 78. A guide to a selection of sea stack areas can be found in localities nos. 3, 4, 5, 18, 24, 25, 26, 70 and 98.

Rocky shores

Rocky shores are the most common type of beach along the Gotlandic coast. The most common and most typical Gotlandic rocky shores are shingle beaches. There are several stretches of beach where you can enjoy the fantastic, completely barren shingle fields that stretch from the water's edge up to several hundred metres inland. The result of constant isostatic rises is more prominent in these shingle fields than anywhere else, in that they often have a very distinct swelling-wave shape. The stones have been thrown up by strong storms to form high ridges. Unfortunately, many parts of the beautiful shingle beach ridge have been defaced by car-driving and quarrying.

The pebbles vary in shape and colour, according to which layer of rock they derive from. The most usual is that they have chipped away from stratified limestone, although sometimes they emanate from reef limestone or from marly limestone beds. The primary rock stones, which can be found in varying amounts on the rocky shores, have all been transported to Gotland by the inland ice.

The rocky shores are probably the best places for fossil collecting. Instead of hammering at the cliffs, you can walk around, turning stones over and looking for beautiful specimens of most types of fossil.

That shingle beaches are often devoid of vegetation is not surprising. Since the sea has washed away all the finer particles of soil between the stones, the beach has become an extremely arid and nutrient-poor habitat for plants. Some plants, which normally belong to other environments, use the rocky shore as a habitat where they avoid competition with carpets of thriving and tall vegetation. Herb Robert often occur in abundance, giving the beach a reddish brown colour. Biting stonecrop, sheep's fescue and woad are some other species often found. Further inland, the barren shingle beach is bounded by a windswept pine forest in which ground vegetation mainly

Opposite: the beautiful arch "Kaffepannan" off the west coast of Fårö at Gamla hamn.

Woad, once a source of blue dye, grow on shingle beaches.

*The oyster catcher is one
of the characteristic birds
of the Gotlandic shores.*

consists of the carpet-forming Alpine bearberry. This is the most
likely spot to find the rare Alpine orchid.

Seaweed provides the rocky shores
with nutrients and life

Long seaweed banks, created at different times by surging
waves, lie along many stretches of beach. In bygone days, the
seaweed was collected and used to fertilize fields. This practice
can still be seen on a small scale at a few places, including the
island of Fårö. When the seaweed decays, nutrients are released,
and the banks can host a thriving population of tall herbaceous
plants, mainly nutrient-demanding species, which can often be
found as weeds elsewhere. Curled dock, nettles, creeping thistle
and various plants from the goosefoot family are plants frequently found on the seaweed banks. Older decaying seaweed
is sometimes completely covered by scentless mayweed, which
abound throughout the summer.

A rich insect life develops in the seaweed banks with sea-
weed-specific flies and many different spiders. The insects are
important food for waders, some perching birds and songbirds.
Apart from the seaweed banks, the rocky shores do not offer
birds much in the way of nutrient sources. Instead, the rocky
shores are breeding habitats for many birds whose feeding
grounds are out at sea. Eider, the common gull, the Arctic tern,
oyster catchers and turnstones are some of the species which
often build their nests on the open beach, and bird-life is thus
very sensitive to disturbance during the greater part of spring
and summer, since the breeding season is lengthy. Eider often

lay eggs as early as in mid-April, while other species like the Arctic tern may still have small fledglings at the beginning of July.

Shingle beaches of particular interest can be found in localities nos. 3, 4, 5, 8, 10, 13, 49 and 82.

Sandy shores

The Gotlandic bedrock contains no primary rock that can produce sand. The sand found on Gotland has been transported to the island from regions with primary rock. Apart from Gotska Sandön and Avanäset on Fårö, where sand is totally prevalent, long sandy beaches are mainly found spread along the east coast of Gotland, but even scattered along the west side of the island.

The sandy shores have often formed where the coastline curves inward and the coast is relatively open. This is where wave motion is sufficiently powerful to wash away the fine-grained material, while allowing sand particles to remain. Just above the water's edge, the waves keep the sand in constant motion, and neither algae nor terrestrial plants can gain a foothold. Slightly further up, where the shore rarely feels the surge of waves, the first herbaceous plants can be found. The light green sea sandwort often form a sparse carpet, sometimes with the odd specimen of sea rocket and prickly saltwort. The plants here draw some of their nourishment from the seaweed remains, which lie embedded in the sand.

When the sand dries, it can easily be lifted by the wind and transported inland, where it accumulates in dunes. The sand is often deposited in small foredunes no more than some ten metres from the shoreline. The foredunes support a series of different grasses, which are adapted to the constant change in shape of the dunes. Both marram and lyme grass have long, tough rhizomes, ensuring the survival of the plants, even if the top sand layer should be blown away. Should the grasses become buried in the sand, they can swiftly send up new shoots to the surface.

The sparse vegetation on the beaches has left space for newcomers to the flora. Both marram and lyme grass, which are now prevalent on the sand dunes, did not spread out on a larger scale until the 20th century. Blue lettuce is an example of a sand plant which first came to Gotland during the 20th century, and which has now achieved wide distribution. Nowadays, blue lettuce is a characteristic plant of many sandy beaches.

On occasions, a flat and open "sand grass heath" occupies the area on the landward side of the foredunes. Here the vegetation is more secluded with grey hair-grass, sand sedge, sand fescue and lady's bedstraw among the most common species. The open sand grass heath is the result of grazing in times past. Wherever grazing has ceased, and providing bathing guests have not trampled too much on the ground, the sand grass heaths will be invaded by pine forests.

Sea sandwort can be found on most sandy shores, often just above the high water mark.

Blue lettuce was first discovered on Gotland in 1929, but has now colonised many of the sandy shores of the island.

Marram is a grass which can survive in mobile sand. It has been planted on Fårö and other places to stabilize the drifting sand.

Little tern, the smallest Swedish tern, breed on the sand banks and pebbly beaches.

White and grey dunes

In areas abundant in sand, where the coast is exposed to strong winds, high dunes have been formed at the back of the sandy shores and way up on land. Further seaward, the dunes are white in colour, since new sand is constantly added from the beach. The sand here is nutritious due to the embedded fragments of dead marine plant and animal tissues. The vegetation is similar to that on the foredunes, and lyme grass and marram are dominant. Further inland vegetation cover has gained a foothold on parts of the dunes, which have acquired a greyish colour due to the concentration of humus. The sand has also been leached by precipitation and become nutrient-poor. Different mosses and lichens have ensconced themselves, accompanied by many of the plants from the sand grass heath. Pioneer plants from the white dunes have been driven away and are extinct. With time, the vegetation will completely cover the area, and the dunes will become pine forests. On Gotland, there are several cases of loss of soil by wind induced by human activity such as overgrazing or forestry in historic time. One example is the "Dead Forest" on Gotska Sandön and at Ullahau on Fårö the sand has formed new dunes which have devastated large areas of forest.

The sandy beaches are the most bird deficient of all coastal areas of Gotland. They are not the favourite haunt of any bird species, and no species is inextricably linked to them. The little tern could possibly be considered as an exception; together with the Arctic tern, they often nest on the sand banks, which have formed at certain places just off the actual shore. During late summer and autumn, Arctic waders can be seen running in front of the waves, picking at the small insects

washed ashore. Waders also appreciate the rich insect life in the seaweed thrown up onto the beach.

The sandy beaches presented in this guide can be found in localities 1, 16 and 65.

Coastal meadows

The typical coastal meadows can be found along the long, flat, shallow coasts of Gotland. Clay particles are deposited in the shallow sea bays, or where the coast is sheltered from the impact of the waves by headlands and islands, forming a substrate for the vegetation of the coastal meadows.

The extension of the coastal meadows is concentrated to the southern half of Gotland, and also to several sites along the coast north of Östergarnslandet in the east.

Gotlandic maritime birdlife is richest in the coastal meadows. The flora is also species-rich, containing several species which seldom thrive in other environments.

In winter, when water-level is high, the coastal meadows are flooded by water which feeds them with nutrients. This increases their productivity, which man has exploited for feeding to livestock. Way into the 20th century meadows were still mown along the Gotlandic coast, and still today many shores are kept open by grazing. Any coastal meadow, which stretches way back from the coastline, has been formed by the activities of man and livestock.

Most of the plants found in the coastal meadows are adapted to tolerate grazing. Conversely, this means that their survival prospects are dependent on grazing. Many of the plants are ground-creepers, thus escaping grazers' muzzles. Trees mainly perpetuate vegetatively by releasing dendritic, creeping shoots. Some plants, including the sea wormwood, defend themselves from grazing animals by exuding a strong aroma.

Vegetation in coastal meadows is often divided into clearly distinguishable zones, whose plant composition is determined by the particular conditions prevailing at different distances from the water's edge. At the upper end of the coastal meadows, which rarely floods and is hardly affected by saline sea water, red fescue is the dominant grass. Red fescue varies greatly in shape and can be found in most varied environments; in coastal meadows, where it is favoured by grazing, it often forms a sward, and regenerates by forming ground-creeping shoots. Thrift, another typical plant of coastal meadow habitats, is most profuse in red fescue meadows.

Many Gotlandic coastal meadows are kept open by grazing.

Seaward of the red fescue belt, the shore is wet and often flooded. Here, saltmarsh rush prevails, often along with the grass creeping bent and a series of other plants, such as saltmarsh grasses, lesser sea spurrey, sea-arrow grass, sea milkwort, sea wormwood and sea plantain.

The constant flooding of the lower end of the coastal meadow means that many plants must protect themselves from salinization (high salt content of the soil). Sea milkwort, for

Long, shallow beach on the east coast of Näsudden. Sea mayweed can be seen in bloom in the foreground.

Glasswort is one of the most halophytic plants in the coastal meadows.

example, has special glands which can secrete the excess salt contained in the water it has absorbed.

In the zones where saltmarsh rush is prevalent, shallow, almost unvegetated depressions are formed. They are known as salt pans or pond holes. These form when seaweed, which is washed ashore, smothers the vegetation cover, making the ground more sensitive to trampling animals, and facilitating erosion of the soil cover by storm waves. The brackish sea water collects in the salt pans, and when it later evaporates, salinity is greatly increased. Glasswort and annual seablite, which are the most halophytic plants of the coastal meadows, are often the only vegetation that can survive in the hyper-saline salt pans. Glasswort have roots which are able to repel the salt in the surface water.

Further down, the saltmarsh rush area is replaced by a narrow belt of slender spike-rush, which indicates the position of the normal waterline. Seaward of the slender spike-rush border, where the beach is more or less constantly flooded, tufts of sea club-rush, grey club-rush and sometimes even common reed grow. In this area the late-blooming sea aster can also be found.

The coastal meadows have a richly varied vegetation, and a throng of insects thrive in the fine-grained, nutritious soil. This attracts multitudes of birds to the coastal meadows to breed or rest during migration. The coastal meadows are by far the most bird-rich coastal habitats on Gotland. Several of the coastal meadows, which have been surveyed, have proved to support up to about forty different breeding birds. Waterfowl, waders, gulls and terns are by far the most richly represented species. Bird life in the coastal meadows is, however, sensitive to disturbance, since they are all ground-nesting birds. The birds become agitated when humans are present in their habitat, and even if the grass is not particularly tall, birds' nests are often not discovered until they have been trodden on.

Of the migrant birds that use the coastal meadows for feeding, the barnacle geese are the most well-known. The barnacle geese which nest around the Arctic Ocean are completely dependent on the rich pastures of the coastal meadows of Gotland, when migrating to their breeding habitats, and when beginning to nest.

Nowadays, agriculture is undergoing a swift rationalisation process, and in the future there is a great risk that pastures along many parts of the coast will cease to exist, or at least become less efficient than earlier. When livestock no longer crop vegetation, the grazing-adapted plants will find survival difficult, and many coastal meadows on Gotland have already shown initial signs of reverting to scrub. Tall grasses, such as tall fescue, reed foxtail, and common couch are the first to take over from the low-growing coastal meadow plants. Common reeds and common club rush migrate from the waterline, and gradually trees and shrubs from the the forest margins encroach on the former open grasslands. The flora and fauna of the coastal meadows are thus completely dependent on continued grazing for survival.

Artificial fertilisation, which is sometimes used in coastal meadows so as to obtain better pasturage, has imposed a further threat to many of the plants of this habitat type. When the ground is fertilized, some of the natural flora is swamped by new fast-growing plants which are able to absorb high levels of nutrition and grow quickly.

Superb coastal meadows can be found at sites nos. 66, 83, 86, 87, 90 and 97.

Avocet prefer to breed in open, level shore meadows.

Lakes and watercourses

Lakes, watercourses and other wetlands are pure oases in the landscape, and numerous animals and plants are dependent on them for their existence. When water is drained off, either to provide new arable land or to extend forest land, something which has been done on a large scale on Gotland, this always leads to a depletion of natural resources. Many large lakes, which formed open water surfaces in the large marshes, disappeared when they were drained off. Whereas Gotland was formerly well endowed with wetlands, today not more than some twenty reasonably large lakes are left. Several of the lakes, locally known as "marshes", are very shallow, seldom more than two to three metres deep. The deep lakes in and around Lojsta form exceptions; Rammträsk, for example, is 18 metres deep.

The groundwater, which empties into lakes, leaches calcium bicarbonate from the ground and bedrock. When the calcium bicarbonate-saturated water reaches the lake, the calcium

Bästeträsk, Gotland's largest lake.

Water mint is a common plant beside many Gotlandic watercourses.

bicarbonate is precipitated and deposited on the lake beds as lake marl, calcareous mud or sludge. Charales, which can occur in abundance, are often the only plant to thrive on these calcareous substrates. They are adapted to the calcite-rich environment and their tissues are impregnated with calcite. Another form of life are blue-green algae, which often carpet stones on the beds of the lakes. The algae absorb calcium bicarbonate from the stones, leaving pits on their surfaces.

The marshes on Gotland display nothing of the richness of plant species that can be found in the shallow eutrophic lakes on the mainland. The high level of calcium carbonate in the water means that many important nutrients appear in forms that plants find difficult to absorb, and the lakes of Gotland therefore have a singular type of nutrient-deficiency.

Great fen sedge and common reed are the most common plants in the marshes. The common clubrush, the common cattail and lesser bulrush are also found, as well as floating leaf plants such as white water lilies and broadleaved pondweed. In shallow water, the floor may be covered with the small grass-like leaves of shoreweed. In some lakes, nutrient supply from surrounding, fertilized agricultural land has caused the rapid growth of common reeds.

Bird life is often rich, but varies with the nutritional level of the lakes. Ducks, waders and gulls all build their nests on the ground, and the shores are thus extremely sensitive to disturbance during the breeding season. Tower hides have been built beside some of the richest bird lakes, in order to provide the visitor with a better all-round view. The advantage of tower hides is that they concentrate visitors to one place, thus reducing disturbance of bird life.

Few natural watercourses left

Most watercourses on Gotland are small and not even Gothemån, the largest stream on Gotland, is particularly impressive in size. Watercourses have all been strongly affected by human activity. Most natural streams and brooks have been straightened and deepened to ditches and canals. This, along with the drainage of marshes, has led to a very uneven water supply through the year. During the mild and precipitous winters, the water flow is even and high, and spring floods are therefore not particularly prominent. The drained marshes have lost their water-storage capacity, and towards late spring, the flow rapidly abates. At the height of summer, there is often a danger of total dehydration.

In many watercourses, nutrient supply from agricultural lands has provided a lush vegetation. The lesser water parsnip is an example of a species which was not so common earlier, but which has now migrated along most watercourses, and whose leaves sometimes form a green carpet. The tall vegetation which fringes the stream channels is largely similar to the vegetation around the nutrient-rich lakes on the mainland. There is often an abundance of meadowsweet, common cattail, common club rush, common reed, flowering rush and

unbranched bur reed. Less-assuming herbs like brooklime, water mint and narrow-leaved water plantain are also common. Hard substrates, where herbs cannot root, are often carpeted with aquatic moss.

Many Gotlandic streams are bordered with a lush vegetation of lesser water parsnip and meadowsweet.

Several of the watercourses on Gotland harbour either breeding or resident kingfishers. Many dippers also spend the cold months by the ice-free streams.

Nineteen different, indigenous species of fish live in the Gotlandic lakes and watercourses. Five of these – lamprey, brook lamprey, bullhead, ruffe and reindeer bull (rudd), are pure freshwater fish, which have probably migrated during one of the freshwater periods in the history of the Baltic Sea. The most common freshwater fish are pike, perch, roach and rudd. Sea trout wander up and play in many brooks and streams.

It is of utmost importance that the few remaining streams, which have not been straightened, are protected. Descriptions of relatively natural watercourses can be found in localities nos. 16, 36, 48, 55 and 76. A selection of lakes are described in sites nos. 6, 7, 11, 22, 50, 51, 73, 95 and 97.

Flush fens

Soligenous, or flush fens offer the botany enthusiast a whole host of plants, which are rarely found in any other habitat. Gotland harbours Sweden's richest treasure of flush fens; elsewhere they can only be found in calcium-rich areas in Östergötland, Västergötland, Jämtland and on the island of Öland.

Flush fens are normally formed in sloping terrain beneath the large Ancylus and Littorina shingle beach ridges. In the cliff faces, and even other places, the ground water may be

conducted to the surface of impermeable bedrock. This spring water maintains an even and low temperature throughout the year, and since water flow is often profuse, even at the height of a very dry summer, a constantly humid environment is created in the flush fen. On its way through the bedrock, a large amount of calcium carbonate is precipitated, and the spring water is therefore very rich in calcium bicarbonate.

The chilling effect of the spring water, along with the fact that the flush fens are largely wide open and treeless, provide the fens with close similarities to the vegetation habitats that can be found in the Swedish mountains and other European mountain areas. Several of the plants, which were part of the tundra-like flora that migrated just after the latest glaciation, have thus managed to survive in the Gotlandic flush fens to the present day. Alpine bartsia and Alpine butterwort are examples of species that are normally part of the Swedish mountain flora, but which also grow in the flush fens of Gotland. It is widely believed that the latter represent remnants of a former much wider distribution. Typical flush fen plants such as short-spurred fragrant orchid and German asphodel have not spread to the Swedish mountain range, but are Alpine in character, with a main distribution in the mountain areas of Central Europe.

Another plant which is mainly found in the flush fens is the birdseye primrose, which often bloom by the thousand all across the flush fen at the end of May and beginning of June. Apart from the short-spurred fragrant orchid, fragrant orchid, pugsley's marsh orchid and marsh helleborine are the most frequently found orchid in flush fens. Long-stalked yellow sedge and broad-leaved cotton-grass are two sedges which seldom grow in other habitats. In the wettest parts of the flush fen, you will find the small and elusive variegated horsetail and also the blunt-flowered rush, which will reach a height of about a half a metre before blooming at the end of August.

Irish eyebright bloom in August-September. This eyebright can only be found on Gotland. It has probably evolved from other similar eyebright forms, which grow in the Swedish mountains and in the mountain areas of Europe.

The grass of Parnassus is the most prominent plant of late summer, when it blooms abundantly in most flush fens. Brown mosses grow at the bottom of the flush fens, where they thrive particularly well in the constant-flowing, calcareous water. Great sundew are loosely rooted in the brown mosses. They catch insects with the help of their long sticky hairs. The most characteristic plant of the flush fens is the brown bog-rush, which flourishes in flowing water, forming dense communities.

In bygone days, when outlying lands were grazed, the flush fens were important water holes where livestock gathered. The trampling and grazing of the animals kept the flush fens open, providing a favourable effect on the weaker plants. At the flush fen at Grausne (site no. 19), the significance of grazing for the flora, can easily be studied. Where the fen is still grazed,

Short-spurred fragrant orchid thrive in the Gotlandic flush fens.

Opposite: Flush fens support many beautiful and rare plants.

German asphodel, one of the characteristic plants of the flush fen.

a rich flora has been retained, whereas the ungrazed areas have become overgrown with brown bog-rush and purple moor-grass, which has led to a decline in the number of flush fen plants, some of which are even extinct.

Today, overgrowth poses a threat to the rich flora in many of the Gotlandic flush fens. A large number of flush fens have been completely destroyed by farmers who have drained them off, to make way for forest extension.

Some easily-accessible flush fens with a rich flora are described in sites nos. 14, 19, 30, 37, 39, 42 and 71.

Fens and bogs

In the summer, tourists on Gotland are often greeted by a seemingly drought-afflicted island. The landscape would appear to be lacking in lakes and fens, and after weeks of the typical early-summer dry spell, the ground tends to be bone dry as early as in mid-June. This drought is often quite natural. The thin soil cover on the bare limestone inland rock is quickly parched, and rainwater is conducted downwards through the cracks in the rock. Although Gotland has relatively low rainfall, the island has earlier supported a wealth of fens and lakes. Since the landscape is flat, the water runs slowly to the sea, and is easily trapped in large, shallow wetlands. It is difficult to visualize prehistoric Gotland, a tenth of which was probably covered with marshland, which was a significant natural resource, utilized and tended by man. Sedge fens provided reliable harvests of hay. The great fen sedge was used as prime roofing material, and could even be used to eke out fodder in adverse times. Despite their shallowness, fens supported a rich fish life, and bird life also provided a significant contribution to food supply.

The population explosions of the 18th and 19th centuries necessitated extensive land reclamation. Drainage of marshlands provided large expanses of new arable land with the minimum of labour. This drainage operation was first seriously initiated in the 1810s, and by the turn of the century the main part of the large fens had been completely drained off, leading to the disappearance of features such as surfaces of open water. Drainage is still in progress, despite the fact that only a quarter of the original wetland areas is still in existence today. The first areas to be drained off were the nutrient-rich fens with a relatively thick peat cover, leaving only the more nutrient-deficient sedge fens in the forest areas. Thus very little is known today of the prehistoric Gotlandic large fens, although we can surmise with great certainty that they supported very rich plant and animal communities.

The drainage of fens led to varied results. In some cases, when total drainage was not attained, the wetland stagnated and was abandoned. In other cases, when the wetlands were completely drained off, the soil on the fen beds proved to be too thin to be cultivated. Some of these exposed beds became habitats for some rare insects. One example is the bath white butterfly, a continental species which colonised the marl of the

Great fen sedge is prevalent in many fens.

former Mästermyr fen at the beginning of the 20th century. Its caterpillars fed on wild mignonette.

Bogs

Mires are often divided into two categories – fens and bogs – according to their relation to surrounding lands. Bogs, which are nutrient-deficient, are formed when white moss grows so tall that it is higher than surrounding grounds. The moss loses contact with the water moving through the mineral soil and becomes dependent on atmospheric precipitation for both water and nutrients. Since precipitation is low on Gotland, and white moss does not flourish in calcareous habitats, bogs are far and few between. Plants such as labrador tea, cranberry and cloudberry are common on the mainland, but can only be found in bogs on Gotland. Avanäset on Fårö, where sand is prevalent, also supports quite a number of calcifuge wetland plants.

Crane breed in many Gotlandic sedge fens.

Sedge fens

The Gotlandic sedge fens are provided with nutrients from the water which flows from the surroundings. After the latest glaciation, all of the present day sedge fens were shallow, unvegetated lakes. Since then, open water surfaces have decreased due to overgrowth. Thanks to the climate and limestone bedrock, the great fen sedge is very competitive, and common reed, which dominate the corresponding shallow, eutrophic lakes on the mainland, are of less significance when overgrowth converts the Gotlandic lakes into fens. In a typical sedge fen, the sedge is able to encroach on almost all other plants, and only a handful of other species survive the competition. Down amongst the densely-growing sedge stems, the semi-parasitical marsh lousewort can be found. On Gotland, the marsh lousewort has developed a subspecies, which is specialised in absorbing nutrients from the sedge roots. In the fen lagg, i.e. the belt between the fen and firm ground, the sedge is sparse. Here, black bog-rush forms a narrow belt, which divides the sedge wetland from the shorter brown bog-rush verdure and the short sedges closest to firm ground. Several species of orchids also thrive in the lagg belt. The dense-flowered southern marsh orchid bloom in June, while July heralds the blooming of the flecked marsh orchid, marsh helleborine and fragrant orchid. These orchids can also be found in other habitats. The rare loose-flowered orchid, however, are inextricably linked to the black bog-rush belt in the sedge fens. The bright yellow flowers of the greater and other bladderworts add splashes of colour to the fen lagg. The leaves of the bladderwort are divided into numerous thread-like green segments, with tiny underwater bladders used to capture small aquatic insects.

Southern marsh orchid is often found in the margins of the sedge fens.

The sedge fens do not exactly flourish in bird life. Since the remaining fens are often surrounded by barren land, they often become refuges for shy bird species. During the past few decades, a small flock of cranes has established itself in the isolated sedge fens. Leeches are an interesting component of the fauna of the sedge fens.

Since the largest and most valuable wetlands have fallen to

the plough, it is of utmost importance today that the surviving fens remain intact. Even the fens, which have already been drained off, pose a threat to the fens which have never been improved. As the tilled land in the drained fens is worked, the peat is decomposed, causing a depression in the ground surface. This leads to the need of increased drainage, and demands are raised to dig ditches through the undrained fens, which form "bottlenecks" downstream in the water system. At Träskmyr, Gotland's largest undrained fen, the water level was finally regulated by pumps and a dam, so as to retain a "natural" fluctuation in water level.

A special type of Gotlandic wetland are "ephemeral pools", which are formed in shallow depressions on impermeable, flat inland rock. These are described under the heading "Flat inland rock pine forests and alvar".

Sites nos. 9, 21, 50 and 99 decribe a selection of sedge fens.

The forest hay-meadow

The Gotlandic forest hay-meadows offer the visitor a superb nature bonanza. Here you can enjoy the brilliantly coloured floral meadows and a profuse birdlife. But while we admire the meadows for their beauty and rich plant and animal communities, we should not forget to appreciate them for what they really are – the final remnants of an ancient rural landscape. The meadows help us to understand how hard, and with what precision people once worked, so that natural production capacity was exploited to the full in the quest for subsistence. The custom of cultivating meadows probably started in the Iron Age, about 1500 years ago, when the climate deteriorated, livestock could no longer graze in the open all year round, and people were forced to gather fodder for winter use. Forest meadows were created by the clearance and thinning out of deciduous forests which grew on the most fertile soils, thus creating glades which facilitated the harvesting of herbs and grasses. Meadow cultivation gradually led to the extinction of natural deciduous forests.

In the meadows, the combination of hay-making and fodder pollarding resulted in several consecutive centuries of good harvests. Trees and bushes acquire nutrients from greater depths in the soil. The ground surface acquires nutrients from falling leaves, thus replacing any nutrients removed during harvesting. Meadow management was refined and developed through the ages, resulting in traditions still in existence today.

Meadow management

When the wood anemone – known locally as "raking flower" – is in bloom, the annual maintenance work on the meadow begins. Twigs and old leaves are raked together so as to make room for the freshly sprouting hay. These are then burned on the same spots in the meadow every year. Although it may be argued that a lot of nutrients go up in smoke, it should be remembered that the leaves have been lying on the ground since autumn, during which time the most beneficial nutrients have been imparted to the soil. In bygone days, the hay in the

The meadow is raked in May, when wood anemone are in bloom. The previous year's yield of leaves and twigs are gathered and then burned.

The Gotlandic forest meadows are remnants of a prehistoric cultural landscape.

meadow was a crop which provided vital winter fodder. Rambling in the meadow prior to hay-making was as inappropriate as trampling about in a cornfield. Even today, ramblers must take care not to trample on the plants in the meadow. If the hay is to be reaped in the normal fashion – a prerequisite for the rich flora – the grass must be allowed to grow freely. Blankets should not be laid out in the meadows, and ramblers should stick to the existing tracks.

When the hay appears to be ripe, which is usually some time in July, it is time to mow the meadow. The yellow rattle is often used as an indicator of when it is time to start mowing – when the seeds in the seed case are ripe, they rattle, and the hay in the meadow is waiting to be reaped. Hay-making was labour-intensive, engaging many farmhands. When the working day was over, it was time for fun and play. When the hay had been cut, which was done in early morning, it was gathered together and then spread out in the sunny meadow glades.

The hay was then tended and turned for about a week. It was often stacked every evening, to protect it from dew and rain. Meadow harvests, by today's standards, would hardly be considered as particularly prolific.

During late summer and autumn, when the hay had been gathered in, grazing livestock (mainly cattle) left the meagre forests and flat inland rock to enjoy the wealth of the meadow. This was also the time for the second fodder harvest in the meadow, namely pollarding. Spindly twigs were lopped off trees, providing winter fodder, which was considered of equal worth to hay. Trees were often kept short, so that they did not grow more than a few metres high, which facilitated pollarding.

37

It took two to three years for a tree to produce new shoots that were worth reaping. Ash and small-leaved elm were the prime trees for fodder pollarding, but birch, aspen, lime and maple were also suitable.

"Manure bashing" was a feature of meadow management that showed how each fodder-producing spot in the meadow was of great concern to the owner. Special clubs were made to break up the dung heaps left by the grazing cattle, which were later spread over the meadow in springtime. This was partly to avoid choking the freshly sprouting grass.

The composition of deciduous trees and bushes in the meadows is not the potluck result of what happened to be left over after forest clearance. Every tree and bush had its own significant task to fulfill. In a well-managed meadow, the trees and bushes form three different levels. Oak trees, which were the property of the Crown for a very long time, were not to be tampered with by the farmers, so they grew freely, forming a canopy over the meadow. Oak trees produced acorns which were excellent fodder for pigs. Other trees were pollarded to a medium height. They provided fodder and timber for various purposes. Whitebeam, for example, produced a hardy timber suitable for tools, and dogwood and hawthorn provided strong rake-prongs. Several species formed the shrub layer. The "fruit-producing" bushes – hazel, crab apple, whitebeam, blackthorn, hawthorn and dog rose – contributed to the diet of the human population, giving them a self-evident place in the meadow.

In this day and age, the greatest value of the forest meadow is its designation as an area of great cultural value and natural beauty. The best time to enjoy this beauty and the rich plant and animal life is between the spring raking session at the beginning of May and Midsummer's Day. At the end of May,

Two orchids often found in forest meadows – the burnt orchid (left) and twayblade (right).

the birdsong can be quite stunning. The structural diversity of the meadows provides suitable breeding spots for a whole range of birds. Certain species do, however, require denser vegetation, and overgrown land in the proximity of the meadow is a good supplement to the well-managed meadow.

Birds and plants

The bird most intimately connected with the Gotlandic forest meadow is the collared flycatcher. In Sweden, they can only really be found on Gotland, and it is the most common fly-catcher on the island. When pollards eventually begin to putre-fy, an array of birds, which excavate holes in tree trunks, easily find a place to set up home in the decayed, hollow trunks. The tawny owl, stock dove, starling and jackdaw are some of the birds which make use of the hollow tree trunks for breeding.

Hollow tree trunks in the meadow provide a home for birds such as the tawny owl.

Meadows are renowned for their spectacular flora. The richness of orchids varies from one meadow to another, although most meadows support several species. The early purple orchid blooms as early as in mid-May. From the end of May to mid June the burnt orchid, narrow-leaved helleborine, twayblade, military orchid, fragrant orchid, lesser butterfly orchid and the greater butterfly orchid succeed one another. Some of the orchids retain their colour until at least Midsummer, but then the grasses shoot up and the succulent orchid stems seem to disappear completely.

Trying to list all the typical meadow plant species would be futile, since the meadow is the habitat which, despite its restricted area, can boast the by far most species-rich flora. In luxuriant meadows 150 or more species of vascular plants are not unusual.

Meadow management was the mainstay of housekeeping for more than 1500 years, not only on Gotland but even in the greater part of southern Sweden. The rapid developments of the latest century have completely changed our ways of utilizing the land.

During the 18th century, farmers began to grow cattle-feed in large fields. During the 19th century, artificial fertilization was introduced, and the meadows gradually lost their economic significance. In the mid 19th century, there were still about 35 000 hectacres of meadowland on Gotland. The thickly wooded and delightful landscape can only be left to the imagination. In 1934, the meadow acreage had diminished to 4 000 hectacres, and to-day only 330 hectacres of improved meadowland remain. Despite this, Gotland does in fact have by far the largest acreage in the country. This is partly due to the islanders' deep emotions and love of old traditions. With the gradual decimation of the rural population, much of the awareness of local heritage has also disappeared, and it becomes increasingly difficult to find volunteers to uphold the annual maintenance work in the meadows.

Improved meadows are described in sites nos. 11, 20, 27, 28, 32, 34, 38, 44, 45, 46, 52, 53, 57, 58, 69, 73, 74, 79, 84, 85, 89, 92, 94 and 96.

Spring pea, a typical deciduous forest plant.

Yellow anemone can be found in the meadows and deciduous forests in the middle and south of Gotland.

Deciduous forests

Deciduous forests were originally widespread on Gotland, especially in the low-lying and fertile marlstone areas, with large continuous broadleaved forests. Throughout the ages, however, the forests on prime land have been transformed into fields or cleared for meadows, so that today there is hardly any truly natural deciduous forest left. On the other hand, there are a number of smaller deciduous woodlands, which have derived from overgrown meadows and pasturelands.

Over the past century, most meadow acreage has been ploughed in or transformed into pastureland. Many meadows have also simply been left to revert to scrub, and these are now developing into deciduous woodland. Most abandoned meadows are at the initial stage of the infill process, and are not of any great interest to the naturalist. Sometimes it can prove quite impossible to penetrate the dense leafy brushwood, and visibility is so restricted by vegetation that it is easy to get lost. Traces of former meadow management are often visible. Broad oak crowns indicate that the forest has been open until recent time. The old meadow glades, easily penetrated by light, are recognisable by the brushwood that forms a remarkably dense jungle. It will take time before the crowns of larger trees merge to such an extent that the growth of shrubs will be curbed. Hopefully in a few generations, leafy groves, easily accessible to roamers, will have evolved.

When the meadow reverts to scrub, the flora quickly becomes more species-deficient. Most meadow plants do not thrive beneath the closed canopy of deciduous forests. They are replaced by typical grove plants, which were previously relegated to the most light-deficient and wettest parts of the meadows. Sometimes the ground is carpeted by ramsons, which are so dense that they swamp all other species. Common cleavers often form long runners, which climb along the branches of the shrubs. In the middle and south of Gotland, yellow anemone can be found among the spring carpets of wood anemones, and when the anemones have finished blooming, woodruff stand in full glory. Spring pea, which bloom towards the end of May, are sometimes profuse in grove habitats. The broadleaved helleborine and twayblade are orchids which thrive best in shady deciduous forests.

Several grasses are grove-specific. Wood melick, wood barley and lesser hairy brome are somewhat rare, whereas wood meadow-grass and bearded couch are frequent.

Some deciduous forests, however, have not derived from overgrown meadows. In the south of Gotland, birch-dominating deciduous forests can be found on sandy substrate. The birch has also found a habitat in some of the mires, which were drained off, but never cultivated, since drainage had not been sufficiently efficient. Here, birch grow along with dense sallow, and with a lush undergrowth of grasses and tall herbs.

Localities nos. 44, 53, 54, 56, 69, 73, 89 and 93 describe some deciduous forest sites.

Coniferous forests

Gotland is very much a wooded landscape. About 45 % of the island is covered with woodland, which can be used in forestry. In the coniferous forests, which answer for almost 90 % of the forest acreage, pine is by far the most dominant tree.

Basiphilous pine forest is the most common type of forest, and in fact the most extensive habitat on Gotland. Basiphilous pine forests grow where loose earth-layer is reasonably thick. In the forests on the mainland, which often grow on lime-deficient substrate, the ground becomes acidy when dead vegetal material from the coniferous trees decays. This ground becomes leached and nutrient-deficient. In the basiphilous pine forests on Gotland, this acidification is counteracted by the highly calcareous soil. Earthworms thrive and contribute to forming highly nutritious humus, comparable to the soil found in deciduous forests. Humus encourages exceptionally lush ground vegetation. The pine forests are sparse, allowing sunlight to penetrate to the ground, which also contributes to the rich herb and grass vegetation. Many species, which normally prefer deciduous forests, are frequent in the Gotlandic basiphilous pine forests. In springtime the grounds are carpeted with hepatica and wood anemones. Lily-of-the-valley and angular Solomon's seal often form dense clusters, in many cases to the exclusion of any other species. Viper's grass, which often grow densely in the meadows, also thrive in the pine forest. Orchids that can be found include the narrow-leaved helleborine, lesser butterfly orchid, greater butterfly orchid and birdsnest orchid. Plants normally found on drier ground, such as bloody cranesbill, dyer's woodruff and dropwort also grow profusely here.

Grass grows almost as profusely in the basiphilous pine forest as in the meadow. Tor grass, false brome, mountain melick and blue moor grass are prevalent. Rough small-reed, which is common in the drier basiphilous pine forests and in flat, inland rock forests in the marlstone areas in the north and middle of Gotland, cannot be found anywhere else in all of Sweden.

In bygone days, most of the forestlands were grazed by cows, horses or sheep. Forest grazing is still practised in many places. These forests are deficient in shrubs, opening up rather like a park. As forest grazing has ceased, the Gotlandic forests have acquired a different character. In some cases, accessiblity has been totally hampered by thickets. Surprisingly enough, juniper, which normally require open, sunny ground, thrive in the Gotlandic pine forests.

When soil cover becomes thinner, there is often a gradual transition to flat, inland rock pine forests, which grow so slowly that any form of rational forestry on these lands would be totally unprofitable.

Bloody cranesbill is a characteristic plant of many pine forests.

Mainland-type pine forests

On calcium-deficient soils, pine forests similar to those on the mainland are found. The substrate normally consists of sand, and these forest types are mainly found on the west and east coasts of the middle of Gotland, and at Avanäset on Fårö. In some of these forests, the spruce rivals the pine for dominance. The trees grow more densely and more quickly, making these woodlands attractive for rational forestry.

Plants, which are frequently found in the coniferous forests on the mainland, are also present in these forests on Gotland, but are restricted to this habitat. Bilberries and whortleberries grow in profusion, but only in calcium-deficient forests. Other typical plants include wavy hair-grass, twinflower, May lily, chickweed wintergreen, small cow wheat and other wintergreen plants.

Over the centuries, the forest has been the mainstay of several of the most important sources of income on Gotland. Tar, which was distilled from wood on nearly every farm, was an important export product as early as in the Medieval Period. When lime-burning for export accelerated in the 17th century, vast amounts of wood were devoured as fuel. At the same time, Gotland answered for a significant proportion of Sweden's export of sawn timber.

Ruthless exploitation of the forests led to large-scale clear-cutting. Since tall, straight trees were the first to be selected, only inferior trees were left to become the forefathers of today's forests, which still bear the stamp of this time. As a reaction to this uninhibited forestry, Gotland was granted Sweden's first Forestry Act in 1869.

It is difficult to visualize a Gotlandic forest without anthropogenic impact. No forest area on the island has escaped either grazing, or the axe and saw of man. In some places, however, there are forest areas that have been left unimproved for a long period of time, and which can be characterized as "natural forest".

Road directions to the natural forest areas are described in sites nos. 1, 17, 59 and 75.

Flat, inland rock pine forests and "alvar"

"Alvar" means treeless areas of bare, or almost bare limestone bedrock.

The inland ice deposited no more than a thin layer of soil across large areas of Gotland. Where the bedrock consists of pure limestone rock, which crumbles very slowly, you will find the typical Gotlandic areas of flat, bare limestone rock. These are largely distributed over the entire island, although really large, continuous areas of flat inland rock are mainly found in the northwest and north of Gotland.

It is very difficult to make a distinction between basiphilous pine forest and the pine forest growing on flat inland rock. When soil cover becomes thinner, the trees no longer form a closed canopy. The inland rock forests consist of a mosaic of treeless areas, where the flat limestone rock lies fully exposed, and of groups of trees which have grown on the same spots, in cracks in the rock, or on surfaces covered by thin soil, generation after generation. The Gotlandic inland rock forests have very little in common with the flat inland rock pine forests on the primary rock on the mainland. "Limestone pavement pine forest" would be a more suitable name for this habitat, pinpointing the significance of the limestone bedrock to wildlife.

Plants in inland rock forests are locked in a hard struggle for existence. The forest is sparse, providing little shade to the thin soil cover, which quickly becomes parched. Many plants on the flat, bare rock are adapted in various ways to the heat and aridity of the summer. Even in wintertime, the plants are severely put to the test. The thin, fine-grained soil quickly becomes saturated with water in the autumn rain, and when temperatures fluctuate around zero in the winter, movements in the ground can sever the roots of the plants.

Cushions of calcium-tolerant mosses, mainly grey-cushioned grimmia and frizzled crisp moss grow on the completely bare limestone slabs. The cushions of mosses retain a certain amount of moisture, enabling a supergrowth of sulphur lichen and stonecrop. The rock is greyish black in colour, due to the various crustose lichens. The surfaces of most flat rock areas are crisscrossed with karst grykes. These were formed during geological periods of unrest, when the bedrock was exposed to tension. They expanded at a later stage, when the carbon dioxide in rainwater dissolved the calcite.

In many inland rocky areas, vegetation is confined to the pockets of soil in fissures and depressions. The rock is otherwise completely bare.

At the height of summer, flowers such as spiked speedwell and reflexed stonecrop add splashes of colour to the inland rocky ground.

Wall-rue is a fern, which often grows in fissures in the outcrop.

Blooming flat inland rocks

Despite the harsh environment, the flora in the flat rock areas is species-rich and often invites the visitor to a flowering bonanza. Annual, centimetre-high plants, including the rue-leaved saxifrage, common whitlow grass, little mouse ear and dwarf mouse-ear herald the new season with a prolific display of blooms in April and May. These plants germinate in autumn and blossom while the ground is still wet in the spring. They survive the aridity of summer by their existence as mere seeds. The karst grykes offer a shady habitat for the hepatica, which are often accompanied by the ferns wall-rue and maidenhair spleenwort, which are green all year round. Globularia, which bloom in June, have a lignified stem which tolerate alternate contractions and expansions in the ground during the winter. Globularia have an isolated occurrence on Öland and Gotland, probably as a remnant of a flora which could be found during a previous warmer climate. They can otherwise be found in the south of France and Spain, and even farther afield.

The areas of flat inland rock bloom most intensively around Midsummer, when the flowering bouquets of the bloody cranesbill cast red shades over the dry limestone rock pine forest, and the flowers of the dyer's woodruff cover the ground with a white veil.

Then, during the summer a whole series of different plants bloom in a wonderful riot of colour. The carpets of white and yellow stonecrop are striking. Stonecrop are able to survive the arid months due to their thick, succulent leaves designed to store water in rainy periods. Vincetoxicum have leathery leaves which minimize transpiration. When the vegetation has become scorched in the driest of summers, the vincetoxicum still retain their healthy, dark green colouring. At the end of July, we suddenly notice the frequency of ciliate melick. By then, the unassuming spikes have ripened and transformed into a beautiful, white shimmering fleecy brush.

Ciliate melick is one of the many plants which is very sensitive to grazing, and did not become widespread on the inland rocky areas until outlying pasture-grazing was abandoned. It is difficult to imagine that even flat inland rock has been an important source of fodder for sheep and cattle. Intensive grazing has in fact occurred on these meagre soils well into the 20th century. Within the areas where grazing has ceased, the vegetation has changed, although progress has been slow in this nutrient-deficient habitat. Apart from a series of different herbs and grasses, which have increased in number, the most palpable change is the ubiquitous emergence of leafy shrubs. Carpets of bush-like lichens, such as Iceland moss and reindeer moss, which were once destroyed by trampling cattle, have now been able to spread again.

In late summer, spikelets of ciliate melick resemble silvery-shimmering bottle brushes.

It would often be tempting to call these areas of treeless and sometimes widespread areas of flat inland rock in the limestone rock pine forests "alvar" (see p. 42). Vast, completely treeless areas, however, similar to those that characterize the south of Öland, are few and far between on Gotland. In the very south of Gotland there is an area known as "Alvar". The ground here has been exposed to such intensive grazing, and the trees to such intensive exploitation that the area today is practically treeless. Fires have also helped to create this open landscape.

The surfaces of flat limestone sometimes develop shallow depressions with no run-off channels. Here water collects during the wet seasons, forming a special type of wetland. During the summer, these depressions are normally completely dry. There are but few plants that tolerate long-term immersion, followed by desert-like summer droughts, and vegetation is thus always sparse in these depressions. The floor is almost always carpeted with charales; other typical plants include shoreweed, glaucous sedge, water germander and great burnet. Great fen sedge often grows in a circular tuft in the deepest part of the depression.

The nightjar find their natural habitat in flat limestone rock pine forests. At dusk and at night in the summers, their bewitching, churring trill can be heard. In early spring, at the same places, the black grouse can be heard at dusk, performing their courtship display. The sparse flat limestone rock pine forest is also a habitat that is appreciated by the woodlark, which still have a vigorous population on Gotland.

Butterflies and other insects

Thanks to the profusion of different types of flowering herbs, the sunlit inland rock is also the habitat of a large number of different species of insects. The most frequent, and easiest to recognise is the firebug, which can often be seen sitting on top of the inflorescence of the vincetoxicum. The firebug is

The eye-catching firebug (left) is common on the Gotlandic limestone outcrops. The blue-winged grasshopper (right) is far less discernible.

known locally as the "church bug", since they can be found by the thousand in churches, defence towers and other tall buildings during the winter.

Areas of inland rock are the favourite habitat of several butterflies. Species include the grayling, which flies in July-August, and the large white Apollo, which flies in July, and whose larvae feed on white stonecrop. Apart from the common blue, which is frequent throughout Sweden, two other blues can be found here – the large blue and the turquoise blue – both of which are only found in southeast Sweden.

The blue-winged grasshopper also thrives on the Gotlandic "alvar". This species can only be found on Gotland, Öland and Bohuslän. It is extremely difficult to spot, when it is sitting on the ground, but when it suddenly flies off, its sky-blue wings immediately attract attention.

The first time you walk in a Gotlandic inland-rock pine forest, you will be struck by its barrenness and desolateness. But as you gradually discover the rich flora, and learn to appreciate the dappled shade of the extremely varied forest of dwarfed pine trees, you will discover a habitat that you can't resist returning to.

Superb areas of flat inland-rock are described in sites nos. 17, 25, 29, 30, 40, 41, 61, 62, 63 and 100.

Orchids on Gotland

Of all the Gotlandic plants, orchids, with their almost exotic colours and shapes, and their singular life history, attract greatest attention.

Orchids are probably the most species-rich of all plants in the world – more than 20 000 species are known, and there are almost certainly many more waiting to be discovered. Of the orchids that can be found in Sweden, the majority prefer calcareous soils. It will thus come as no surprise to learn that the limestone islands of Öland and Gotland are extremely rich in orchids. Of the slightly more than 40 species of orchids that exist in Sweden – the exact number depends on how different species are defined – at least 35 have been seen on Gotland, and of these at least 33 are still in existence today. This means that Gotland is the province in Sweden which can boast of the largest number of orchid species. Three species – the white helleborine, loose-flowered and Alpine orchid – cannot be found anywhere else in Sweden.

Several of the Gotlandic orchids, such as early purple orchid, fragrant orchid, broad-leaved helleborine and twayblade, can be found in varying habitats and in great profusion. Others are more particular about their choice of habitat, making them more difficult to find. Habitats which support many species of orchids are wet meadowlands and land which has not been too heavily grazed.

Orchids have a complicated classification system, and scientists are – as mentioned above – not always agreed on how different species should be categorised. The most difficult of the Gotlandic families are the *Dactylorhiza*. Cream early marsh orchids and flecked marsh orchids are sometimes counted as species in their own rights, sometimes as subspecies of early marsh orchids. Heath spotted orchids and common spotted orchids are sometimes considered as two different species, sometimes subspecies of a single main species. Moreover, it is not uncommon to find hybrids of the two different species within the same family. Hybrids are also common within other Gotlandic orchid families.

The Gotlandic orchid season begins as early as in mid-May, and lasts until the end of August. Most species bloom from mid-June to early July, but the mass blooming of the elder-flowered and early purple orchids must be seen at the turn of the months of May-June.

The schedule below indicates the seasonal flowering periods of the different Gotlandic orchid species. The times given, must be interpreted as "normal year" times. If summer comes unusually early, or late, the time for the early bloomers must be adjusted accordingly.

Fly orchids mimic the shape and smell of female aculeata insects, so as to attract males to mate with them and pollinate the flowers.

Time of flowering

Species	May	June	July	August
Military orchid		———————		
Burnt orchid		———————		
Green-winged orchid	———————			
Loose-flowered orchid		——————	———	
Early purple orchid	——————	———		
Alpine orchid		———		
Elder-flowered orchid	——————			
Early marsh orchid		———————————		
Pugsley's marsh orchid			————————————	
Heath spotted orchid		——————————————		
Common spotted orchid			——————	
Pyramidal orchid[1]		——————————	——————	
Fragrant orchid			——————	——
Short-spurred fragrant orchid		——		
Frog orchid		———	——————	
Lesser butterfly orchid		———	——————	
Greater butterfly orchid		———	————	
Fly orchid		———	————	
Musk orchid				———————
Creeping lady's tresses		———		
Red helleborine				
Narrow-leaved helleborine		———		
White helleborine		———		
Broad-leaved helleborine			———————	———
Dark red helleborine			———————	
Green-flowered helleborine				———————
Marsh helleborine			————————	
Twayblade		———	————	
Lesser twayblade		———————		
Birdsnest orchid		———————		
Ghost orchid			———————	
Coralroot orchid		——————		
Bog orchid			———————	
Lady's slipper		——		

[1] Two types on Gotland, an early and a late blooming type

Military orchid, one of the orchids which bloom in June.

Faunal Life on Gotland

Mammals

In common with many other islands, Gotland has a relatively species-deficient mammal fauna, and of the larger mammals only foxes, which have a thriving population on the island, and a number of implanted deer can be found.

One of the most multitudinous mammals on Gotland is the wild rabbit. They are not native to the island, but were introduced at the beginning of the 20th century. In the 1960s the Gotlandic rabbits were struck by myxomatosis, a virus infection, which at first was highly virulent, wiping out the greater part of the then large rabbit population. Later outbreaks were less virulent, but in 1990 the rabbits were struck by RHD, a swiftly spreading disease, which has further decimated the population.

Two other Gotlandic Leporidae are the alpine hare, which is native to the island, and the common European hare, which has been shipped in. The latter is the most common of the two.

The hedgehog is still common on Gotland, despite the fact that many fall victim to inattentive car drivers. Hedgehogs are part of the order *Insectivora* and closely related to the pygmy shrew.

Of the eleven species of bats found on Gotland, the northern bat is by far the most common.

On Gotland, there are only five species of rodents: the squirrel, brown rat, yellow-necked and long-tailed fieldmouse and house mouse. Strangely enough, none of the various species of voles, which are common on the mainland, have managed to colonise Gotland.

The only marten on the island is the mink, which derives from animals which have escaped from mink farms. There are actually no badgers on the island.

Of the three species of seal in the Baltic Sea – the ringed seal, grey seal and harbour seal – only the grey seal is frequent along the Gotlandic coast.

The Gotlandic pony, known as "russ" (cf Old Norse *hross;* English "horse") was introduced by the Stone Age population, probably from Eastern Europe. The ponies ran wild in the Gotlandic forests until the beginning of the 20th century, when the last of the wild "russ" were captured. They now live in a semi-wild state on the wooded moors at Lojstahajd, part of which has been fenced in for them.

Sheep were introduced to Gotland by man at a very early stage. The primordial Gotlandic sheep are all horned – rams, ewes and lambs alike. They are officially called "gutefår" (Goth sheep), although locally they are called "hånnlamb" (horned sheep). The breed was an endangered species during the 1930s

Goth sheep – both rams and ewes are horned.

and 40s, but today there is a secure population. One of the largest flocks of "gutefår" on Gotland can be found on the small island of Lilla Karlsö. Most sheep on Gotland today belong to a more modern, hornless breed. They remain outside all or most of the winter, and are sometimes called "outdoor sheep".

Opposite: The hedgehog is still common on Gotland.

Birds

The birdwatcher would find the contrasts between the different habitats much more striking on Gotland than anywhere else. In the meadows and other woodland areas, as well as in the coastal meadows, the bird communities are extremely profuse in numbers and species. The inland rural areas, on the other hand, are often dry and nutrient-deficient, attracting very few birds.

It soon becomes quite apparent that several birds, which are common on the mainland, are completely absent on Gotland: the green woodpecker, crested tit, marsh tit and willow tit are examples of species that have never immigrated to the island. An example of the contrary – a bird species which is common on Gotland, but which cannot be found on the mainland is the collared flycatcher; it does, however, breed locally on the island of Öland. Collared flycatchers breed predominantly in gardens, meadows and areas of older deciduous forests, but also occasionally in mixed forests or pure coniferous forests, provided they have access to suitable nesting trees. Although the pied flycatcher is also a species often seen on the island, it is nowhere near as numerous as the collared flycatcher.

Collared flycatcher, Gotland's "official provincial bird".

The male collared flycatcher is easily distinguishable from the male pied flycatcher by its wide, white neck-band. Its upper rump and forehead are also whiter. It is, however, very difficult to distinguish between the females and juveniles of the two species. During May and the first part of June, the persistent song of screeching tones can be heard from collared flycatchers in pretty well every leafy grove on the island.

For some decades, the roller established a reputation as a Gotland-specific bird; from the mid 1930s to 1967, the roller bred in the open pine forests of southern Fårö. The occasional roller is still observed on Gotland, mainly during spring and early summer.

The golden eagle has a thriving population on Gotland.

Even the shortest account of characteristics of birdlife on Gotland must mention the fantastic bird islands Stora and Lilla Karlsö. They are the only bird-cliffs in Sweden, and the breeding site of most of the guillemots of the Baltic Sea, as well as about half of the Swedish razorbill population.

Of the birds of prey of southern and central Sweden, neither the honey buzzard nor the osprey breed on Gotland, nor is the kestrel a loyal annual breeder any longer. On the other hand, the hobby is more common on Gotland than in the rest of Sweden. This is particularly true of Fårö, which the hobby favours as a habitat with its open landscape and proximity to lakes and mires.

Barnacle geese are new-comers to the Gotlandic bird fauna.

About 150 bird species breed on Gotland each year. A further 60 species are regular passage migrants, and during the course of one year, just over 350 different species have been observed on Gotland. Although the flight of birds is not quite as concentrated anywhere on Gotland as on the southern tip of Öland, numerous birds are nevertheless caught and ringed every spring and autumn in the south of Gotland, and on certain days, thousands of migrating birds can be seen flying past.

Gotland is of great value as a resting place for numerous barnacle geese. During the 1920s, these small, beautiful geese began using Gotland as a staging area on their way to and from their breeding grounds on Novaja Semlja in the Artic Sea. Earlier, the migration passage had taken a more easterly route across the Baltic Sea. From the beginning of April until the end of May, the barnacle geese graze on the bare islets and shores of the eastern coast of Gotland, and at the beginning of May, the number of grazing geese can exceed 40 000.

During spring, the feeding areas on the Gotlandic grass-lands are of vital importance to the geese. When they arrive at their breeding grounds in the Arctic Sea regions, the gro-und is still covered with snow and frozen. This means that during the initial period they must sustain themselves on the body reserves which they laid down on Gotland. When the geese pass Gotland on their southbound flight in October-November, they do not stay as long as in the spring. At the beginning of the 1970s, and to everyone's amazement, some barnacle geese actually stayed on to breed on some of the islets off the east coast of Gotland. Since then, the group has grown quickly, and now several thousand pairs of barnacle geese breed on Gotland.

Some birds, such as grey plover, curlew sandpiper, knot, little stint, dunlin, sanderling and bar-tailed godwit embark on their southbound flight at the height of summer. Female waders lead the way, leaving their progeny in the care of the males in June/July.

Species of a southern or eastern range often stray up to Got-land in May-June. Many rarities have been sighted. Of these, the red-footed falcon, hoopoe, golden oriole, river and greenish warblers and penduline tit are virtually annual visitors.

The sea around Gotland seldom freezes over during winter, making it an important winter habitat for sea birds. Most of the winter auk birds of the Baltic Sea, spend their winters off the Gotlandic coast. Other birds, which gather in large flocks, are the mallard, tufted duck, scaup, goldeneye and cormorant; in this situation, these birds are particularly vulnerable to oil emis-sion. On several occasions thousands of auk birds have been fatal victims, when oil has been emitted from wrecked ships or from ships that have cleansed their tanks.

In the descriptions of the different habitats, bird species, which are typical for each habitat, have been named. Birding enthusiasts are recommended to study sites nos. 1, 6, 7, 9, 22, 35, 37, 47, 50, 51, 66, 80, 81, 83, 86, 87, 88, 90, 91, 95, 97, 99 and 100.

Reptiles and Amphibians

Only nine of the country's twentyish different species of amphibians and reptiles have been found, with all certainty, on Gotland. Of these, only five species are common, and these are the smooth newt, common toad, common lizard, grass snake and moor frog. Others which are of rather rare occurrence are the smooth snake and adder, and on very rare occasions the green toad and slow-worm have been observed.

The Gotlandic moor frog differs in some ways from the mainland moor frogs. They usually have dark markings on the throat and belly, while the mainland moor frogs have a plain white abdomen. Blotches on the flanks are normally joined to form a band along the length. Fully-matured Gotlandic moor frogs have longer legs than their counterparts across the sea.

The green toad, which once had its home on Gotland, completely vanished for a period of time. Attempts to reintroduce the species to the island have been in progress since 1994. The common toad, on the other hand, is more frequent.

A large number of the Gotlandic grass snakes are almost completely black. Of those which are not black, many can be distinguished from the mainland grasssnakes by large dark blotches along their flanks. These grass snakes are similar to certain subspecies of grass snakes, that can be found in southern Europe. Whenever light blotches occur on the throat, these tend to be orange on Gotland, rather than yellow as on the mainland.

One explanation for this development of special Gotlandic types of grass snakes and moor frogs, might be that only a few specimens of each species colonised the island. A certain degree of adaptation to the unique environment could have taken place within a relatively short space of time, since the number of colonisers was small. Random genetic changes are more likely to succeed in small, isolated communities than in larger populations.

The smooth snake, which would appear to have a stable population on Gotland, prefers to warm up by lying on rocks heated by the sun, rather than by actually sunning themselves. This would explain why it is so rarely seen.

Adders are rare in most parts of Gotland, probably since they normally prey on voles, which cannot be found anywhere on the island.

There are very few suitable habitats for the glow-worm on Gotland, and it has only been spotted on a few rare occasions. Its current existence on the island is, in fact, very doubtful.

Both the grass snake (top) and the moor frog (bottom) are common on Gotland.

Salvorevs
naturreservat

Sälskydd

94

107

36

6

8

Langhammars-
hammaren **3**

Norsholmen
9

Ajkésvik

13

Skärsändan
Aurudden

Skär

4 Digerhuvud

23

Lang-
hammars

Nors

2 Ekevik
Ullahau

Avanäs
Holm

Fårö

Skogsbo 7

Norrsund

Åke

14

4

22

L. Gasmora

Släthällar

Lauter

Kalbjärga

Ava

Fårö

1

Broskogs
St Hoburga

Ringvida
St Gasmora

Sudersandsviken

10

5

Friggars

21

2

Avagrunn

40

Hammars

9

Svens

Mölnor Alnäsaudden

51

Saxriv
25

Falholmen

Aurgrunn

Marpes

7 Fårö

Ar

Nors

Trälgar

Lansa

10

Verkegards
Hammars

Svärvnäset
Medebys
Bläse

Bästeträsk
6

II

Håu

8

22

Oce-
hoburga

29

Fårösund

Limmo-
träsk
18

9

5

Lundar-
hage

Nors

Strå

8

Dämba

3 Djupvik

Skymnings

Fleringe

25

Hägur

Broa

2

14

6

KA3-5 Fårö-
sund

Mil övningsomr

Utoje 27

10 Ryssnäs

kers

Mölner

Bunge

Bunge fpl.

Ryssudden

orugns

148

Änghult

Broungs

12

Rute

Bräntings

Hult-
ungs

Bungenäs

Bunge aur

7

Gerpungs

Ale

Alby

Kauparve

Risungs

Talings

Bräntings

Skjutfält
Skenholmen

32

Krogen
Käll-
städe

23

Vallevikeñ

Fardumeträsk

Ire

22

Hellvi

Lergrav

24

Furilden

22

Herrvik

Källst

Kajlungs
Norrbys

Stengrinde

Känn-
ungs

Längere

Malms

18

27

51

Klasen

Kyllaj

25

6

27
Hammars

Hide

Lörge

14

Suderudd

rlästi

Nystugu

Smöjen

Lörgeskär

32

terby

St. Olofsholm

Slite

26

Asunden
16.

Enholmen

Majgu

16

12

jstudden

64

rviken

holm

39

49

30

nhammar

58

Botvaldvik

Medebys bodar

Kyrkebinge-
grunn

34

50

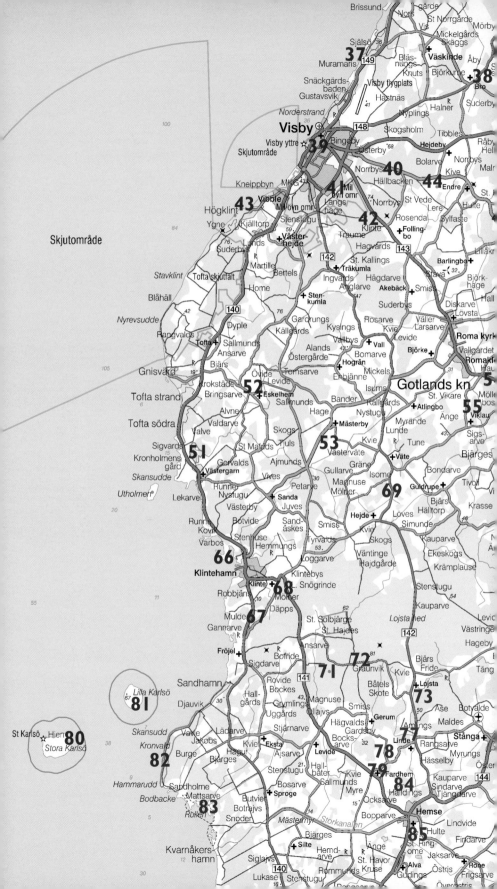

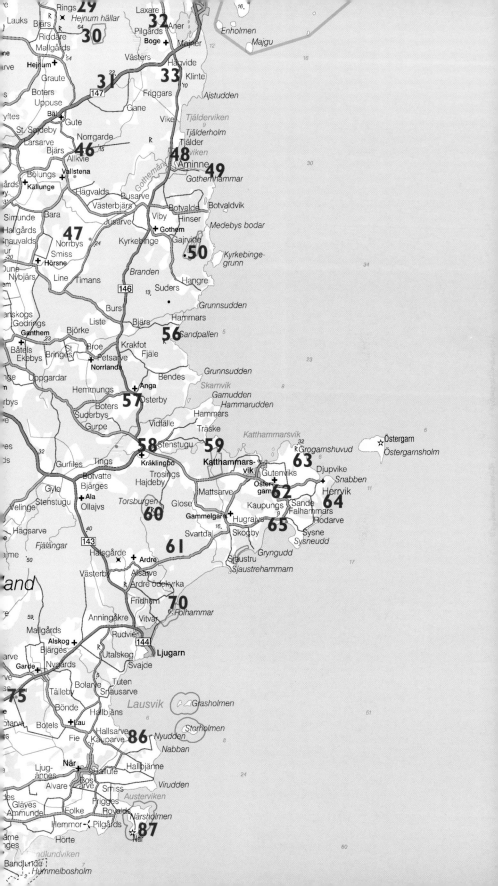

Field Guide

Ⅰ Gotska Sandön, the only national park on Gotland, is incorporated in the parish of Fårö, and lies 38 km directly north of Fårö. The position of the island has nothing to do with the nature of the bedrock, but is the result of the activities of inland ice, which deposited enormous piles of loose till. Gotska Sandön is part of a long, narrow ridge of gravel, stone and sand, which stretches from Avanäset in the north east of Fårö, across Salvorev and all the way up to Kopparstenarna, 18 km north of Gotska Sandön.

Practically the whole island is covered with a thick layer of sand. The coarse gravel beneath the sand can only be seen at Höga land in the south, where sea waves constantly erode the steep slopes. The bedrock, which consists of Ordovician limestone, making it older than the bedrock found at the surface of the main island of Gotland, lies at an awesome depth of 75 m.

Present-day visitors to Gotska Sandön experience the island as one large, unimproved, virginal area. It is difficult to imagine any form of lively human activity. Stray finds have been found from the Neolithic Period and Bronze Age, and two Medieval settlements with substantial yields have been unearthed. During the 18th century, the farmers of Fårö used the island as pastureland for their sheep, as a sealing base and as a base for wood distillation for tar production. On occasions there has been a residential population of about 100 people with both livestock and arable fields. A shipyard was established in the south west of the island in the mid 19th century.

Forestry was carried out on an intensive scale during the 19th century and at the beginning of the 20th century, and a small railway was laid down for the transport of timber to Hamnudden. Since the island was simultaneously grazed by sheep, the vegetation cover was drastically reduced, and flying sand became a serious problem. At the end of the 19th century, the lighthouse station, which had been built at Bredsand in 1859, was under the imminent threat of being buried in sand. Sand trapping grasses and trees were planted to baffle the drifting sand. Although many of the surface shapes of the sand on the island are of ancient origin, many of the dunes along the coasts and towards the inland have formed as the result of tree-felling and grazing. At several places, the forest has been killed off by sand. At Arnagrop, the parched trees stand as a large and beautiful collection of ruins. During summertime, the grounds are extremely parched, and several large fires have ravaged across the island, causing sand mobilization.

The majority of the island is dominated by pine forests. Since intensive forestry has been carried out right up to the 20th century, there is no hope of finding any true primeval forest there. Most of the forest is rather commonplace, and lacks the gnarled pines that fire the imagination in the calcareous ground of Gotland. The once prevalent oak forests, that were widespread across the island, have decimated considerably due to ship-building and as a result of the cessation of grazing and hay-making. Deciduous forests cover small areas, and the largest deciduous areas are around Kapellet, at Idemoren, at Gamla gården and Höga land. Aspen and hazel, along with oak are prevalent in these stands, although yew is also abundant.

No less than 500 vascular plants have been found on the island, although not all of them can be seen today. Many of them were introduced by man, only to disappear shortly afterwards. The characteristic plants on the open shores outside the beach dunes are sea rocket, prickly saltwort

Parched pine and red helleborine, almost buried in sand, at Beckrevet.

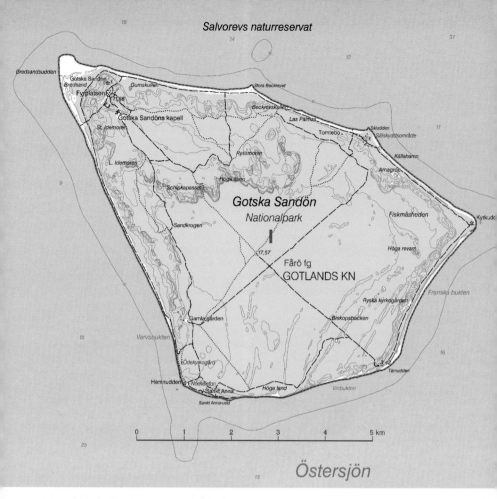

Map of Gotska Sandön on a 1:77 000 scale. All the subsequent detailed maps are on a 1:50 000 scale.

and sea sandwort. The rare and protected sea kale emerges from time to time. The coastal foredunes reach a height of five metres, and are mainly covered with marram and sea pea, which trap and baffle the sand. There are profuse communities of sea holly along certain stretches of the shore. Rarities of the island include hairy milk vetch and thyme broomrape, both of which grow in the proximity of Hamnudden.

On the landward side of the low foredunes, parallel dunes stretch along most of the coasts of the island. These dunes are 10-15 metres high and form a 300-metre-wide belt. On the parallel dunes, the marram has become sparse, having been invaded by sand sedge and grey-hair grass, which grow profusely. Mosses and lichens have gained a foothold on the sand. The intervening elongated swales can be very moist, encouraging a profusion of birdseye primrose and marsh helleborine.

Since Gotska Sandön is built up of sand which is calcium-deficient, orchids are not as abundant as in the rest of Gotland. The pine forests, how-

ever, are home to a number of vigorous red helleborine. Tall narrow-lipped and dark red helleborine grow on the lee side of the dunes, and at Bredsandsudde military orchid can be found.

In the pine forest, which starts on the landward side of the longitudinal dunes, ground cover is species-poor. Heather, whortleberry and Alpine bearberry are interspersed with various forest mosses, mainly stair-step moss, as well as carpets of lichens, where Northern reindeer lichen and white and grey reindeer moss are prevalent.

A chain of tall sanddunes, known as "Tall Ridges", stretches straight across the northern part of the island. One of the ridges boasts the highest point on the island – 42,2 metres above sea level. There is a very large area of flat ground south of, and even to a certain extent north of the ridge. The pine forests here are rather commonplace. Even with a map, it is easy to get lost as soon as you stray from the trails.

Gotska Sandön is a popular attraction for all insect-lovers, although it is prohibited to collect

60

Windswept pine at Las Palmas.

these six-legged creatures in the national park. Some twenty species can only be found here in all of Sweden, and seven species in all of Scandinavia.

There are two main reasons for this singular insect fauna. Firstly, the climate – dry summers are followed by long, mild autumns. Secondly, several of the beetle species are dependent on a supply of dead pinewood, of which there is plenty, since the flying sand has killed off much of the forests. The beetles will also have a constant supply of decayed tree-stumps in the future, since forestry is no longer practised, and the forest will thus be able to develop into a primeval-forest-like habitat. The most remarkable of all of Sandön's beetles must be the longhorn beetle *Ergates faber*, which often reaches over 5 cm in length, and has its strongest foothold in Sweden on the island. In July and August, they can be seen on occasions at night, swarming round the lighthouse, attracted by the strong light.

Prerequisites for birdlife are not so good on Gotska Sandön. The landscape is uniform, offering a limited range of habitats. There is no supply of freshwater during the summer, which excludes a large number of species of breeding birds. Since there are no rodents whatsoever, owls and birds of prey have nothing to feed on. The Alpine hare and northern bat are the only mammals on the island. In the pine forests the prevalent bird species are the chaffinch, coal tit, spotted flycatcher and crossbill. Since the island is extremely isolated, it is a very attractive spot for migrating birds. During springtime, when the flight of birds is most intensive, Bredsandsudde is the best place from which to observe divers, ducks, Brent geese and waders in flight.

At the end of May and beginning of June, the island is often visited by an array of rare birds. One of the island's few freshwater reservoirs – a small pond – can be found at Kapellunden, where early-summer morning treats of listening to such rarities as the greenish warbler, golden oriole and red-breasted flycatcher can be enjoyed. A list of all the rarities which have been observed on the island would be very long indeed.

As early as in 1909, one tenth of the island was brought under national park protection. This status was not extended to the whole island until 1963. Gotska Sandön is now administrated by the Swedish Environmental Protection Agency, and there are two wardens on the island all year round. National Park regulations mean that all wildlife on the island is protected. Visitors may move freely around the entire island. Camping is only permitted

Longhorn beetle, *Ergates faber.*

at designated places close to the lighthouse. Accommodation is also available in purpose-built baracks and cabins. There are regular boat tours from Fårösund and Nynäshamn (south of Stockholm) during the summer. Further information on timetables, regulations, etc can be obtained from Resestugan (telephone +46 498 24 05 50) or on the website: www.gotskasandon.com (Swedish only).

A stay on Gotska Sandön is an experience to be remembered forever. Although Sandön may seem faraway and inaccessible, the trip is not exactly full of hardships, nor is it very expensive, so all naturalists should yield to temptation.

Map on p. 60

2 Ullahau is situated at Avanäset in the north east of Fårö, an area consisting almost entirely of sand. The boundary of this large, sandy area runs largely along the road from Sudersand to Ajkesvik. Since the sand at Avanäset is totally lacking in calcite, its quartz and feldspar composition supports a vegetation which is completely different to the rest of Gotland, where non-calcareous habitats are rare. An array of plants, common on the Swedish mainland, but not found anywhere else on Gotland, occur at Avanäset. Large parts of the sandy area support forests of tall and unusually fast-growing pine trees. Wherever you walk in the forests, you will stumble over carpets of bilberry and whortleberry undershrub, in the company of crowberry and twin-flower.

Originally, all the sand at Avanäset was prone to drifting. Avanäset has emerged from the sea, and since the sand was initially unvegetated, it was easily entrained by the wind, to form dunes of various shapes and sizes. Today, Avanäset is vegetated to such a degree that sand can only really drift along the beaches. Ullahau is a clear indication of the fact that conditions have not been stable for all that long.

Ullahau harbours the epitome of a so-called parabolic dune (at least in Sweden). The dune is shaped like an enormous horseshoe, with its opening facing north. In the north, the arms, which cover an area of 1.3 kms, are narrow, whereas in the south, the dune is up to 300 metres wide. The eastern part of the dune is the best-developed, reaching a height of more than 15 metres above its surroundings. Ullahau has been shaped and positioned by strong northerly winds, which have entrained the sand, shifting the dune in a southward direction.

Ullahau emerged in relatively recent times. The dune began to form during the 18th century, following a period of over-intensive forestry and overgrazing. Ullahau is not recorded on maps from the beginning of the 18th century, but has been drawn in roughly the same shape as today on the Land Reform maps of 1824. The dune drifted in a southward direction, at a velocity of about 3 metres per year, killing large areas of forestland and submerging croplands in its path. An intensive planting campaign was initiated towards the end of the 19th century, in order to stabilize the shifting sand. Pine, birch and alder were planted on the plain on the downwind side of the dune, and thousands of marram grass plants were introduced on the upwind side of the mobile dune. Forestry and grazing were simultaneously regulated, and shortly after the turn of the last century, the dune became inactive.

There is a car park at the southern end of Ullahau, almost a kilometre along the newly-built road to Holmudden. Numerous people visit the dune every year. Trampling impedes the vegetation from getting a proper foothold in the sand, so that those parts of the dune, which are most frequently visited, have never progressed further than the initial overgrowth stage. On the part of the dune, which is first reached from the car park, vegeta-

Open space at Ullahau.

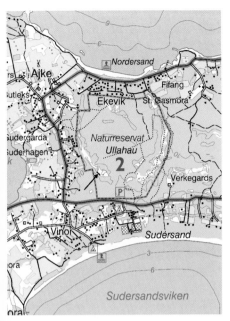

tion is sparse, consisting mainly of various grasses. The most vigorous grass can be found on the crest of the dune; marram colonised this area at the end of the 19th century. Since marram is able to grow and spread quickly, trapping the sand, it is also extensively planted. Another very common grass on the open sandy surfaces is the grey-hair grass, which is easily recognisable by its stiff, often densely tufted and greyish-red stems. Another sand-loving plant which blooms profusely at Ullahau is the sheepsbit scabious with its globular blue heads of flowers. At the end of July/beginning of August, the yellow flowers of the leafy hawkweed can be seen wherever the sand is open. Here and there, low sallow grow, with leaves bearing dense white hairs on both sides. This is creeping willow (moondancer), which is most frequent along the sandy shores of Fårö.

Vegetation at Ullahau is largely species-deficient and dominated by a handful of species. On the downwind side of the dunes, where the forest is dense, only ground-carpeting vegetation can be found. Stair-step moss forms large continuous carpets, with the occasional patch of reindeer moss. Here and there, leaves of the common polypody emerge from the moss carpet. Yellow birdsnest, a small yellowish-brown herb, is not uncommon in the the arid pine forest. This saprophyte has no chlorophyll, but derives its nutriment from mycorrhizal fungi, which live on pine roots. Two orchids, which are rather infrequent on Gotland, but which both grow in the forests of Ullahau, are the lesser twayblade and creeping lady's tresses.

The funnel-shaped pitfall traps of the ant-lion can be found in the open sand. The ant-lion is the larvae of the ant-lion fly, which resembles the dragonfly. It lies in wait at the bottom of its trap for its prey. If an ant or some other insect tumbles into the pitfall, the ant-lion flicks sand on it, making it even more difficult for the victim to climb up the steep walls. Finally, the ant-lion seizes its prey with its large, serrated jaws.

Other insects found at Ullahau include the longhorn beetles and *Ergates faber*. The latter, with a body length of up to 6 cm, is Sweden's largest longhorn, and is only found on Gotska Sandön, Fårö and Gotland. Other beetles found at Avanäset include the 5 cm long longhorns *Prionus coriarius, spondylus buprestoides,* and the Buprestis 8-guttata, an iridescent blue beetle with eight bright yellow spots on its elytra.

Fårö is renowned for its bathing-friendly beaches, where dune vegetation has been severely damaged by bathing guests. The 3 km long beach at the Bay of Sudersand is one example, although its eastern end supports a plant community similar to that of Ullahau.

Bird life is sparse at Ullahau. The monotonous song of the coal tit is the most frequent sound to break through the sighing of the wind blowing through the pine treetops. On spring and summer evenings at about dusk, the roding display of the male woodcock can be experienced as he flies just above the treetops.

Map on p. 63

3 The vast sea stacks on the beach at Langhammarshammar can be seen from a great distance. The sea has chiselled these sea stacks out of the ancient cliffs, which are now flat and evenly rounded, and covered with shingle ridges. By the sea stack field, the slope is steeper, and from the car park, you look down on these fantastic giants of stone. Most impressive is a group of tall, slender sea stacks towards the south – several of them are over 8 metres tall.

On a sunny summer's day, when the sea lies as smooth as a millpond, and the shingle beach is dazzling white, the beautifully sculpted sea stacks are a peerless aesthetic experience. When autumn approaches, with its dull, windy days, the sea stacks take on another dimension. The hissing sea and the whirling wind enhance and give life to the ruggedness of the sea stacks.

The landscape is extremely barren out at Langhammarshammaren. Juniper bushes, restrained by sheep-grazing and the relentless westerly wind, crouch firmly down on the shingle substrate. A large colony of lesser black-backed gulls breeds at Langhammarshammaren, and sometimes the

Tall sea stacks at Langhammarshammar.

melancholy whistle of the golden plover can be heard from the open juniper grounds.

Langhammarsvik can be seen beneath the farm Langhammars, which is passed on the road out to the sea stacks. This bay is in the throes of becoming an isolated lake, due to isostatic rise. A substantial beach ridge already separates the bay from the sea, but storms still cause salt water to flow into the lagoon.

On the way to Langhammars, some sites of natural interest are passed. The road runs largely along a depression, and soon passes Alnäsaträsk on the east side, while Norrsund is in view further to the north, and Bondansträsk to the west. The stretch where these lakes now lie isolated from each other and from the sea once formed a strait that divided Fårö in two. The strait existed way into historic time.

The countryside along this road, is strongly characterized by sheep, which keep herbs and grass well-stunted. The sheep do not touch the vincetoxicum, which are toxic and grow profusely in certain places. The forest is mainly sparse, containing a large number of dead trees.

East of Norrsund, the ground is wide open. Just a few occasional pines remain, while numerous tree stumps bear witness to a former thick forest. The storms at the beginning of the 1930s, and the harsh arid summers at the end of the 1950s claimed many victims among the pine trees. Sheep-grazing subsequently impeded regeneration. Although the landscape of Fårö would appear to resemble a large clear-felled area, there is still beauty in the open landscape, interspersed with an occasional, majestically towering pine tree.

Once all the gates had been removed from the road to Langhammars, and replaced with cattle grids, car drivers have increased their speed, and many sheep get run over. It is vital to drive cautiously and keep a watchful eye on the freely-roaming sheep.

4 The sea stack field at **Digerhuvud** harbours both Gotland's and indeed Sweden's largest collection of sea stacks. A roughly 50 metre-wide field of sea stack-shaped reef limestone stretches from Släthällar, just north of Lauterhorn, northwards to Helgumannens fishing hamlet. A total of several hundred sea stacks stand along the 3.5 km long coastal stretch, the majority of which are rather squat, although some rise to a height of 8 metres. The reef limestone continues outwards beyond the shoreline, so that the sea stacks furthest out are standing in water, and are still being sculpted by waves. At many places, small lagoons have formed in the wide belt of reef limestone. The sea stacks are standing on an underwater ledge of stratified limestone. Slightly offshore, the underwater ledge ends in a perpendicular cliff, where the sea plunges to a depth of 50-60 metres just beyond the sea stack area, making this an ideal spot for cod-fishing from land.

Sea stacks were once part of a cliff, until waves eroded weaker sections, exposing pillars of reef limestone. The corresponding cliff is now a softly rounded formation on the landward side of the sea stack area. The bedrock is covered with loose, sharp chips of eroded reef limestone. At certain places, you can see how the limestone chips are none other than remnants of stromatoporoids. Whole blocks of reef limestone lie scattered along the backshore, where they were washed up after breaking away from the sea stacks.

Vegetation is very sparse in the sterile environ-

ment above the sea stack field. Vincetoxicum, sheep's fescue and herb Robert are most frequent. The rare sandwort *Arenaria gothica* is rather abundant among the limestone rocks at Digerhuvud. It mainly blooms in June, but the occasional specimen can be found in bloom in late autumn.

The beach ridges alongside the sea stack field have earlier been damaged by cars driving off the designated roads. It is of utmost importance that visitors in cars keep to the asphalted road, and only park at designated places.

5 South east of Lake Farnavik there is a rough road leading to the sea stack area of **Gamla hamn**, on a headland south of Lautervik. One of the sea stacks there has been given the name "coffee pot", due to its singular and beautiful shape. The lower part of the broad sea stack has been eroded by waves, leaving an arch, and above the arch there is a loose limestone slab. Normally, sea stacks are composed exclusively of reef limestone, but at Gamla hamn, the sea stacks are rather unique, in that they stand on a base of stratified limestone. Many of the sea stacks stand on the plane bedrock surface of the underwater ledge, slightly offshore.

Reef limestone out on the headland is highly fossiliferous. Apart from stromatoporoids, corals, bryozoans (moss animals), crinoids, snails and brachiopods can also be found. Despite the fact that the sea stack area at Gamla hamn is a protected nature reserve, people still break up reef limestone to extract a fossil, something which obviously is prohibited.

The shingle beach north and south of the sea stack area is of outstanding beauty. The beach is almost totally deficient of all forms of vegetation, and shines dazzling white in the sunlight.

In the forest on the landward side of the sea stack area, there is a small basin, which is the remnant of the harbour which has given the area its name (Gamla hamn means Ancient Harbour). The harbour was probably in use during the Viking Age and Medieval Period, but became cut off during the 14th century, due to isostatic rise and to high beach ridges thrown up by the stormy sea, which blocked the entrance to the harbour. Today, it is a long, narrow, shallow wetland, with a profusion of aquatic insects. A greyish green carpet of charale covers the floor. Slightly to the south are the remains of the Church of St Olof and its former churchyard, probably contemporaneous with the harbour.

Map on p. 65.

6 Some kilometres north east of the Church of Fårö, where the main road runs alongside the sea at Alnäsaviken, the lake **Alnäsaträsk** lies a couple of hundred metres towards the north. The lake is concealed from the road behind an enclosed field of sheep and a piece of woodland. The lake is most easily accessible from the path which runs northwards from the east side of Alnäsavik. The public road ends at the cattle grid, and here you can park your car and continue on foot. From the cattle grid it is only a short walk to the grazed littoral meadows on the eastern side of Alnäsaträsk. Since the sea is highly nutritious and shallow, it harbours a large field of common reed and great fen sedge.

Alnäsaträsk, along with Mölnorträsk, is Fårö's bird-richest lake, and is considered to be Gotland's best birding site, supporting breeding birds such as the horned grebe, March harrier and bittern. The great reed warbler has sung from the lake reeds for a number of years, and little crake have also been observed on several occasions.

Alnäsaträsk, one of Gotland's best lakes for birds.

To date, no tower hide has been built to provide opportunities to view across the lake, but the best view of the open water surface of the lake is from the littoral meadows on the eastern side. Bird life, however, is very sensitive here during the breeding season, i.e. during spring and early summer until mid July. Visitors to the lake during this period, should show utmost caution. Thanks to grazing, the littoral meadows are of botanical interest, not least for their orchids.

East of Alnäsaträsk lies a large alvar-like area, where the occasional pine tree and some windmills without their sails dominate the landscape. This area is called Vinngardsalvaret and has a slightly vaulted shape, due to the content of reef limestone in the bedrock.

Map on p. 65

7 One kilometre north of Fårö church, down in a marked depression, lies **Mölnorträsk**, a shallow and highly nutritious lake. In a very short space of time, it has become clogged with a profusion of common reed along with lesser bulrush and great fen sedge, which are now totally prevalent in the western half of the lake. Open water can only be found at the south east and northern ends of the lake. Towards the west, the lake almost unnoticeably transforms into a large fen, where sedge and reeds are prevalent.

The dense vegetation and high nutritious content have attracted a large number of bird species to reside by the lake. Apart from a series of characteristic flatland lake birds such as the great crested grebe, pochard, mute swan and reed warbler, the greylag goose, crane, ruff and bittern also breed here. The great reed warbler, the largest of our Swedish warblers, was regularly heard during the 1970s and 1980s. During early summer a few little gulls can be seen hunting insects above the lake.

At the very south east tip of the lake, nearest the road, the shore is fringed by a belt of sedge and black bog rush. In the adjoining wet littoral meadow, birdseye primrose bloom in early summer, and several species of orchids can be found later in the summer.

The main road passes across an elevation adjacent to the south eastern end of the lake, and it is possible to park beside a gate in the sheep fence. This is the best viewing point of the lake. On the slope descending to the east side of the lake, where sheep have grazed, there are some thriving Swedish service trees. The vegetation has been cropped by grazing, with the exception of some musk thistles, shunned by sheep. Scattered outcrops of reef limestone, which forms the elevation east of the lake, protrude from the slope.

Map on p. 65.

Little gull can be seen at Mölnorträsk.

8 On the way to **Norra gattet**, the route traverses typical Fårö landscape – barren ground. Only occasionally is the soil cover sufficiently deep for cultivation. A closer look at the croplands reveals that the ground mainly consists of stones. In common with large parts of the rest of Fårö and northern Gotland, much of the land has not been suitable for anything other than sheep pasture. On Gotland, sheep have retained their significance as a source of income, and most of the island's woodland is still used as pasture. When the grass on the dry land becomes too sparse, the sheep start work on the juniper bushes. Those bushes that manage to grow beyond the reach of sheep are normally grazed clean from below, forming what is known as a grazing horizon, which corresponds to the height the sheep can reach.

All grounds, however, are not as intensely grazed. When the ears of the ciliate melick have ripened at the end of the summer, it is easy to distinguish between slightly and intensely grazed grounds. Ciliate melick is the favourite food of sheep, and wherever it grows in profusion, this must mean that grazing has diminished or ceased.

Many of the pines fringing the road are old and beautiful. The tree trunks are slanted, and the crowns are often large, with branches hanging almost right down to the ground.

At the farm Lansa gård, the landscape suddenly becomes wooded and lush. Beyond the farm, the grounds are used as hay meadows. A lot of the deciduous trees, especially the ash and birch, which have been preserved, are a reminder of the times when there was a real meadow here, with trees that were pollarded to provide fodder for the livestock. The last part of the road up to Norra gattets pilot station is surrounded by open land.

Occasional pine trees stand out majestically among numerous stumps. The habitat encountered here is unique for Fårö, and has sometimes been called "pine savannah". Many of the trees, which once stood here, were ravaged in a heavy storm at the beginning of the 1930s. Extremely dry summers, especially during the 1950s, but also at the beginning of the 1980s, later finished off most of the remaining trees. Since sheep have no inhibitions about grazing on young pine saplings, it takes a long time for a forest to regenerate.

A couple of so-called lambgift can be seen on the pine savannah. These are huts that have been built to provide the sheep with shelter in bad weather. These sheep huts are roofed with sedge thatch, and the pairs of twigs attached to the top are to ward off evil spirits.

The area around the pilot station was the main haunt of the roller, which bred on Fårö for a number of consecutive years. Many trees were damaged and left dying after the heavy storm at the beginning of the 1930s. The black woodpecker excavated nest holes in the dry pine trees, which later became excellent homes for rollers. From the 1930s until the 1960s, a period of about 30 years, the roller had a stable population on Fårö with up to some ten pairs breeding there.

Beneath the pilot station, a gently sloping coastal moor takes over. A long series of beach ridges with sparse vegetation stretch right down to the sea. By the narrow strait, Norra gattet, just over a kilometre south of the pilot station, Fårö stretches so far west that only a few hundred metres separate Fårö from the main island of Gotland.

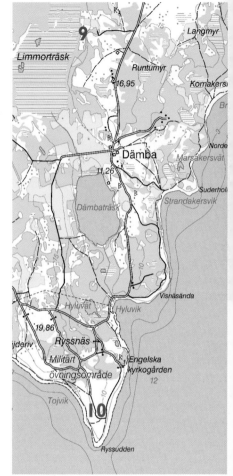

9 When travelling southwards from Fårö church, the terrain ascends slightly a couple of kilometres north of Dämba. With the wink of an eye, you suddenly find yourself on a large inland cliff. In the west, a few hundred metres from the road, the cliff plunges steeply towards the plateau below. About 3 kms south of Fårö church, a small road leads south west to the low cliff above **Klint-ängarna** (Clifftop Meadows). There is a car park in front of the first gate.

From the cliff edge there is an expansive view. Beyond the sea of sedge in Limmorträsk in the southwest, the main island can just be seen in the distance. Between the lake and cliff is a large area of deciduous forest, interspersed with open land, known as Klintängarna. A footpath leads down from the cliff to an open area at the southern end of Klintängarna. Traditional meadow management has not been practised for a long time. Instead, the land is kept open by grazing and well-managed clearance. Hazel is prevalent, although there is an unusually large element of birch. In the north, the

wooded grounds are replaced by hay meadow and some areas of juniper that have been grazed by sheep.

On a windy spring day, Klintängarna is a prime place for a day out. The meadows are sheltered from wind by the towering cliffs, and in mid May thousands of cowslips shimmer in the tender green grass.

Towards the north, Verkegardsänget forms a continuation of Klintängarna. This former meadow is so choked with weeds that it is almost impenetrable in places.

Limmorträsk, west of Klintängarna, is often called "The Former Limmorträsk". Its level was lowered at the end of the 19th century, and today it rather resembles a fen with extensive sedge fields. All that is left of the former lake is a small area of open water in the north east.

The lake and the varying surroundings are unusually bird-rich. Breeding birds include the greylag goose, crane, corncrake, spotted crake and marsh warbler. A few barred warblers can be found in the juniper areas. The scarlet grosbeak

View of Klintängarna from high elevation, east of Limmorträsk.

immigrated to Sweden from the east in 1938, and when it bred on Fårö, it was the first recorded breeding of the species in Sweden. Nowadays the scarlet grosbeak is one of the most common birds at Klintängarna. The nutcracker, which is otherwise a very rare bird on Gotland, is frequently seen in the surroundings of Limmorträsk. The hazel groves at Klintängarna offer a well-stocked larder of hazelnuts.

When the level of Limmorträsk was lowered, new land was created. Orchids are examples of plants which are the swiftest colonisers of virgin land. In the wet meadowlands on the borders of the lake, early marsh and fly orchids, dark red and marsh helleborines are often found. The only community of loose-flowered orchids on Fårö also grows here. *Map on pp 65 and 68.*

10 Some hundred metres north of the ferry station at Broa, a road runs in a south easterly direction from the main road. The road leads down to the vast and magnificent landscape at **Ryssnäs**, the southernmost point on Fårö.

Arriving at Ryssnäs, all that can be seen are sparsely growing pine trees and juniper bushes along the slopes down towards Fårösund. Then, all higher forms of vegetation seem to cease, and vincetoxicum and sheep's fescue seem to be the only plants growing on the beach ridges. These plants are adapted so that they are resilient to the intensive sheep grazing which goes on here. Vincetoxicum is toxic and is left in peace, whereas sheep's fescue survives by growing so thickly tufted

that the sheep never manage to crop the plants.

The road down to **Ryssudden** passes a low cliff of reef limestone and sea-stack-like sections, and the reef limestone projects from the ground here and there, forming hummocks. Ryssudden itself has no trees or shrubs whatsoever, making the beach ridges, which are in fact high and well-developed in themselves, very conspicuous. The desolate and barren landscape at Ryssudden is awesome, especially since the area is entirely exposed to the sea and the persistent winds. Only traces of military activities somewhat mar this experience of being close to nature.

One kilometre north of the southern point of Ryssudden lies the "English cemetary", a cholera cemetary from the Crimean War, when the British fleet was stationed at Fårösund. *Map on p. 68.*

11 (a) **Burgbackar** – The road which runs north west from Fleringe church passes through "Burgbackar", a long, narrow and completely barren area, just over ½ kilometre past the church. At a height of 20-25 metres above sea level, there is a shingle "field", 2½ kms long and 50-150 metres wide. The shape of the beach ridges is very distinct, and the area bears every feature of a typical coastal habitat. It is, however, 1½ kms from the sea and completely surrounded by forest.

Burgbackar was formed when the Littorina Sea, one of the earlier stages of the present Baltic Sea, reached its highest point about 7 500 years ago, and the sea waves cast up stones quarried from the bedrock by strong wave action. The stones were

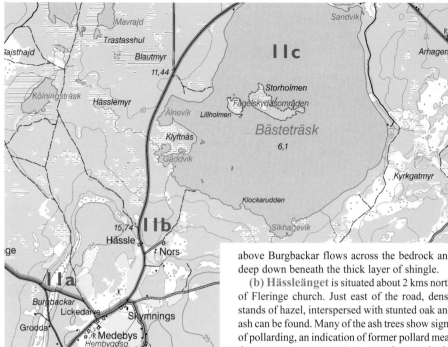

then rounded by abrasion as they lay rubbing against each other. Simultaneously, the backwash dragged finer particles back out to sea, leaving the shingle beach ridges at Burgbackar very dry and nutrient-deficient.

Vegetation is practically non-existent in the area. A few pine trees and blackthorn bushes have migrated out to the shingle beach ridges. Herb Robert, common toadflax, dark red helleborine and toothed wintergreen are some other plants which, amazingly enough, have survived on this stony ground. At other places, richer vegetation can be seen forming a narrow strip beyond the slopes, an indication that water from the ground

above Burgbackar flows across the bedrock and deep down beneath the thick layer of shingle.

(b) Hässleänget is situated about 2 kms north of Fleringe church. Just east of the road, dense stands of hazel, interspersed with stunted oak and ash can be found. Many of the ash trees show signs of pollarding, an indication of former pollard meadows, now overgrown. A gate can be seen in the sheep fence, leading to a path into the area. Having passed the hazel-prevalent area, more open ground is reached; this is sheep pastureland, supporting an unusual mixture of oak, pine and juniper. The stunted oaks with sparse crowns are indications of meagre soils. The topsoil is a mere thin sheet on top of limestone rock and shingle. The flora as a whole is rather poor, and certain patches of ground bear very little cover other than moss. Between the drier sections, there are belts of wet, humid depressions. Here, the vegetation is more lush and includes meadowsweet, marsh thistle and tall true sedges (*Carex*).

(c) Bästeträsk is a large, but nutrient-deficient and rather desolate lake, situated some kilometre from the wooded grounds at Hässle. The surface of the water at the south east end of the lake can

Bare shingle field at Burgbackar.

A multitude of eider breed on the islets in Bästeträsk, and the rare swordleaf inula can be found on the west shore of the lake.

be glimpsed from the road through the pine forest at Älnevik. A small forest trail will take you to the lakeshore, and here it is worth stopping to take a look at some interesting xeric plants. Immediately beside the main road, just north of the forest trail leading to the lake, grows a large community of the rare swordleaf inula, which is similar to the common Irish fleabane, but has lanceolate, parallel-veined leaves, and blooms at the height of summer. Carline thistle are also abundant here, and there are quite a number of pale St John's wort; the latter bloom at Midsummer.

Down on the shore at Älnevik, the vast water surface of Bästeträsk can be viewed. Bästeträsk is Gotland's largest lake, with an area of just over 7 km². It lies in a very sparsely populated area and is completely surrounded by forest and fens. The lake is thus remarkably unsusceptible to sewage or seepage of fertilizers from cultivated land. The water is highly calcareous, but deficient in most other substances which are of vital importance to plants. Apart from a certain amount of reeds and sedge which grow along some of the shallow shore areas, the lake seems almost lifeless. Charales, however, carpet the lake bed a few metres down.

As a result of plant deficiency in the lake, bird-life is also under-developed. The two islets in the lake, known as Storholmen and Lillholmen, support a remarkable colony of birds. Several hundred pairs of eider breed on these islands. Eider feed almost exclusively on common sea mussels from the Baltic Sea bed, and are not normally found in lakes. The islets in Bästeträsk have provided the eider with a sheltered breeding site at a comfortable distance from the marine larder. It is prohibited to go ashore on the islets between 15th March and 15th July, so that the eider may breed undisturbed.

North of Bästeträsk, the road runs right alongside the shoreline. Here you can see how the winter ice has created a "shore-barricade" – a high bank of earth and stones. At some points, water furrows

have formed between the former shore and the shore barricade, which is about one metre tall.

12 Hallshuk is the name of the high marine cliff, which is situated just east of Hall fishing hamlet, at the end of the main road at the northernmost point of the promontory. The top of the 25-30 metre-high cliff is a superb viewing point. In the east you can see Fleringe and Rute parishes, where the church spires soar above the coniferous forests. On a clear day, and with the help of field glasses, you can see the sea stack field at Langhammarshammar and Digerhuvud on Fårö, more than 20 kilometres away!

The land on the clifftop was grazed until a few decades ago, and you can now see how the young pines are gradually invading the open juniper bushland. The numerous visitors and wild rabbits fulfill the same function as the sheep – they keep the grass and herbs well cropped. Those who dare to venture out to the cliff edge will be rewarded with the sight of ardent, chirping house martins. House martins, which normally construct closed mud nests on outsides of houses, find cliff faces a natural site for breeding. The foreshore beyond the beach at the foot of the cliff is shallow, due to a flat limestone rock, known as an underwater ledge, which stretches some hundred metres out from the beach, whereupon it plunges down as an almost perpendicular underwater cliff.

The beautiful road which follows the coastline southwards from Hallshuk is hardly suitable for any heavier form of transport than a bicycle.

The landscape on the Hall promontory is mainly very barren with pine forests on inland rock and bare flat rock. Since the infertile land has attracted few people, large areas are singularly unaffected by human activity.

In 1967 the almost 22 km² Hall-Hangvar area was brought under the protection of a nature reserve, as a measure to preserve a large area of

Cliff face at Hallshuk.

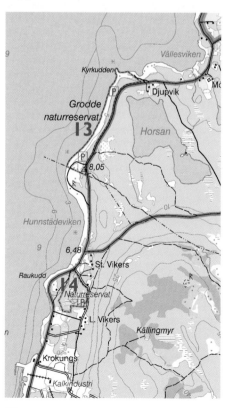

land untouched by human activity. The nature reserve comprises the entire marine cliff coastline in the west, as well as a large landward area. Apart from the pine forest on flat inland rock, which is prevalent within the nature reserve, there are also several unimproved sedge fens.

Some of the wilderness qualities of the nature reserve have disappeared, due to difficulties in regulating limits of landowners' rights to engage in forestry. Regulations have mainly targetted casual visitors. Vehicles are prohibited on the smaller roads, camping is also prohibited, in common with firelighting which is not allowed between May and October.

The road to Hallshuk passes Hall church. The small parish meadow is situated next to the road on the east side. The meadow is dominated by majestic pine trees, which have a lush undergrowth of hazel. The northern edge of the meadow supports an enormous community of dogwood.

13 On the east side of the bay "Kappelhamnsviken", a beautiful stretch of coastline with shingle beaches, which have been singularly unaffected by human activity, has been preserved. **Grodde nature reserve** was established in 1981, and comprises a stretch of coast which is 1½ kms long and about 150 metres wide. The landscape is characterized by a wide, totally barren shingle beach with a long series of well-developed beach ridges.

The road to Bläse runs alongside the coast, forming the eastern border of the nature reserve. Between the road and the shingle beach, there is a low, slowly-growing pine tree forest. The ground is carpeted with Alpine bearberry undershrub, which enhances the shape of the beach ridges (even in the forest). The transition from forest to barren shingle beach is distinctly marked. Although more than a thousand years have passed since the upper part of the still treeless beach emerged from the sea, only occasional junipers and pines have managed to gain a foothold in the shingle beach ridges. The lack of fine-grained soil has rendered the beach a parched and nutrient-deficient habitat. This, in combination with the strong westerly winds, which often torment the coast, has led to a very slow colonisation of the beach.

Vincetoxicum is the most prevalent plant on the beach ridges, and almost the only plant to grow vertically. It's leathery leaves, which impede transpiration, enable the plant to grow in dry conditions and exposed to the elements. The sparse vegetation of the low-growing herbs comprises just a few species, and occurs in patches. The most common plants are sea campion, lady's bedstraw, wild thyme, biting stonecrop and mouse-ear hawkweed. The tiny carline thistle, which look withered and parched even

Shingle beach at Grodde nature reserve.

when in full bloom at the end of July, also thrive between the shingles on the beach.

Closest to the beach, the long series of beach ridges terminates in a low cliff, which is mainly covered with shingle. Different species of crustose lichen and algae, growing on the stones, give the shingle beach a greyish and in certain places a distinct reddish colour. Beneath the cliff, where the sea swells over the shingle, the beach is dazzling white.

North east of Grodde nature reserve, both limestone kilns at Bläse can be seen. These abandoned limestone works have been converted into an industrial museum. A very conspicuous, over 30 metre tall slag heap can be seen beside the limestone kilns. *Map on p. 72.*

14 The beach ridges on the slopes on the eastern side of Kappelshamnsviken are the source of a spring called **Vitärtskällan**. After a 500-metre drive along the road leading south east at Raukudd, water can be seen flowing from some buried pipes to the right of the road. When the sea thrust up beach ridges, it retrieved finer material in the backwash, leaving coarse sand and shingle behind. The beach ridges thus comprise similar material to the gravel, which formed the large eskers and can therefore sometimes accumulate and conduct water in much the same way.

Even in dry summers, the beach ridges produce an abundance of water, which creates several small furrows that meander down the slope. In the running water, plants like fen pondweed, marsh pennywort and a profusion of water mint can be found. Beside the brook, the ground is flushed by the nutrient-rich water, and a series of different grasses and sedges form healthy green meadows. The cold water from the spring delay the development of the flora. Birdseye primrose, for example, which grow abundantly beside the brook, bloom unusually late, and many flowers remain in bloom some time after midsummer.

The flora at Vitärskällan contains many typical flush fen plants. German asphodel and brown bogrush grow just beside the brook channel. At the end of June, a profusion of Pugsley's marsh orchid bloom in the constantly flushed meadows. Caution is vital when walking here, so as not to damage the fragile orchids, which at first stay concealed in the grass. Fly orchids, marsh helleborine and fragrant orchids are all part of the flora of the flush fen, but none are as profuse as the Pugsley's marsh orchid. In some of the meadows, a white shimmer can be seen, emanating from the long hairs in the drooping inflorescence of the broad-leaved cottongrass. Tall marsh thistles can also be seen alongside the brook.

At several places, you can see how the blue-green algae have formed calcareous nodules on the bed of the brook. The nodules comprise several nubbles, and where colonies of algae are still active, they form a slimy, dark green coating on the stones.

Where the slopes flatten out, the brook discharges into a small lake, in which a carpet of bogbean blooms during early summer. *Map on p. 72.*

Pugsley's marsh orchid.

Beautiful and dramatic cliffed coastline at Sigsarvestrand.

15 A very beautiful piece of cliffed coast can be found in the south of the large Hall-Hangvar nature reserve. From road 149, just over 2½ kms north east of Ire farm, there is a smaller gravel road, about 2 kms long, which leads down to the coast at Sigsarvestrand. Having parked on the clifftop, take time to enjoy the view of the beach and the cliffed coast, stretching out both to the north and south.

At Sigsarvestrand the sea has cut back the outer layers of the cliff, so that a remarkably wide shingle beach has formed at the foot of the cliff. A perpendicular wall leads down to the southern end of the beach. The tall cliff faces fringing Sigsarvestrand give the beach an enclosed, almost exclusive atmosphere. At first it seems as if the fishing hamlet to the north of the beach is in a very sheltered position, but it is soon discovered that it lies completely exposed to the prevailing west winds. Apart from the projecting cliffs which demarcate the beach in the north and south, there is also a distinct "visor" – a projection of reef limestone in the middle of the cliff face, east of the beach, where, the sea has sculpted it to a gentle shape. At several places shallow cave-like depressions can also be seen in the cliff face.

Sigsarvestrand is at the height of its beauty in June and July, when the sparse cluster of viper's bugloss adds a splash of colour to the shingle beach with its otherwise species-deficient vegetation. Down on the water line you will notice a large number of extraneous rock types, mixed with the calcareous shingle. These stone were carried here from northerly regions by the latest inland ice.
Map on p. 75

16 The road down to Irevik passes through an area with weekend cottages. On the left hand side of the road you can see the cliff face and occasional sea stacks through the sparse pine tree forest. On the western side of the bay, where the road ends, there is a fishing hamlet and dwelling houses, with an impressive backdrop of tall cliffs to the west and south.

The beach at Ireviken is open and roamer-friendly with a narrow belt of beautiful pine forest. Red helleborine bloom among the pines in the latter half of June, simultaneously with the dark red helleborine. Two typical sea shore plants, the woad and sea rocket, grow between the shingles just above the shore line. To the east, the high coastline continues northwards from the east side of the bay of Ireviken.

Much of the water in Ireån, the river which discharges into the middle of the bay of Irevik, is from Tingstädeträsk and from the drained off mire Elinghemsmyr. From the main road at Ire farm and out to the sea, Ireån follows a natural meandering path, which is sometimes steep and torrential. Here, the river has carved its way down through deep beds of loose soil, which partly consist of former dunes of flying sand. The river is mainly fringed by a dense, almost impenetrable vegetation, which makes it difficult to roam alongside

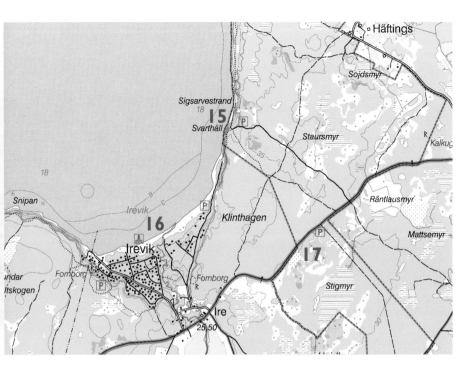

the river channel. By the old mill, a few hundred metres northwest of the main road, however, there is a gap in the verdure, where it is easy to access the river shore.

In autumn, sea trout wander up the river Ireån to play. At first, the fish gather in dense shoals beyond the river mouth. To protect the sea trout from poaching, a protective zone has been proclaimed beyond the river mouth. Within this zone, fishing is prohibited between 1st October and 31st December.

The insects which can be found in the river are not only eaten by sea trout and other fish. They are also food for the dippers which usually overwinter here each year.

The beach, which has become increasingly popular for bathing, is beginning to take its toll; damaged or removed vegetation has resulted in blowouts. On the flat, sandy beach at the mouth of Ireån, numerous common fumana grow on a substrate most unusual for this species. In the long run, this community is threatened by the increasing number of bathing guests. *Map on p. 75.*

17 Two kilometres northeast of Ire farm, the main road passes **Stigmyr**, which is about 600 metres to the southeast. Stigmyr cannot be seen from the road, but when abreast the fen, you will notice the large, dry, long-boled pines in the forest on inland rock, which borders the road. You are now in a 100-hectacre area which is part of

the southernmost section of the Hall-Hangvar nature reserve, where you can see an old pine forest surrounding Stigmyr.

The soil cover is mainly very thin, entailing slow growth of the forest. At certain places the forest is very sparse and the pine trees are low and knotty.

Red helleborine.

Knotty pines make useless timber, which might explain why the forest has been left more or less unimproved during the last few centuries. The Gotlandic forest has been exploited extensively for a very long time, and still today it tends to be over-exploited. Areas of ancient forest are therefore unusual on Gotland, and the area around Stigmyr is considered to be one the most valuable natural forest areas on the island.

Frost heave structures can normally be seen just west of Stigmyr. Water carrying soil from adjacent land accumulates in shallow depressions in the flat rock during autumn and winter. There are also small stones in the thin soil cover. When winter comes, and the water in the soil cover freezes to ice, the ground expands, and numerous stones in the soil are forced upward to the surface, where they often accumulate in various patterns, including polygons, which is why this phenomena is often called "polygonal ground".

A tractor road, straight as an arrow, leading north from the main road, north west of Stigmyr, passes some wetland around the outlet of the fen. The grass here grows vigorously and lush, and an abundance of lesser butterfly, early marsh, late-blooming fragrant orchids, as well as a number of fly orchids can be found. From the fringes of Stigmyr, about 100 metres to the south along the outlet, there is a good view of a sedge fen, much resembling most other fens in the north of Gotland. The entire expanse of the fen is totally dominated by great fen sedge, although the borders of the fen support a richer vegetation with black and brown bog-rush. With a stroke of good luck you might see the cranes which usually frequent the fen.

Map on p. 75.

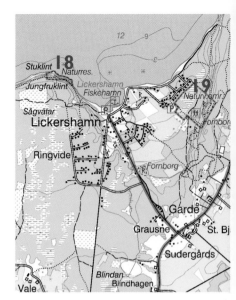

Jungfrun, Gotland's tallest sea stack.

18 Lickershamn, in common with Irevik further to the north east, sports no high marine cliffs, but the coastline has been cut back to form a shallow bay.

A 600-metre walk from the fishing harbour at Lickershamn will take you to the cliff **Jungfruklint**, which forms a projecting section in the high cliffed coastline, which is resumed west of Lickershamn. Jungfruklint is a nature reserve, mainly because Gotland's tallest sea stack, Jungfrun (transl. Virgin), is situated at the head of the clifftop. Jungfrun rises over 11 metres above the clifftop, and 27 metres above sea level. This giant sea stack was sculpted by the Littorina Sea, whose highest level was one metre above the crown of Jungfrun.

From the cliff edge in the pine forest south east of Jungfrun, you can see that the reef limestone, which constitutes the sea stack, continues some metres down the cliff, which otherwise consists of marlstone. Large blocks have tumbled down to the foot of the cliff. Some of them consist of reef limestone, and have earlier been part of Jungfrun. Inland from the cliff-top which you are standing on, there is another cliff ledge of stratified limestone. On the slope between the two cliffs there is a distinct series of beach ridges, which were thrust up by the waves of the Littorina Sea.

On the shingle beach north of the car park at Lickershamn, a large number of dark red helleborine can be seen at the end of June and in July. One hundred metres to the north along the beach, you will reach a place where water flows from the hill above. A carpet of yellowish-brown mosses grow in the trickling water, which is supersaturated with calcium bicarbonate. When the water emerges from the slope, it is heated. On contact with the air, some of the carbon dioxide is gasified, and a solidified deposit of calcium carbonate (tufa) forms a crust on the moss, which finally becomes completely embedded in a thick calcareous coating. The moss and calcite thus combine to form a several-decimetre-thick coating of porous rock known as tufa, or travertine. Flush fen plants, such as birdseye primrose, Alpine butterwort and German asphodel grow adjacent to the tufa formation.

A few hundred metres south east of the harbour, the main road passes a section of reef limestone with several shapely sea stacks. This small sea stack area is so embedded in the verdure that it is almost invisible from the road. *Map on p. 76.*

19 At the foot of the cliff east of Lickershamn are a couple of flush fens, which are constantly flushed by spring water which forces its way up to the surface. Beside the holiday camp east of the harbour Lickershamn, a sign points to **Grausne flush fen**, which is a protected area. Grausne flush fen harbours a species-rich flora, and apart from the characteristic flush fen plants like brown and black bog-rush, birdseye primrose, Alpine butterwort and German asphodel, rarities such as Irish eyebright and blunt-flowered rush also thrive here.

Having led the visitor to the actual flush fen, the nature trail then passes through an area of pine forest on inland rock, later continuing through more lush forest with a significant amount of spruce, and on to a hillfort on the cliff-top. In the hillfort, the forest has been thinned and the ground is covered with a dense undershrub of Alpine bearberry. From the hillfort you have a good view of the bay of Lickershamn with the cliff Jungfruklint in the background.

The final stretch of the nature trail passes the upper part of Grausne flush fen, where both the fragrant orchid and short-spurred fragrant orchid thrive at the height of summer.

At the beginning of the two-kilometre-long nature trail, there is a small box containing a guide to the flush fen and the surrounding varied forest. *Map on p. 76.*

20 **Ekebysänget** is a small but very beautiful meadow, which is part of a larger oak-dominating deciduous forest area. The meadow is characterized by free-standing, vigorous and wide-crowned oak trees. Hazel is the dominant bush, but is not as dense as in other meadows.

The large oak crowns cast a deep shadow on parts of the meadow. Several plants, which are otherwise associated with shady glades are thus able to survive in this meadow. When trees come into leaf, the ground is covered with cowslips and

Typical flush fen plants such as birdseye primrose (above) and Irish brighteye (below).

wood anemones. Later, towards the end of May, the intensive purplish-red flowers of the spring pea can be seen everywhere. Wood melick is an uncommon glade grass which is profuse in Ekebysänget, and in the densest shades of the corners of the meadow you will find the fragrant woodruff.

Of early summer's orchids, the most common is the early purple. Later, fragrant orchids can be discerned in the profusion of grass-green twayblades.

Ekebysänget is on the left hand side, about 2 kms along the road leading northeast from Stenkyrka church to the abandoned church at Elinghem. Immediately west of the meadow, there is a small road which leads to a suitable place for parking and turning the car.

Träskmyr, Gotland's largest undrained marsh.

21 **Träskmyr**, covering an area of 197 hectares, lies in the forests between Hangvar church and the bay of Kappelshamnsviken, and is Gotland's largest undrained fen. It is situated at the far end of a water course which originates in Verkmyr at the northern end of the Hall promontory.

Formerly, Kyrkbys myr, Stormyr and Väsnings stormyr were fens which acted as a reservoir for the water on its way to Träskmyr. Since these fens are now drained off, the spring flood is short-lived and intensive. Träskmyr, which is undrained, was formerly a bottle-neck which halted the water,

causing croplands further up in the watercourse to become waterlogged. Voices were raised to have the fen drained off, but to counteract this threat, the fen was placed under the protection of a nature reserve in 1981. Since then, the troubles have been dealt with, to the satisfaction of both agriculture and nature protection.

During 1983, a pump station with very high capacity was installed at the western end of the fen. Once the spring flood has passed, water is now pumped into the fen from the canal which drains the croplands in the west. At Vasteån, the

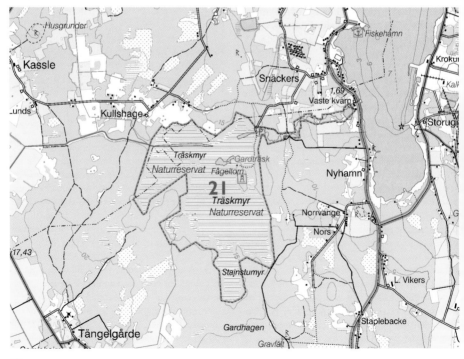

river which is the outlet of the fen in the east, a dam has been built to regulate the water level. In this way, the croplands can be drained in time for spring tillage, while the water level in the fen can be kept at a relatively natural level.

Träskmyr is dominated by great fen sedge, although tall true sedges (*Carex*) and black bog-rush are abundant. In the fen there are some fifty small open water areas, of which Gardträsk in the northeastern part of the fen is the largest. Around Gardträsk and along the canal which was dug into the fen in the 1960s, highly nutritious water from the croplands has encouraged a dense community of common reed.

Along the edge of the fen, there is a wide belt of black bog-rush, which is sometimes replaced by slender sedge. This is where you can find the rare and protected loose-flowered orchid, which is the main attraction at Träskmyr at the height of summer; some years, up to 2 500 specimens of this majestic orchid, which can reach a height of a half a metre, have been observed. Between the black bog-rush belt and the forest land is the fen lagg, which is wetter than the rest of the fen, and overgrown with low grasses and true sedge (*Carex*).

Bird life at Träskmyr is rarely particularly lively. The fen has been surveyed, and about 17 different species breed out in the actual fen. When including the immediate surroundings, the number is doubled. Among the resident species are the crane, March harrier, spotted crake, water rail and corncrake.

On a headland at the eastern end of the fen there is a tower hide providing a good view of the vast range of the fen and the mirror surface of the water of Gardträsk.

A newly- built road leads right down to the north eastern corner of Träskmyr. If you take this road, which leads in towards Snäckers, about 500 metres south of the harbour at Kappelshamn, you will eventually arrive at the dam construction beside Vasteån. *Map on p. 78*

22 The 3.5 km² **Fardume träsk** is the third largest lake on Gotland (Bästeträsk and Tingstäde-träsk are larger). The lake receives water, super-saturated with calcium bicarbonate, from the surroundings, and when this calcium carbonate precipitates as bog lime into the lake, vast banks of sediment are gradually formed on the lake bed. Since the level of the lake was lowered at the end of the 19th century, and is now very shallow, the banks of bog lime sometimes almost reach the water surface. The sediment banks are a suitable hotbed for plants, and both common reed and great fen sedge grow in extensive continuous fields, covering almost the entire lake.

Loose-flowered orchid.

At the beginning of the 20th century, ruthless bird-hunting was carried out in Fardumeträsk. In 1937, however, the landowners themselves proclaimed the lake a protected area on their own initiative. Since then, bird life has developed uninhibited and today the lake is a renowned birding site. A wide range of common sea birds breed in Fardumeträsk.

Two later additions to the Gotlandic bird fauna – the mute swan and great crested grebe – both arrived on Gotland and started nesting here at the end of the 1930s. Several species in the lake are slightly less common; the March harrier is an old faithful, and a few pairs of little gull breed here. For several years now, the loud, strident song of the great reed warbler has been heard from among the lake reeds. The lake is one of the few places on Gotland harbouring the bittern on a regular basis, and several pairs of greylag goose also breed here. There are fair chances of hearing the corncrake in the proximity of the lake.

Fardume träsk is not only attractive as a breeding site. Flocks of greylag geese gather here in spring, and in autumn the lake reeds are used as stop-overs by large flocks of starlings on their way south. The crane, grey heron, raven and a number of birds of prey also find their way to the lake in search of food.

The best view of the lake is from a rubbish dump beside the northeast flank of the lake. Northeast of the lake, a small road leads from Valleviken village past Fardume farm. The first junction on the left, after leaving Valleviken, leads to the dump. Since the lake is large, birders will find a birding scope useful.

From the dump you can see Storholmen, an islet in the middle of Fardumeträsk. This islet supports

Greylag goose.

a somewhat unusual formation on Gotland – a raised bog, dominated by bog moss. In the moss on Storholmen, several species of calcifuge plants can be found, which is uncommon on Gotland. These include Labrador tea, crowberry and cranberry. Storholmen is a nature reserve, and admittance is prohibited from 1st February to 15th July.

The fly orchid, and in late summer large communities of marsh helleborine can be found on the marshy lakeshore, northwest of the dump. The lake is fringed with a sparse mixture of reed and sedge, interspersed with marsh lousewort and brown bog-rush. Marsh lousewort has beautiful dark red stalks and pink flowers. It is a semi-parasite and acquires some of its nourishment from the roots of sedge. Early marsh orchids bloom in early summer in the sparse vegetation fringing the lake, followed by the bright yellow flowers of the great bladderwort. *Map on p. 81.*

23 Anyone interested in geology and wishing to hunt for fossils and rocks in the bedrock is advised to visit one of the numerous stone quarries on the island. The stratification of the bedrock is most distinct in quarries. The fossils have been weathered away from the quarry walls.

The richness of fossils varies from quarry to quarry. **Fardume marlstone quarry** is situated northeast of Fardumeträsk. Here you will find a rich and varied fossil fauna.

Part of the stone quarry is filled with sparkling clear water, although most of the quarry floor can be negotiated dry-shod. Fossils of a great variety of animal groups can be found in the limestone and the loose marlstones in the quarry walls. The most common fossils are of brachiopods, snails and tabulate corals. *Map on p. 81*

24 (a) **Lergrav**, about 6 kms southeast of Rute, harbours one of Gotland's largest and most beautiful sea stack areas. Several roads lead to Lergrav from road 148, both to the north and south of Rute Church. Having arrived at the northern edge of Lergravsberget (= hill), keep to the edge of the cliff, and walk straight on to Lergravsviken (= bay), where the sea stacks stand on the slopes west of the road.

Some of the groups of high sea stacks form exciting and beautiful shapes. "Lergravsporten" (= gateway), towards the south, is one of the largest and most singularly shaped sea stack.

Some Gotlandic sea stack fields are embedded in thick verdure. At Lergrav, bushes and trees have been cleared, exposing the sea stacks in all their glory. Since there are no trees to shade the ground, the flora mainly consists of species that thrive in open, sun-drenched, dry soil, such as common rock rose, spiked speedwell, vincetoxicum and mouse-ear hawkweed, which can be found in abundance here. Moon carrot is a tall, umbelliferous plant, which is most common on the northeastern coast of Gotland, and which thrives on the slopes at Lergrav. It is mainly recognizable by its ridged, woody stems.

(b) From Lergrav the road continues south, passing "**Husken**", a long, narrow headland projecting into the eastern side of the bay of Valleviken. The headland offers a variety of natural features,

Lergravsporten, one of the many sea stacks at Lergravsviken.

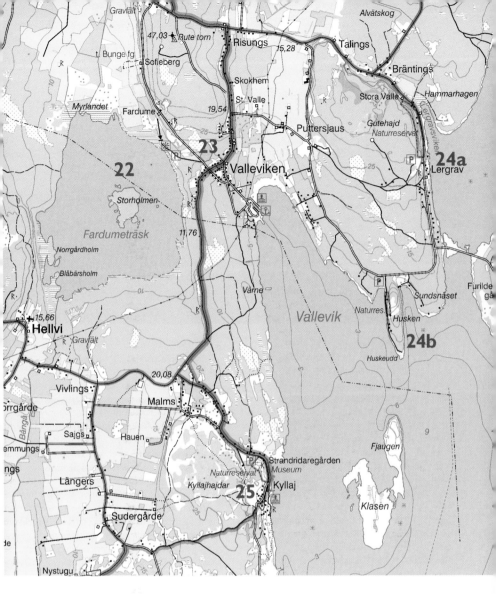

an enticement to the walker. A suitable starting point is from the car park, just north of the headland.

The northern part of the headland is a nature reserve and is dominated by a 20-metre-tall hill of reef limestone. Sea stacks cluster in small groups on the slopes of the hill. A thick spruce forest encircles a few tall, solitary sea stacks on the east face of the hill.

The road out to the south point of the headland follows the west face of the hill, which is shaped like a high cliff, with large blocks of limestone resting at its foot. On the south side of the headland, pebbles have accumulated to form prominent banks, partly overgrown with thickets of Alpine bearberry.

Map on p. 81

25 From the road between Hellvi Church and Valleviken, a road leads south east to Malms and **Kyllaj**. From Malms and down to the sea, the road descends a steep hill. Strandridaregården, the former home of a former customs officer, is situated a few hundred metres north of Kyllaj, where the gradient of the cliff face decreases. The slopes rising above Strandridaregården harbour the sea stack field Malms-Kyllaj, which is a nature reserve.

Strandridaregården was built at the beginning of the 18th century, and was the residence of the customs officer and "lime baron" Johan Ahlbom. The interior of the house is well-preserved and is normally open for guided tours in the mornings in summer. Carl von Linné sought accommodation here when travelling around Gotland, and made drawings of the tall sea stacks.

Sea stacks surrounded by lush early summer verdure at Kyllaj.

The ground on the slopes above the sea stacks is covered with shingle, and vegetation is sparse. The tall golden yellow false oat-grass is prevalent, and ragwort are also abundant. There is a good view of Valleviken from the slopes. About one kilometre out at sea, you can see the two islands of Fjaugen and Klasen, which have now been united following isostatic rise.

A young and dense spruce forest has developed west of the sea stack field. Luxuriant dark red helleborine grow in the glades in the month of July. "Kyllaj hajdar" is situated beyond the spruce forest; this large and almost completely flat outcrop of pure limestone harbours a fascinating biota, as well as traces of small, scattered, shallow limestone quarries. Limestone from Kyllaj hajdar may have been burned in the kilns bordering the road south of Kyllaj. Fuel for limeburning may also have been gathered from this inland-rock area since the rocks are now practically treeless. The only plants here of any height are small juniper bushes, and the area resembles an "alvar" (p. 42).

Breckland speedwell.

The western part of the area largely lacks soil cover, and the only flora are crustose lichens, furnishing the naked rocks with a greyish black surface. In the thin soil layer, which has been formed under the protection of the juniper bushes, lesser meadow-rue grow in abundance. St Bruno's lily grow in scattered groups. At many places the limestone pavement is criss-crossed by deep and narrow grykes, harbouring small ferns, such as wall-rue, maidenhair spleenwort and occasional brittle bladder fern. Wild pansy, which are rather uncommon on Gotland, have been found in this area of limestone outcrop. The rare Breckland speedwell, which bloom as early as in mid-May, have one of their few Gotlandic haunts here at the north end of Kyllaj hajdar. *Map on p. 81*

26 At the far end of the headland separating the bays of Hideviken in the west and Aurskallviken in the east lies **St Olofsholm**, today a promontory, but formerly an small island (hence the name holm = islet). The promontory consists of reef limestone with gently undulating slopes, terminating in a low cliff in the east. About 15 moderately tall sea stacks, rising from the nearshore zone, provided arguments for bringing St Olofsholm under the protection of a nature reserve. A long series of high shingle ridges stretch right up to the crest of the promontory. Intensive grazing characterizes the vegetation, which consists of grassy moors with low juniper bushes. Although it has not been used as pastureland for a very long time, no more than an occasional pine, spruce or whitebeam have managed to colonize the area. When winter storms rage, dispersing the snow cover, saplings lose the shelter they need for survival. The dry-rock flora on the south side of the promontory is very colourful. Bright yellow plants, such as common rock rose, hop trefoil and biting and tasteless stonecrop border the luxuriant viper's bugloss and spiked speedwell. A windmill without sails and a small house surmount the highest point of St Olofsholm. Remains of Gotland's first church are incorporated into the house. According to the Gute Tale, in 1029, Olaf the Holy of Norway stopped off at Gotland on one of his journeys and erected a church, which was later given the name The Church of St Olof. The marsh west of the church might have been the harbour that was in use at that time.

Off the east coast of St Olofsholm you can see the islet Ytterholmen, where black guillemots breed; they can sometimes be seen fishing just off St Olofsholm. The beach situated south east of the promontory consists of a wide abrasion limestone platform, which every now and then is covered by seawater. Beyond the platform, the sea floor suddenly plunges to a great depth.

The area west of St Olofsholm is characterized by scars from intensive limestone quarrying. Limeburning has been carried out here ever since the 17th century. Limestone was shipped from the harbour on the northern side of St Olofsholm right up until the 1950s. Remains of one of Gotland's oldest limekilns can be seen here. It was built at the beginning of the 17th century.

27 The beautiful **Hammarsänget** is bordered by forest and overgrown meadowland. A narrow, signposted road leads south from the road between Hellvi and Othem, to the meadow.

This is one of the few larger meadows in the north of Gotland; its beauty lies in its large open meadow plain, surrounded by a backdrop of magnificent, wide-crowned oaks.

The field layer is lush and relatively species-rich. The most common orchids are early purple, military and burnt orchids, with a peak blooming time at the beginning of June, when you will also find numerous narrow-leaved helleborine growing in the shade of shrubs.

During early summer, yellow and white buttercups and meadow saxifrage shine on the meadow plains. Communities of lily-of-the-valley, often growing next to viper's grass with similar leaves, can be very dense.

In the northwestern part of the meadow, there is a "pond", which is a water hole, once dug out to provide water for grazing cattle. Ponds are common in the Gotlandic meadows, reminiscent of times when livestock were released into the meadows during late summer, so that they could enjoy the fresh growth after haymaking. In the area

Hammarsänget, a forest meadow.

around the pond, the ground is waterlogged, harbouring a completely different vegetation from the drier meadow plains.

The wood warbler, which prefer tall-tree forests with little dense thicket, feel at ease in Hammarsänget, and usually accompany the collared flycatcher in the late spring chorus.

West and southwest of Hammarsänget, there is an area housing a large number of ancient monuments. The remains of an Iron Age farm are worthy of note. Two renowned picture stones, which are now part of the Bunge Museum collection, once stood in Hammarsänget.

28 The well-managed meadow, **Othems korsänge**, is situated about 300 metres WSW of Othem Church, immediately west of the Boge-Hangvar road. The meadow, which is extremely varied, supports a large number of birch and pine. With an almost total lack of shrubs, the meadow has a light and open character. The flora is rich in herbs, and many of the typical meadow plants can be studied here.

Some of the thick aspen at the northern end of the meadow have rotted; as a result of exposure to wind just a few tall stumps remain. The tree trunks have now become home to cavity-nesting birds. When the nesting cavities are abandoned by the woodpecker, they are taken over by other birds, such as tits and flycatchers.

29 (a) **Hejnum hällar** is an elevated area, rising to over 74 metres above sea level in the south. Along with Filehajdar in the northeast and Hejnum kallgate in the east, Hejnum hällar forms the largest area of limestone outcrop on Gotland. Towards the north, Filehajdar merges with Forsviden, a widespread area with large limestone outcrops.

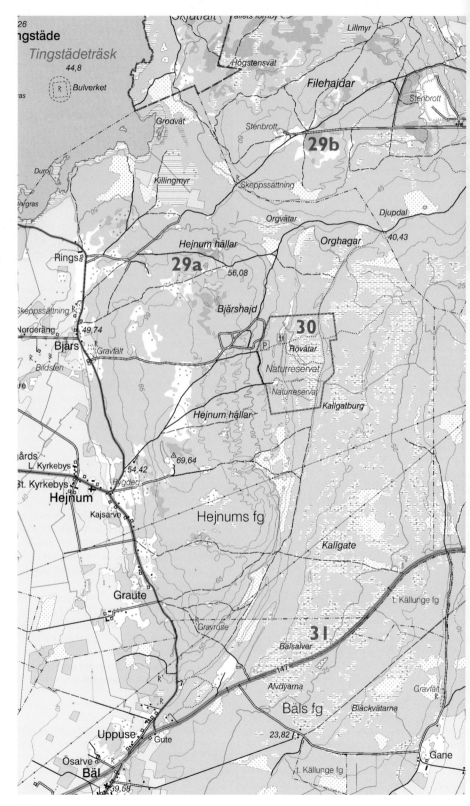

Tingstäde
Tingstädeträsk
44,8
R Bulverket
ras
Duroj
rgras
Grodvät
Killingmyr
Skjutfält
Lillmyr
Högstensvät
Filehajdar
Stenbrott
Stenbrott
29b
Skeppssättning
Orgvätar
Hejnum hällar
Djupdal
Orghagar
40,43
Rings
29a
56,08
Skeppssättning
Norderäng
49,74
Bjärs
Gravfält
R
Bildsten
re
Bjärshajd
P
30
Rovätar
Naturreservat
Naturreservat
Kallgatburg
Hejnum hällar
årds
L. Kyrkebys
St. Kyrkebys
54,42
Bygdeg
69,64
Hejnum
Kajsarve
Hejnums fg
Kallgate
Graute
Gravröse
t. Källunge fg
31
Bälsalver
147
Alvdyarna
Gravfält
Bäls fg
Bläckvätarna
Uppuse
Gute
23,82
Ösarve
Bäl
39,58
Gane
t. Källunge fg

84

St Bruno's lily (left) do not bloom until July, whereas the Eastern Pasque flower (right) bloom at the beginning of May.

The northern part of Hejnum hällar is best reached by following the small blue signs marked "Gotlandsleden" in an easterly direction from the farm Rings, about 1 km south of the lake Tingstädeträsk. The road passes through a sparse inland rock pine forest, at one point cutting through a small area with deeper soil cover, harbouring a vigorous spruce forest which supports a community of the rather rare northern bedstraw.

After about 2 kms along small, narrow roads, there is an open, almost treeless area on the right hand side of the road. This is a good place to stop for a while, since the area shows features typical of large parts of Hejnum hällar. The limestone pavement is largely covered with a thin layer of soil, but here and there it is completely bare, apart from a blackish grey growth of crustose lichens. The vegetation is sparse and consists of species which are typical of the Gotlandic limestone outcrops. During the few weeks from the end of June, when the white stonecrop blooms, the ground is carpeted in pink. A taller lesser meadowrue grows practically everywhere in the dry grounds of Gotland, and is very common at Hejnum hällar. Wild cotoneaster, which blooms in early summer and bears light red berries at the beginning of July, is related to the cultivated cotoneaster, which can be found in many private gardens. Common fumana cannot be found anywhere in Sweden other than on Öland and Gotland, where it is infrequent. A large community of common fumana grows just south of the road; this dry undershrub spreads along the ground and is difficult to discern. It only blooms for a few hours on sunny mornings in June and July.

Today, limestone outcrops are considered as useless and of no economic value. In former times, however, all ground was used. The dry outcrop with its thin soil cover could obviously not be used for cultivation, but was suitable pastureland for sheep, goats and young cattle. Pastures in forests and on the outcrops have existed until quite recently, although they have now mostly been abandoned. Once livestock left the outcrops, vegetation has undergone considerable changes. At Hejnum hällar, several plants which are sensitive to grazing are now increasing in number; St Bruno's lily, with their beautiful white lily petals and long yellow stamens is one example, growing in abundance throughout the month of July. Another example is angular Solomon's seal, which bloom at the same time as the lily-of-the-valley. Ciliate melick is a grass that also returned, once grazing had been abandoned. The grass is hardly noticeable during most of the summer, but at the end of July, when the seeds are ripe, the scale enveloping the floret splits, revealing a fringe of white hairs. The spikelet now becomes light and fluffy, shimmering like a jewel in the sun.

Very few sounds are heard when roaming around Hejnum hällar; in fact the atmosphere is uncanningly desolate. Although woodlark have become rare in most parts of Sweden, there is still a stable community on the Gotlandic limestone outcrops. The clear, somewhat melancholy yodelling song, delivered in flight high-up, can often be heard across Hejnum hällar.

(b) The large limestone outcrop area of **Filehajdar**, northeast of Hejnum hällar, has long had the status of an area of outstanding scientific interest. Included among its priceless treasures is Gotland's largest lek for black grouse and Scandi-

85

Rövätar, marshland at Kallgatburg nature reserve.

navia's largest habitat for the Eastern Pasque flower. Thus, when the Cementa enterprise sought permission to quarry limestone at Filehajdar, they met with great opposition from the public. The battle between Cementa and conservationists became drawn-out, but the government finally granted Cementa permission to quarry. A large road has now been blasted from Slite to the centre of Filehajdar, where quarrying is now in full swing.

The large community of Eastern Pasque flower, growing in the area around a former stone quarry, is still in existence. The east road, which was formerly the pilgrimage route used by nature enthusiasts during the first half of May when the Eastern Pasque flower was in bloom, has been closed off, and Eastern Pasque flower-fans are relegated to a poor road from the west.

Map on p. 84.

30 The nature reserve **Kallgatburg** is situated east of Hejnum hällar. It harbours a large stand of yew and a marsh with flush fen vegetation. An easy, well-defined, 2 km-long nature trail runs through the nature reserve.

The road to Kallgatburg is signposted about 2 kms north of Hejnum Church. It runs east, gently ascending to the centre of Hejnum hällar, then making a gentle descent on the east side of the outcrop area. There is a car park after a little more than 2 kms. You can then roam some hundred metres through the forest, when you will arrive at a small piece of enclosed pastureland, where the nature trail begins.

At the outset, you will notice that the ground slopes rather steeply in an eastward direction. The slope marks the border between two areas with different bedrock. Hejnum hällar, in the west, is part of a large area of pure limestone. Hejnum kallgate, in the east, is part of the large belt of marlstone which stretches across the entire island in a southwesterly direction. The limestone at Hejnum hällar is full of grykes, which quickly drain off all rainwater, leaving a very dry area. The marlstone, on the other hand, is dense, and Hejnum kallgate has all the characteristics of a large swampy area.

On arrival at the marshy area of Rövätar, you will have entered Hejnum kallgate. The flush fen vegetation of the marsh, including birdseye primrose, Alpine butterwort, German asphodel and short-spurred fragrant orchid can be viewed from the causeway across Rövätar, whose east flanks form part of the Kallgatburg nature reserve.

The nature trail leads through the nature reserve to its eastern end, where one of the largest stands of yew in the country grows along a high Ancylus shingle beach ridge, which is composed of coarse sand and small, rounded, flat limestone pebbles, and was formed about 8 000 years ago, when the Ancylus lake, one of the predecessors to the present day Baltic Sea, retained its highest water level for a long space of time.

Formerly, the main road from Fårösund to Visby ran along the top of the Ancylus shingle ridge, which provided a firm substrate through the surrounding swampy ground. A pleasant detour can be made by walking northwards along the Ancylus ridge, instead of sticking to the southbound nature trail. The forest growing on the ridge is a typical example of "basiphilous pine forest". This habitat, which is rare outside of Gotland and Öland, is characterised by a very lush field layer with an abundance of grass and great richness of herbs. Large communities of lily-of-the-valley and angular Solomon's seal grow in the forest on the Ancylus ridge. Heather is also abundant, indicating that the soil is not as calcareous as on the rest of the island. The Ancylus ridge continues a couple of kilometres further north, where it turns off in an easterly direction.

Just south of the point where the nature trail arrives at the Ancylus ridge, there is a wide track leading north east. A 1 km walk will lead you to a community of lady's slipper. This orchid was discovered in 1950, and has become the main object of many day trips at the beginning of June, when it is in full bloom. The popularity of the site is probably the reason why this protected species has never been dug up or picked.

Map on p. 84.

One of Gotland's few Lady's Slipper sites, not far from Kallgatburg.

31 A few kilometres north east of Bäl Church, the Visby-Slite road passes through a large area of ephemeral swamps, promoting a singular landscape, known as **Bälsalvret**. Juniper bushes and small clusters of knotty pine trees grow on the grey ground surface, otherwise almost totally lacking in vegetative cover.

Bälsalvret is part of a large area of flat, limestone outcrop, known as Hejnum kallgate, which continues in a northerly direction along the east flank of Hejnum hällar. Bälsalvret differs from the usual type of Gotlandic limestone outcrop in many ways. The bedrock at Bälsalvret and Hejnum kallgate consists of marlstone, a relatively soft type of limestone, with a high content of clay. The features of the marlstone explain the special character of the area. Most areas of flat limestone outcrop consist of hard, stratified limestone, containing numerous grykes, which drain off rainwater very quickly, leaving a parched area. The marlstone at Bälsalvret, on the other hand, is dense, impeding infiltration.

Marlstone is easily eroded, producing fine-grained soil of calcium-rich clay known as "alvar mo". Bälsalvret is situated in a shallow depression in the terrain, and alvar mo has thus been transported here with rainwater, resulting in a several decimetre thick accumulation. No more than a moderate rainfall is needed for the alvar mo to become saturated, and since almost no water is drained, the soil has a consistency of thick porridge most of the year.

Vegetation is sparse at Bälsalvret – although plants tolerate this extreme habitat, they do not exactly thrive, so they are not able to form continuous carpets of vegetation. The few species that do grow here offer a good display of bloom during the summer. Bälsalvret is renowned for its abundance of great burnet, which cannot be found anywhere in Sweden outside Gotland. Its tiny, dark red flowers on dense, oblong heads can be seen at the beginning of July. Orchids face little competition from other plants and thrive so long as the summers are not too dry. Dark red helleborine and fragrant orchid flourish, and short-spurred fragrant

Great burnet.

orchid are prolific. There is also a profusion of lesser butterfly orchid.

When water in the alvar mo freezes and expands in winter, movements in the ground can sever the roots of more fragile plants, and tree-roots are slowly pressed upwards until they finally emerge above ground surface. Everywhere long, dead roots stretch out from the small pine groves. Even summers can be detrimental to the plants. Since alvar mo forms a relatively thin layer, the ground is swiftly parched. Anyone walking across Bäls-alvret after a long period of drought will notice that the ground is so dry that dust forms underfoot, calling attention to the fact that the plants are suffering from shortage of water.

Map on p. 84.

32 Although oak and ash are prevalent at **Laxare änge**, the meadow is characterized by numerous birch and a remarkably rich stand of magnificent hazel clusters. Some of the oaks are old and the solitary oaks are often strikingly beautiful. At the southern end of the meadow there are a few solitary thick aspen, as well as scattered old crab apple trees and small yew saplings. Profuse dogwood and hawthorn add to the variety of shrubs.

The flora differs greatly from one part of the meadow to the next. The ground is largely rather damp, and the low blue moor grass is the most common grass. Orchids grow in profusion and include early purple, military and fragrant orchids. Grass is more abundant and grows tall in other areas of higher, drier ground. Early summer blooms are dominated by buttercups, meadow saxifrage and cow parsely, whereas orchids play a subordinate role. Narrow-leaved helleborine thrive in the shade of the hazel bushes.

There are several ancient monuments in the meadow, including remains of house foundations.

A former road cuts through the meadow, and is bordered by a double row of hazel bushes just by the entrance to the meadow.

Laxare meadow is situated about 2 kms north of Boge Church, slightly west of the Boge-Othem road.

33 **Bogeklinten**, also known as Klinteberget, is situated adjacent to the Boge-Gothem road, 1 km south of the 147 and 146 crossroads. Boge-klinten is an inland cliff with steep sides, towering 15-20 metres above its surroundings. The eastern side of the cliff is ornamented with sea stacks, which spread a few hundred metres along the slope. The sea stacks at the north end of the sea stack field are tall and narrow, whereas in the south they are more squat and covered with shrubs and trees.

The limestone outcrops at Bogeklinten are largely overgrown with juniper bushes and brush-wood. Some sections are exposed, bearing a colourful, xeric hillside flora. The ground surface here is slightly undulating. When the surrounding less-resistent limestone was firstly eroded by the inland ice, and later weathered by waves and wind, the more resistant reef limestone remained intact, forming small hummocks.

Those of you who are not aware of the fact that there are two types of wild strawberry in the Swedish flora, will have the opportunity of getting to know the less common green strawberry, which grows ubiquitously at Bogeklinten. Although green strawberry exists on the mainland, it is of rare occurrence, since it thrives on dry, calciferous soils. Provided the summer is not too dry, you can pick large berries, which taste much sweeter than the common wild strawberry. Apart from the taste, the green strawberry is also recognisable by the fact that the sepals remain attached to picked berries.

Laxare änge, a forest meadow.

34 The medium-sized, well-managed and beautiful **Lummelunda parish meadow** lies behind Lummelunda Church. It is dominated by ash pollards, which are often wrapped in a "stocking" of vigorous hazel bushes. The meadow also harbours a number of oaks that tower far higher than the manageable ash. A community of small-leaved elm can be seen at the northern end of the meadow.

During early summer, the myriads of cow parsely and wood cranesbill, growing in open spaces, paint the meadow in a blaze of colours. Ramsons thrive in the shade.

Map on p. 89.

35 **Landträsk**, which once lay in the northwest corner of the marsh Martebomyr, was one of the largest lakes on Gotland. When Martebomyr was reclaimed in the mid 19th century, Landträsk was also drained. In 1976, a large dam, about 20 hectacres in size, was constructed on the drained lake bed. It is now used for the irrigation of surrounding farmlands. Vegetation and insects have gradually colonised the dam, providing a valuable incentive to breeding and feeding birds.

When the bird life was surveyed in 1978 – the third summer in the life of the dam – sufficient common reed had grown for about 15 bird species to find suitable breeding spots. Along with the tufted duck and pochard, other breeding birds included the great crested, horned and little grebe. A further 25 species of birds were sighted, although they probably did not breed.

The area around the irrigation dam consists of the former lake bed of Landträsk. The aim of draining off Martebomyr was to cultivate the reclaimed lake bed as well. Today, however, this area provides a striking example of how the hu-

Landträskdammen is a favourite haunt of the grey heron.

man race has failed to reshape nature. The ground is infertile and impossible to cultivate. Although so many years have passed since the lake was drained off, there is still no more than a very sparse vegetation cover. Solitary, gnarled pine trees grow here in a sea of sparse common reed, a vegetation which has appropriately been called pine-reed savannah.

A smaller junction, about 1½ kms southeast of Lummelunda Church along the main road, leads to the north end of the irrigation dam. The dam is best viewed from the top of the bank surrounding it.

Map on p. 89.

36 **Lummelunds bruk** is the site of the entrance to one of Sweden's longest underground caves and of remains of a former industrial complex, housing ironworks, papermill, flour mill, etc.

The mouth of the Lummelunda underground caves was known and written about as early as in the 17th century, but the inner caves remained unknown until present-day. As late as in 1948, three boys squeezed their way through a narrow outer passage, thus becoming the first human beings to enter the part of the cave which today is open to the public. The boys' explorational adventure led to an increased interest in caves, and several expeditions were undertaken during the ensuing years. In 1959 a new entrance to the cave was blasted open, and the public admitted to guided tours. Today, the cave is Gotland's most popular tourist attraction with 100 000 visitors each year.

To date, almost 3 kms of subterranean tunnels have been investigated and documented, making the cave one of the largest in Sweden. However, there are in all probability numerous side tunnels still waiting to be discovered. In the small part of the cave which is open to the public, encrustations of travertine, known as dripstones, adopt many beautiful forms.

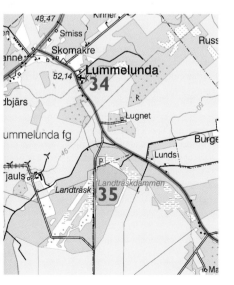

The ground in the park at Lummelundsbruk is carpeted with the white flowers of ramson.

Lummelunda caves were originally formed by water seeking its way through narrow cracks in the rock. The water carved out the rock partly by mechanical wear, but mainly through its solvent action – calcium carbonate was chemically dissolved by the carbonic acid in the water. As the cavities in the rock enlarged, greater quantities of water could flow underground, accelerating the formation of caverns by ever-widening channels. The water which still flows through the caverns disappears into the ground through several so-

Pyramidal orchid in bloom at Lummelundsbruk in the first two weeks of July.

called sink or swallow holes, which today lie at the bottom of a dug canal. The water comes from the marsh Martebomyr, once forming a strong current through the cavern, but since the marsh was drained off at the end of the 19th century, water flow has decreased tremendously, except during the spring thaw. Nobody knows how long the cavern formation took, but it is widely believed that it was scooped out before and during the latest glaciation.

Intensive industrial activity has taken place at Lummelunds bruk. In the 1620s, six water-powered mills were in use beside the stream Lummelundaån. These included sawmills, flour mills, and later iron works and a small paper mill. The stream still generates a large millwheel, open to the public under the name "Northern Europe's largest millwheel".

A grove-like deciduous forest, originally laid out as an English park, grows south of the stream Lummelundaån, beneath the late 19th century manor. High, thick ash, maple and elm trees provide the ground with dense shade. During early summer, ramsons bloom in a thick, white carpet in the park. You will be overwhelmed by the scent of onion as you wander through the grove down to the sea. In the glades, ground vegetation is lush; cow parsely and wood cranesbill compete to secure the lion's share of the nutritious soil.

During early summer, the choir of small birds in the shady park is almost deafening; choristers include the wren, various songbirds and the collared flycatcher. For a number of years, tawny owls have been nesting in one of the old, hollow tree trunks.

The stream, Lummelundaån is fringed by vigorous alder. The kingfisher was once a regular breeder here, but is now only seen on occasions. Every year, at the end of October, dippers arrive to spend the winter by the stream, and in 1981 a pair of dippers stayed on to breed, although this proved to be a one-off occasion. In late autumn, sea trout spawn in the stream.

On the beach, south of the estuary of Lummelundaån, there are a couple of botanical rarities. Hairy milk vetch and fastigiate gypsophila grow on the sandy ground among the juniper bushes. Northwest of the car park beneath the mill, there is a meadow which is becoming overgrown. A large community of pyramidal orchids can be found there.

37 Brucebo nature reserve could be said to contain a consolidation of the wildlife of Gotland. The area harbours good examples of many Gotlandic habitats.

The 2½ km-long nature trail, leading visitors through the reserve, has two starting points. A junction to road 149, signposted "Naturreservat" leads to one. Further north, the road to Själsö fishing hamlet leads to the car park entrance and the starting point north of the nature reserve.

The crown of the cliff, housing the remains of a hill fort known as "Bygdeborg", is a magnificent viewpoint. Directly beneath the cliff is Skansudd – a typical example of a sand spit. Sand-spits are formed by longshore currents which transport particles, depositing them where the shoreline projects seaward, slowing down the wave fronts.

Further north along the coast are the two fishing hamlets Själsö and Brissund, with harbours laid out on similar sand-spit formations. (Visby was

Cave in cliff at Brucebo nature reserve.

actually once built around a large sand-spit. Still today, it is quite apparent that Almedalen, the innermost part of the bay landward of the sand-spit, was the site of the first harbour of Visby).

The calm, shallow water within Skansudd provides favourable conditions for a rich birdlife. Numerous species of ducks, waders and terns breed here, and the calm water within Skansudd is also a resting place for migrating birds – flocks of ducks and waders sometimes gather here in autumn. Skansudd is under site protection legislation; access is prohibited from 15th March-31st July.

The nature trail descending from the crown of the cliff is distinctly terraced. Each ledge reflects the different sea levels following the latest glaciation. The Littorina Sea has carved out caves and left overhanging rocks in the cliff face. The finest example is the 8-metre deep cave, Brucebogrottan. The swell of the waves has also formed several distinct shingle beach ridges along the slopes.

A sparse and stunted flat rock pine forest grows on top of the cliff and other parts of the slopes. Further down, water percolates between different beds of limestone, providing the necessary nutrients for a lush spruce forest.

Ivy can be seen weaving its way up some of the trees and slopes. Mezereon, which is a rare shrub on Gotland, is scattered along the slopes, and blooms at the beginning of May.

At some places, the water flow from the cliff is so strong that small brooks are formed, in which you will find the extremely rare hybrid between

View of Skansudd from cliff top.

watercress and one-rowed watercress. Wherever water from the cliff flows across the ground below, flush fens have formed, supporting the typical flush fen plants, such as birdseye primrose, Alpine butterwort, Pugsley's marsh orchid and common cotton grass.

On the way down to the beach, where a wind-swept pine forest grows, the nature trail passes a small sedge fen.

Within the protected area of Skansudd, the path passes through humid grassy meadows, where numerous marsh helleborine, fly and Pugsley's marsh orchids bloom in July. The tiny, almost imperceptible musk orchid grows just beside the trail at one point.

38 The small parish meadow of Bro is situated just northeast of Bro Church. The managed sections harbour pine trees, many of which are old, thick and very majestic. The undergrowth is species-poor, but rather lush, due to the tall-growing cow parsely, which is one of the prevalent species.

On the mainland, forests growing on calcite-poor substrate mainly have a ground cover of lichens, mosses and brushwood. On Gotland, however, grasses and herbs grow profusely, even in coniferous forests, provided the soil is not too thin and dry. These conditions afford a rich harvest even in meadows supporting large stands of pine. A pure pine forest meadow, such as the one at Bro, must have been of little significance, however, in this large area of deciduous forest, where foliage constitutes an important source of fodder.

Some bird cherry trees are growing in the dense vegetation beside the canal at the east end of the meadow. They probably derive from a garden, since bird cherry does not grow naturally on Gotland.

39 Visitors confined to the town of **Visby**, need not leave without some nature exploration. Below, are some examples of what can be seen in and around Visby.

(a) Intra-mural Visby is actually a sparsely built-up and very green town. The houses bordering the streets give the impression of a built up area, while concealing well-maintained green back gardens. The birdlife of the town was carefully recorded in 1978; about 950 pairs of breeding birds of about 29 different species were found. The most common species are the house sparrow, blackbird, domestic pigeon and collared turtle dove. On summer evenings, nobody can avoid noticing the numerous common swifts, shrieking shrilly, while flying in formation above the town, catching insects on the wing.

In the evenings you will also see hedgehogs emerge from the back gardens and scurry around in the streets. Unfortunately, they are easy prey for inattentive car drivers.

The town wall supports a number of interesting botanical features. The keen-eyed walker will discover patches of ivy-leaved toadflax with their violet petals draping over the wall. Perennial wall rocket is a yellow crucifer, which has attached itself to the wall at several places. The small fern maidenhair spleenwort, normally found in the grykes of the limestone pavements, also grows on the wall.

Ivy-leaved toadflax in bloom on the northern section of Visby town-wall.

(b) Almedalen is a green park surrounding the remains of the Medieval harbour of Visby – today a duck pond. Originally, the harbour was protected by a spit of sand and gravel, created by southbound longshore sea currents. The harbour gradually became shallower, due to isostatic rise, and was eventually abandoned.

Numerous overwintering ducks provide the pond with a rich bird life.

(c) The Botanic Gardens of Visby were laid out in 1855 by a society called DBW (The Bathing Friends). It is one of the oldest botanic gardens in Sweden, and in many's opinion the most beautiful. Its sheltered location just behind the sea wall, and the mild climate, have enabled the growth of many trees which would normally not be found in these latitudes; here they thrive and bear fruit which ripen. The long, mild autumns allow plants to bloom right up until November-December. Birdlife is rich, and you will almost certainly find the collared flycatcher here in early summer.

(d) Östergravar and **Nordergravar**, the areas immediately north and east of the town wall, are known as "Northern Moats" and "Eastern Moats" and are pleasant roaming areas. The dry meadow flora is often rich and interesting here. The large depressions, known as "moats" were formed when building material was excavated for the wall and town. Down towards the sea along Nordergravar, a profusion of the large, rhubarb-like leaves of butterbur can be seen in the summer.

(e) On **Galgberget** (Gallows Hill) there is a rich dry meadow flora with many rare plants which are dependent on, and have been spread by land management. Plants growing here include lady's mantle, white mullein, large speedwell, weld and longleaf. Trees include the whitebeam variations rock whitebeam and Greek ash, the latter originally cultivated, but now widespread, probably due to berry-eating birds. The most rare plant on Galgberget is a Gotlandic variation of salsify, which can only be found at a few habitats on Gotland.

There is a large community of butterbur along Nordergravar.

The rare crocus-leaved goatsbeard (left) is found on Galgberget. The collared turtle dove (right) breed in the town centre at Visby.

(f) Kärleksstigen (Lover's Lane) begins beneath Galgberget, beside the maze called "Troja-borg". It leads up to Gustavsvik through a pleasant roaming area. The path passes some grove-like areas with dense carpets of ramsons. Laburnum bloom in abundance in the meadows in early summer. The rare, protected sea kale can be seen just north of the bathing beach Norderstrand.

(g) Åsbergska hagen is an enclosed pasture owned by the society DBW and consists of open meadows fringed by grove-like forests, in which vigorous, old pines are prevalent.The main attraction here is the unbelievable abundance of ivy, which forms densely carpeted patches on the ground. The ivy often weaves its way up tree trunks, sometimes completely enveloping the tree right up to the crown.

(h) On both sides of the gravel road which forms the northwest boundary of Åsbergska hagen, there are small **flush fens**, suporting an array of sensitive flush fen plants such as common cotton-grass,

brown bog-rush, marsh helleborine, fly, Pugsley's marsh and fragrant orchids. Large clumps of great fen sedge, as well as marsh valerian, which is very rare on Gotland, grow in one of the fens.

(i) Just south of the town wall, on a cliff sloping down to the harbour, is a shady and peaceful park area, known as "**Pallisaderna**". A smaller brook flows through the park; it has cut out a series of small continuous ravines in the limestone rock, where the sequence of strata down to a depth of 30 metres is in full view. At the beginning of the century, a large number of samples were collected from just about every centimetre of the sequence of strata. The samples then remained untouched until the 1970s, when their fossil content was surveyed by a number of experts. A total of about 500 fossilised faunal species were found, of which many were previously unknown. The most renowned of these is a very well-preserved scorpion.

Map on p. 93

Glade in Åsbergska hagen (enclosed pasture).

*Common fumana
in bloom.*

40 Ölbäcks hällmarksområde is an open, almost treeless area of flat limestone outcrop, harbouring a species-rich and typical flora, with occurrences of several rarities. It is situated a few kms outside Visby and about 500 metres before the junction to Follingbo hospital. Öl means beer, and refers to the pub which was once situated just west of the outcrop.

The outcrop at Ölbäck is almost totally lacking in grykes. Most of the outcrop is covered with a thin layer of soil, topped by a layer of eroded calcareous gravel; the remainder is completely bare.

Although the area is practically treeless, it is richer in different species of shrubs. Apart from juniper and blackthorn, bearberry, common and

Thyme broomrape with its host wild thyme.

alder buckthorn, rowan and Swedish wild service tree can also be found. Stonecrop is a succulent plant which grows on very thin soil cover. In order to survive the long arid summers, stonecrop have thick, fleshy stems and leaves designed to retain water. Ölbäck harbours three species. The low, creeping tufts of biting stonecrop bloom at the beginning of June. White stonecrop, which form large, continuous carpets, have white flowers, but are also recognizable by their red stems. Reflexed stonecrop can reach a height of ten centimetres, and bloom with bright yellow flowers in July.

Different plants attract attention at Ölbäck at different times of the year. In April and the beginning of May, while the thin soil cover is still damp, the small annuals bloom; Rue-leaved saxifrage, dwarf mouse-ear, little mouse ear and common whitlow grass are some of the plants casting a white veil over the outcrop. At the beginning of June, the abundance of light purple chive flowers draw attention. At, and about a fortnight after Midsummer, dyer's woodruff and bloody cranesbill bloom, despite the fact that the soil is often bone dry, following a long period of drought. When the blue breckland speedwell bloom in July, at the same time as the yellow lady's bedstraw, the outcrop takes on the colours of the Swedish flag.

Areas of thicker soil cover, mainly consisting of sand, can be found scattered around the outcrops. This is the haunt of the sheepsbit scabious and the greater butterfly orchid. The small Pasque flower also thrive here. The rare proliferous pink require dry, sandy soils, and the occasional specimen can be found on the outcrops at Ölbäck.

Some rather profuse communities of common fumana grow in the northern part of the outcrop. In June and July the common fumana are in bloom an hour or so each day, most often early in the morning.

Thyme broomrape is a rare plant, which can be found in the proximity of the outcrop at Ölbäcke. As the name suggests, this plant is parasitic on thyme, and can be found in carpets of wild thyme, south of the road at the western end of the area. *Map on p. 93.*

41 Some kilometre southeast of Visby there is a long, narrow area of flat limestone outcrop, which is quite different from any other outcrop on Gotland. A wide gravel road, leading from **Langs hage**/road 142 to **Slättflis**/road 143, runs along its border.

Limestone in the Gotlandic bedrock has been formed by the deposition of lime mud, layer upon layer, at the bottom of a shallow sea, normally producing flat, horizontal outcrops. The outcrops between Langs hage and Slättflis deviate completely from this rule. From the gravel road, you can see how they rise to a "vault" towards the south east, and at some places they are distinctly hummocky. Bedrock geologists took an early interest in this area, and measured up to a 30° gradient in the layers, a feature that remains unexplained to this day. The bedrock has probably been compressed from the sides, and crumpled into folds, as the result of tectonic collision.

The outcrops in the area have been particularly susceptible to weathering. Calcium carbonate has been chemically dissolved and removed by rainwater. At certain places, intense weathering has widened the original deep joints to half-metre wide rills. Near Langs hage, erosion has worked on the joints in several crossing directions, creating a system of large blocks, arranged in a symmetrical pattern.

The outcrops between Slättflis and Langs hage support many of the common outcrop plants, some of which thrive particularly well adjacent to the rills. The small fern wall-rue is common at the tops of the grykes. Hepatica grow in the constant shade of the deep grykes. Some of the pines, which grow sparsely on the outcrops, are of a great age. At some places, there are also many dead trees.

The long, narrow outcrop leads to sandy soil in the southeast, where the trees have better access to nutrients and water, and the trees shoot tall, straight trunks in a much denser forest than on the outcrops. The ground is thickly carpeted with heather.

At Slättflishage, south of the outcrop area, a large community of eastern Pasque flowers grows in a protected area. This is the grandest of all Gotlandic anemones, standing in full bloom from the end of April until mid-May. *Map on p. 93.*

Karst formations at Langs hage.

42 The **flush fen at Klinte in Follingbo** supports typical flush fen vegetation and a very large community of short-spurred fragrant orchid about 5 kms SE of Visby and 2 kms NW of Follingbo Church. On the Visby-Roma road, you will notice that the scenery suddenly changes. Some kilometre before the road passes Follingbo Church, the terrain slopes downwards, and the forest is transformed into agricultural landscape. Here you pass the border between an area of stratified limestone in the north west, and marley limestone in the south east. Where the slope at Klinte is steepest, water emerges from a joint between the permeable stratified limestone and the less permeable marlstone, forming a border-like flush fen.

From the middle to the end of July, the scent of hundreds of fragrant orchids and short-spurred fragrant orchid hangs heavily over the fen at Klinte. This is an excellent opportunity to compare the short-spurred fragrant orchid with the tall and late-blooming type of fragrant orchid. The short-spurred variety is not as tall as the fragrant orchid, and is often more faded in colour. The three lobes of the lip of the fragrant orchid are of equal length, whereas the lip of the short-spurred variety has an elongated middle lobe. The short-spurred variety also has a shorter spur than the fragrant orchid, as

Brown bog-rush is a characteristic plant of the flush fen.

the name suggests. The difference between the light fragrance of the fragrant orchid and the musky scent of the short-spurred variety is palpable after a while. The early summer blooms of birdseye primrose and German asphodel have by now been reduced to withered stems.

Brown bog-rush is prevalent in the flush fen, although there is a large community of purple moor-grass. Rough small-reed grows around the margins and on certain tussocks out in the fen; this grass is otherwise mainly found in drier coniferous forests. Yellow-flowered tormentil creep between the tussocks of brown bog-rush in the fen, and there are scattered small clusters of broadleaved cotton grass.

Fragrant orchid with long, slender spurs.

The flush fen follows the slope westwards for about 600-700 metres, although it has now largely lost its natural character. At some places pine forest has wandered in, and the brown bog-rush has been completely outstripped by dry soil grasses. In areas which are still open, the brown bog-rush has been joined by a large community of common reed.

Overgrowth has mainly been caused by deep ditches which were dug along the slope to collect and lead off water. Although flush fens are of but marginal economic significance, they are often subjected to drainage, aimed at increasing forest growth. Many of the finest flush fens on Gotland have been destroyed in this way.

Map on p. 93.

43 One of the highest cliffs along the Gotlandic coast can be found at **Högklint**, about 7 kms south of Visby. This is reached by turning off the southbound road 140 from Visby towards Kneippbyn and Högklint. The road leads right up to the renowned viewpoint, which is part of a small nature reserve.

At Högklint, the cliff towers 48 metres above sea level, providing a magnificent view towards the north east, where Fridhem, Knieppbyn and Visby are situated. Towards the south you can see the steep-cliffed coast and the coniferous forest-clad terrain towards the inland. Do not venture too close to the edge, as the overhang presents an ever-present danger of rockfall.

From the clifftop, steps lead down to a ledge called "Getsvältan". Goats, which once grazed at Högklint, were often lured to the succulent grass on the ledge; unable to return to the clifftop, they remained to starve to death. By Getsvältan you can see cave formations in the cliff face.

Up on the cliff plateau, where the forest has been thinned and cleared of undergrowth, there are numerous specimens of the vigorous and large-leaved umbellifer, sermountain.

From the viewpoint, you can walk southwards through the nature reserve. Quite a number of the toxic red-berried elder, and even occasional common elders grow along the path. At the height of summer dark red helleborine bloom on the dry ground. Rock whitebeam can be seen here and there; they are recognized by their whole, unlobed leaves, with silvery white undersides. Rock whitebeam grows in a few coastal areas in our country. On Gotland they are mainly found along the west and north cliffed coasts, where they have probably been favoured by the mild autumn maritime climate.

In the middle of the nature reserve, there are two clefts, the results of landslide in the soft, marly limestone. At the south end of the reserve, the

Cliffed coast at Högklint nature reserve.

sliding of a whole stretch of cliff has formed a large "false sea stack" on the beach. The cleft left behind is known as " Lilja the Bandit's Den". The thief Jonas Lilja sought his final refuge here in the mid 18th century, before being captured. The top of the talus, where a few small pines grow, still contains pristine pebble deposition.

From Högklint, the nature reserve stretches about 1 km to the south along the coastline. If you feel like a longer walk, keep going south along the path, and after about another 500 metres you will arrive at a picturesque fishing hamlet at Ynge.

44 A signposted junction about 2 kms west of Endre Church on the Visby-Endre road leads to **Allekvia meadow**. When traditional management was restored in the 1940s, Allekvia had been abandoned for a very long period. The meadow is one of the largest on Gotland, and was brought under the protection of a nature reserve in 1980.

Shapely oaks and small-leaved elms are prevalent in the meadow. Ash are also common, and these, like some of the small-leaved elms are often pollarded. Contrary to common practice in most meadows, where trees are clustered in groups, the trees in Allekvia meadow are rather evenly distributed. The glades are therefore small and shady, especially at the east end of the meadow.

The flora varies from place to place in the meadow. At the entrance, the meadow is open.

Dropwort, common rock rose and bloody cranesbill are indicators of rather dry ground. In the central parts of the meadow, wood cranesbill, buttercups and common cow-wheat are most frequent in the shade of the trees. At the south end, the meadow has become overgrown and taken on a grove-like character, with a ground-carpet of ramsons.

A nature trail has been laid out through the reserve. Signs describe the history, management and wildlife of the Gotlandic forest meadows.

45 South of Ekeby Church, the surroundings are particularly shady. **Mangsarveänget**, a medium-sized, oak-prevalent forest meadow is situated east of the road, and just over 100 metres south of the church. Just inside the entrance there is a sign board describing the history of the meadow, and presenting a list of the plants which have been discovered there.

In the part of the meadow facing the road, vegetation is dense. The ground is damp, and meadowsweet, buttercups and water aven thrive. Herbs like twayblade and herb Paris flourish in the dense shade. Wood sedge with hanging female spikes is very common.

The east end of the meadow is drier and more open. Large glades are fringed by groups of oaks and small-leaved elms with a few pines. The large glades were created so that the mowed hay could be spread out to dry in the sun.

Dropwort in bloom in late summer in Mangsarveänget (forest meadow).

In Mangsarveänget, ash are not as numerous as in most Gotlandic meadows. They have been replaced by the small-leaved elm which are abundant. Small-leaved elm are recognisable at a distance by their short twigs and foliage which is attached to the trunk.

The open meadows have an abundance of dropwort, which along with numerous tall, vigorous spotted catsear and large harebells, add splashes of colour to the meadow at the end of June. Communities of crested dogstail (a grass mainly found on enclosed pastureland) also occur.

North of the meadow and west of the road, sheep graze in the open and beautiful oak grove.

46 The road to Alvena lindaräng runs eastward, about 300 metres north of Vallstena Church. The meadow, which is surrounded by cultivated fields, is one of the largest managed meadows on Gotland. Gotland's largest stand of small-leaved lime grows in the meadow, where they are prevalent; they occur only sparsely on the rest of the island. Oak, ash, small-leaved elm and occasional shrubs and aspen also grow here. Many of the lime and ash trees are low-cut pollards.

Fungi often invade pollards, seeking their way into the sores in the sawn-off branches. As the trees rot, cavities are formed, which are used as nesting

places by a series of different birds. In Alvena lindaräng, numerous starlings and jackdaws nest in the pollards. Both starlings and jackdaws thrive here, since the surrounding fields offer rich access to nutrition. Collared flycatcher also nest in these cavities, and are as common here as in most forest meadows. The tawny owl has also been a long-standing regular in the meadow.

The flora in Alvena linaräng is usually characterized as poor in grass but rich in herbs. The meadow is not least rich in orchids, and twelve different species have been seen here, which is a large number for a single meadow. Fragrant orchids are particularly abundant during the weeks prior to midsummer. At the same time, numerous lesser butterfly orchids are in bloom. Viper's grass is very common in the whole meadow; its leaves can be found not only in meadows but even in coniferous forests with luxuriant ground vegetation.

Alvena linaräng displays distinct traces of prehistoric human activity. Apart from several house foundations from the Iron Age, there are a number of remains of dry stone walls, which may have been built to keep animals in or out, or as demarcation.

47 Lina myr was the last large marsh to be drained off on Gotland. Before drainage, it was not only one of the largest remaining marshes, but also the unsurpassably richest as regards bird life and vegetation. The drainage of the marsh was thus preceded by a long campaign to preserve it. Prior to drainage, the marsh covered an area of over 900 hectacres and included the two lakes of Råby and Lina. The enormously rich bird life in the marsh, prior to cultivation of the land, has been documented in various connections. At that time, about one hundred species of birds nested in the marsh or in its proximity. In 1940, the best bird lakes of Sweden were ranked, and Line marsh was placed among the top eight on the list.

Once the marsh was drained off in 1947, the rich bird life became a thing of the past. Web-footed birds stopped breeding as soon as the two lakes were emptied of their water. Ducks do sometimes stay in the canal, which drains the former marshlands, or in the fields during springtime flooding. Several waders returned temporarily some decade after the drainage operation. Ruffs had several leks at that time, but they have now completely disappeared. The black-tailed godwit once had its largest community in Sweden at Lina myr, but has decimated concurrently with the deepening of the canal, which dried out the land. The curlew, which has been a resident of Lina myr for a very long time, has adapted to the new cultivated landscape and now breeds on the fringes of the cultivated fields.

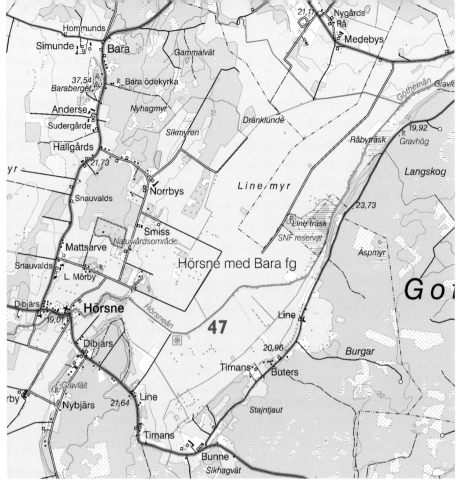

The numerous corncrakes are probably the most highly appreciated feature in the present bird life of Lina myr. On summer nights, it is a remarkable experience to go out to the grasslands and listen to the persistent nightcall – a gruff, two-syllabled "crek crek". Although the corncrake population has decimated somewhat over the past few years, there are still sufficient numbers to form an almost deafening choir. The best way of approaching corncrakes and other birds at Lina myr is to use the northbound "Hörsne marsh road", which projects into the south end of the marsh. At the end of this road there is a large area of lush sallow shrubbery which is rich in small birds. This is where you are most likely to meet the grasshopper and marsh warblers. River warbler have also been heard singing in this area.

Although bird life has most to offer during early summer, exciting observations can be made at other times of the year. In early spring, you can, if the fields are flooded, see flocks of up to one hundred whooper swans, sometimes accompanied by a few Bewick's swans.

The buzzard and great grey shrike often spend the winter out on the marsh. Sometimes occasional golden eagles come to hunt. The best view over the former enormous area of Lina myr can best be gained from the 15 metre high precipice, which forms its eastern border, and also marks the border between two rock strata with differing degrees of resilience. There are also good viewpoints in

Curlew still breed beside the drained-off Lina myr (marsh).

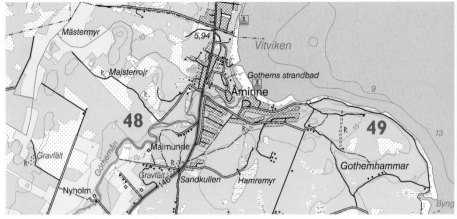

the north, where the forest on the slope has been clear-felled, and in the south, where the grounds around Line farm have been cultivated.

Map on p. 101.

48 Gothemån is Gotland's largest watercourse, draining large areas of central Gotland. The distance from its source, at its highest point, north-west of Etelhem, to its estuary, is 50 kms. Having passed the canal in the drained off Lina myr, the stream flows north east in a natural meandering channel through forests. Gothemån empties into Vitviken at Åminne (meaning "estuary"). One of the meander bends of the stream runs just beside the road, a few hundred metres south of the bridge at Åminne.

The deep stream channel is largely the result of heavy spring flooding. During late winter, the stream is transformed into a swift rapid, but in

Meadowsweet.

summer the water flow is moderate, and sometimes the stream channel is completely dry. In the steep riverbanks (the result of landslides) the soil consists mainly of sand. A large area around the upper reaches of the stream is covered with a very thick layer of sand, providing a very suitable habitat for a thriving coniferous forest and a large number of spruce.

Gothemån is rather rich in fish. Around March/April ide swim upstream, and ide-angling becomes a popular past-time. In former times, ide was an important contribution to household fare.

On its way through the agricultural lands, the water of Gothemsån becomes highly nutritious, which has led to a luxuriant growth of tall herbs and willow in the stream channel. Down among the metre-tall plants, you feel as if you have been transported to a tropical river. The bright clusters of hairy spurge bloom at the beginning of June, and these are later accompanied by the bright yellow flowers of yellow iris. The tall reed canary grass, along with meadowsweet, which is very similar to its relation dropwort, form a dense border along the stream channel. Dropwort begin to bloom on dry soil in June, and meadowsweet bloom one month later.

Beneath all the tall herbs, the leaves of the lesser water parsnip form a dense carpet, semi-immersed in the water. Here and there in later summer, you may notice the beautiful flowers of the one metre tall common reed. The large pink flowers crowd together to form an umbel-like inflorescence.

The wren is a bird which thrives beside watercourses fringed by dense vegetation, and with spruce forests nearby. Here at Gothemån, there are good chances of hearing the harsh grating call of the wren, which is Sweden's smallest bird. In the cold months of the year, the open water of Gothemsån is the haunt of the dipper.

Map on p. 102.

Shingle beach ridges with windswept pine and carpets of Alpine bearberry at Gothemshammar.

49 Just south of the bridge across the stream Gothemån at Åminne, a road leads east to the beautiful shore habitat at **Gothemhammar**. Once the road has passed through a weekend cottage area, it reaches the coast, where a sparse and beautiful coastal pine forest is situated between the road and the beach. A long series of distinct shingle beach ridges are completely carpeted with Alpine bearberry sprigs.

Landward of the road which leads eastward alongside the beach on top of the beach ridges, a coniferous forest rises from a slope, which at certain places is more like a cliff. A small road towards the south east leads up to a hill fort, a few hundred metres up the slope. Around the ramparts (the remains of the hill fort), the forest has been cleared to accentuate the hill fort, which was built on a former promontory, connected to the main island at the point where the ramparts were built. The sparse forest around the ramparts supports a rich community of red helleborine.

The rough, narrow road continues a couple of kilometres along the beach with no possibilities of turning or parking a car. It is thus advisable to leave the car as soon as you arrive at the open beach, and continue on foot.

The road leads along the beach landward of a low cliff which is highly eroded and partly covered with pebbles. Beneath the cliff there is a shingle beach, patches of which are tinged a shade of brownish red, due to the dense communities of herb Robert, which are in bloom from late spring right up until autumn. They thrive on all types of stony ground, and are the characteristic plant of the shingle beach.

One of Gotland's most esteemed fossil localities is by the cliff at Gothemhammar, where you can find well-preserved representatives of the primitive fish which evolved during the Silurian.

As you walk along the beach towards the south east, you will notice that the beach gradually widens. Beneath the windswept pines, which form beautiful small groves, the soil cover is sufficiently deep for the Alpine bearberry sprigs to take root. The surrounding beach is quite barren. Small spruce growing in clusters on the bare shingle ridges resemble those found above the tree-line in the mountains – short and with several trunks sharing a common root.

Map on p. 102

Herb Robert thrive on barren pebble beaches.

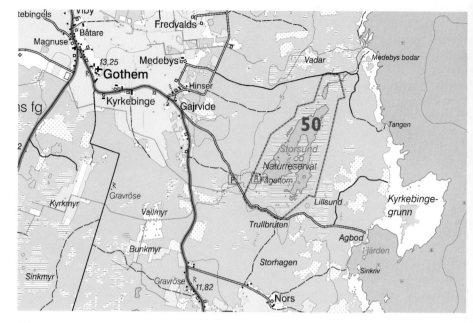

50 Lake **Storsund** is situated just one kilometre from the sea and no more than a couple of metres above sea level, which means that it has been isolated from the sea in historical times. The lake is remarkably nutritious, considering that it is completely surrounded by woodland, and is becoming clogged; like so many other lakes it is being transformed into a marsh. A good population of bog myrtle has spread along the border between the lake and the woodland, and its fragrance is already noticeable as you approach the tower hide.

From the hide you can see how the lake, which is about 100 hectares in area, including the shore, has already been largely colonised by reeds and sedge. The belt of great fen sedge is widest in the south, where there are also some pine-wooded islets. The common reed is sparsely interspersed among the sedge, but is most luxuriant in a narrow belt between the sedge and open water. Great fen sedge often form small islands and islets surrounded by open-water surfaces. A large area at the east end of the lake is totally engulfed by tall, dense common reed.

The well-balanced mosaic of plants and open water provides an ideal habitat for birds to breed or just stop over for a while. Storsund must be counted as one of the most interesting birding localities of the inland areas of Gotland. Permanent residents include the little grebe, great crested grebe, March harrier, mute swan, gadwall, pochard and sometimes even the grey heron, bittern and crane. The goshawk, which can sometimes be seen hunting across the lake, have nested nearby for many years. Water rail rarely make an appearance

View from the tower hide at Storsund.

on open water, but they blow their cover with their pig-like squealing.

The proximity of Storsund to the sea can be deduced from the prescence of Caspian and little terns, which have come in from the coast to fish. During late summer and autumn, flocks of several thousands of starlings overnight among the reeds in Storsund.

The trail to and from the tower hide passes through some lush, meadowy pine forests, interspersed by spruce. Narrow-leaved helleborine, birdsnest orchid and dark red helleborine grow along the path.

Since 1951, Storsund has been in the ownership of the Swedish Society for Nature Conservation, which partly financed the acquisition with the compensation received from the company that drained off Lina myr. Storsund was brought under the protection of a nature reserve in 1974.

To reach Storsund, choose the road to Hangre at the crossroads north of Gothem church, and continue for just over a kilometre until you reach a junction on the left, signposted "Fågeltorn".There is a carpark just over one kilometre along the forest road. A path, a few hundred metres long, leads from the carpark through the forest to the tower hide beside the southeast flank of the lake.

Map on p. 104

5 I Paviken was once a shallow, nutritient-rich seabay, which later became an isolated lake, following isostatic rise. During the Iron Age, Paviken was utilized as a sheltered harbour, and east of the lake, by the outlet of the stream Idån, there are remains of a trading station from about 600-950 A.D.

Today, Paviken is one of Gotland's best birding lakes. Birds which breed regularly in the lake and its proximity include little grebe, gadwall, garga-

Garganey.

ney, corncrake, spotted crake, grasshopper warbler and marsh warbler. Although no tern breed in the lake, four different species (common tern, Arctic tern, little tern and Caspian tern) can be observed simultaneously in summer, when they fish in the lake.

A good viewpoint is the tower hide just beside the southeast shore of the lake. A car-park has been laid out about 100 metres southeast of the lake.

Paviken is drained by the stream Paån, which discharges into the sea immediately north of Västergarn harbour. Avocet and little tern breed on the sandbanks seaward of the estuary, and many different waders stop to feed in spring and autumn. This area is best viewed from Västergarn harbour.

Map on p. 105.

52 Maldesänget is a larger-sized parish meadow opposite Eskelhem church, sporting unusually large open-canopy areas. The south end of the central section is dominated by yellow rattle, wood cranesbill, meadow saxifrage and meadow buttercups. The main orchids are fragrant and early purple orchids.

Clusters of birch, ash, oak and hazel grow at the east end of the meadow, alternating with small glades. The ground here is damper, and there are numerous twayblade, wood anemone and various types of sedge.

The shady areas at the western end of the meadow support a profusion of lily-of-the-valley and bitter vetchling.

53 From the main road south of Mästerby Church, looking south, you will see how the wide oak crowns of Mästerbyänget clearly demarcate the extensive arable fields north of the meadow. The oak is the most common tree in Mästerbyänget, which is one of Gotland's largest managed meadows.

The meadow is relatively open-canopied, and solitary oaks are often thick and have had space to spread their crowns. Ash often form small groups, surrounded by hazel bushes. In some places small-leaved elm are prevalent.

By and large, the meadow is rather meagre with sparse, low-growing grass, leaving space for the orchids to thrive. Twayblade and early purple orchid are ubiquitous. Some parts of the meadow support large numbers of fragrant, lesser butterfly and military orchids. When the orchids eventually fade at about midsummer, the meadow flora retains the bright colours of its flowers a little while longer, thanks to the low-growing grass.

Early purple orchid.

A wide path leads directly into the meadow. A vigorous dogwood bush grows by the bridge over the ditch that runs through the entire meadow. Dogwood is quite common on Öland and Gotland, but rare elsewhere in southern Sweden.

The path through the meadow continues into an area which was formerly managed, but is now overgrown. The vegetation here is more luxuriant but more species-poor than in the meadow. The path runs through the overgrown area, eventually leading back to the well-managed meadow.

54 Halla klosteränge, the monastic meadow at Halla, which is one of Gotland's largest deciduous woodland areas, covering almost 30 hectacres, is situated a couple of kilometres northwest of Sjonhem Church, and mainly surrounded by cultivated fields. It is densely overgrown and largely inaccessible. Just a few thick, broad-crowned oaks live to tell the tale that this was once an area of open-canopied deciduous woodland; today the oaks stand widely scattered in the thicket. Birch and small-leaved elm can also be found here. The forest is mainly dominated by dense communities of oak saplings.

In the mid-1940s, when the area had long been abandoned, the hazel bushes were cleared, and replaced by oak and some unfamiliar tree species the following year. The aim was to produce an economically viable oak forest. The area was then left to its own devices, and necessary maintenance measures were never carried out.

Interest in deciduous woodland management has been rekindled over the past few years. This has resulted in a management plan for Halla klosteränge, drawn up by the Nature Conservation Section of the County Administrative Board and the National Board of Forestry. In the future, sound forest management will be combined with the protection of the flora and fauna of the habitat. The deciduous forest will, however, remain somewhat inaccessible even in the future, so as to induce the oaks to grow tall and straight; it may not be cleared to form a park, nor may it be left to develop freely into a grove-like natural forest.

The springtime flora in Halla klosteränge is magnificent. Hepatica are succeeded by an abundance of wood and yellow anemones. When the cowslip eventually fade, it is the turn of the spring pea to add a splash of colour to ground vegetation. In summer, when the ground lies in dense shade, not many plants can be found in bloom. Instead, a range of interesting grasses hide in the meadow. Wood barley, which is scattered about in the meadow, was once regarded as extremely rare, but has lately been discovered at several different places in central Gotland. This is also true of the lesser hairy brome, which grows in one spot in this deciduous forest.

Soft-leaved sedge has only been found at a few places on Gotland, but where it grows it flourishes. In parts of Halla klosteränge, it is the prevalent field-layer plant. Woodruff is a typical grove plant, which grows profusely here.

As in most dense deciduous forests, Halla klosteränge supports an interesting bird life with breeding birds such as various warblers, tits and flycatchers. Many of the old oaks are hollow, providing nesting space for stock doves, starlings and jackdaws.

Map on p. 107.

55 In Viklau Parish, the stream **Dalhemån** has largely retained its free and natural course, an unusual feature for larger watercourses on Gotland. Dalhemån, which drains parts of the moor Lojsta hajd, flows northwards to join the streams Hörsneån and Gothemån.

About 1 km east of Viklau Church, the road crosses the stream Dalhemån (locally known as Möllebosån). From here the course of the stream can be followed northwards. The first point of interest is a stone bridge beside the road, which once supported the former main road.

Since **Möllebosån** overflows its banks every spring, the floodplain tends to be swamped way into early summer. When visiting the stream at the height of summer, it is advisable to walk downstream to the farm Möllebos, about 2 kms to the north. The first hundred metres north of the bridge

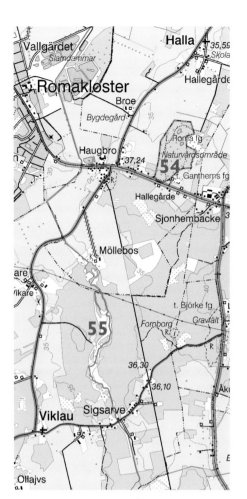

Wood barley is a rare grass found in Halla monastic meadow.

Cowslip is a common spring flower in meadows.

have been dug up and straightened. Then the stream flows along its natural, narrower, deeper channel, meandering all the way down to Möllebos.

Meandering (a sinuous river course) occurs when water flows across a flat substrate. When a river meanders, it constantly changes the shape of its own channel. It might be interesting to ponder over how this happens. When water flows in a curved channel, the current will be swifter along the outside concave bend than along the inside convex bend. Material will thus be eroded from the outer bends, to be deposited along the inner bend of the next curve. On the outside, the channel shifts laterally to make a curve of larger radius, while a long, curving deposit of sediment accumulates on the inside. Eventually, the meanders are so sinuous, that the bends almost meet. The river will then cut across this narrowing neck of land between the meander bends, shortening and straightening its course. The former channel will remain as an isolated, semicircular lake. Several of these so-called oxbow lakes, which have been filled in with deposits and hydrophilic vegetation to form a marsh, can be seen along Mölle-bosån.

The type of vegetation and its luxuriance indicate that the water is rather nutrient-rich. The dense foliage of lesser water parsnip, which do not bloom until late summer, carpets some parts of the river bed.

In late summer, the stream channel is decorated with the flowers of purple and yellow loosestrife, while yellow water lily bloom in the slow current of the stream. Bittersweet, a poisonous relative of the potato, cling to the sallow beside the stream.

Unbranched bur reed, whose prickly fruit resembles a small mace, and water speedwell form part of the luxuriant vegetation here, at some points almost completely engulfing the stream channel.

Map on p. 107.

56 Just north of the junction between the road from Hörsne and the main road 146, a minor road leads down to Hammars fishing hamlet. There is a car-park beside a wooden fence, just before you reach Hammars. **Liste meadow** is situated to the south, and was traditionally managed by raking and mowing right up until the 1930s. Liste ängar then had a reputation of being the haunt of Gotland's richest community of orchids. The flora is still rich, despite the fact that the area has largely lost its meadow character.

Slightly south of the car-park, there is an open area which is cut with a mowing-machine every year. The flora here contains typical dry-land

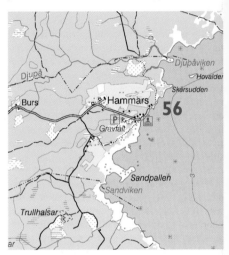

plants such as lesser meadow-rue, mountain clover, dyer's woodruff, common rock-rose and bloody cranesbill. Down towards the sea there is an undulating piece of ground which has been thinned and cleared to enhance some prehistoric graves.

Fine-leaved vetch bloom along a small, rough path running west from the open area and through the meadow, as well as on the slopes descending

Managed section of Liste forest meadows.

to the sea. They are similar to tufted vetch, but have narrower leaflets, and the thick stalks grow densely tangled like small shrubs. Narrow-leaved helleborine produce a magnificent bloom at the beginning of June.

Parts of the former meadow are grossly overgrown, particularly with aspen scrub. Liste ängar is divided into several ownerships, and just south of the northernmost, overgrown parcel lies "Jakobsson's meadow" which is still meticulously managed. A shed, once used as sleeping quarters during hay-making, is still standing in the meadow.

In bygone days, when the pollard meadows were still managed to provide winter feed for the livestock, the animals grazed in the forests during the summer months. Even the coastal meadows were used as hay-making meadows. Nowadays, the coastal meadows may occasionally be used for grazing, although they have been largely left to overgrow. Beneath the northernmost parcel in Liste ängar, grazing was not abandoned until quite recently. The beach has now been invaded by enormous blackthorn bushes, juniper and creeping thistle. Bird life along the wide, shallow beach is rich, and the characteristic bird of the Gotlandic shores, the avocet, can often be seen among the redshanks, oyster catchers and shelduck.

If you walk along the littoral paths in a northerly direction, passing Hammars fishing hamlet, you will arrive at Hammars watermill after about one kilometre. There were seven different sawmills and other mills in the upper reaches of the stream Djupån in the mid 19th century. Hammars mill, which is situated a few hundred metres upstream from where Djupån spills into the sea, is the only mill that has been preserved and restored. The former dam above the watermill is densely overgrown with hydrophilic flora. The majestic hairy spurge bloom in June, and the flecked marsh orchid can also be found here. The woodland immediately south of Hammars mill is known as Hammars kraklunde.

Hammars and Liste are situated in an area which houses numerous ancient monuments from various prehistoric periods. The renowned prehistoric site Trullhalsar lies about 1½ kms south of Liste ängar. Trullhalsar is a burial ground with more than 400 graves, many of which have been excavated and restored. The main part of the site has been dated to 600 A.D. (the "Vendel Period"). The road leading to Hammars fishing hamlet from road 146 passes a number of large cairns, mostly dating from Early Bronze Age, although Bjärs Mound, the largest mound on Gotland, is probably Iron Age.

Just beside the crossroads between the road to Fjäle farm and road 146 there is rather a large

The tall fine-leaved vetch.

community of Alpine orchid; this species cannot be found anywhere in Scandinavia, except on Gotland. Its nearest neighbour grows more than 1 000 kms to the south in the Austrian alps. The flowers of the Alpine orchid vary in shade from dark purple to white. At this particular spot they bear the most common shade – pink. Their most common habitat on Gotland is among Alpine bearberry carpets in sparse coastal pine forests.

Alpine orchid bloom in the last week of May and the first two weeks of June. They are distinguishable from the similar early purple orchid partly by their spur, which points downward in the former, but upward in the latter, and partly by their brownish-green hood.

Map on p. 108.

Common rock rose.

Alpine orchid.

57 Anga parish meadow, which is situated just over 300 metres south of Anga church, west of the Anga-Kräklingbo road, is small but beautiful and orchid-rich. The canopy layer is composed of pine and birch, which is unusual in a meadow. The meadow also supports ash trees which are regularly pollarded. The ground is nutrient-poor and damp in springtime. The low-growing blue moor grass is prevalent, and a number of herbs, not least orchids, are able to grow in abundance. Myriads of fragrant orchids bloom in June, joined at midsummer by numerous yellow rattle. Other orchids growing here include early purple, military and burnt orchids.

Gotland is the only province in Sweden to host great burnet. One variety, which blooms at midsummer, can only be found in a few wooded meadows in the east of Gotland, but here in Anga parish meadow it is abundant. The common variety of great burnet can be found in the ephemeral swamps on limestone outcrops, where they bloom two to three weeks later than the meadow variety.

The Swedish variety of eyebright was once a character plant of the Gotlandic wooded meadows. Now it only occurs at a few sites and is not known outside Gotland. In Anga parish meadow there are some communities which are prolific. Contrary to most other varieties of eyebright, they bloom before hay-making. Great burnet and fragrant orchid have also adapted to the practice of early haymaking in pollard meadows.

58 Kräklingbo prästänge – North and northeast of the road at Kräklingbo church, there is a deciduous woodland which largely consists of heavily overgrown wooded meadows, although a small part of this area just opposite the church is still managed as a meadow. A splendid broad-crowned oak grows in the meadow; it is protected as an object of great scientific interest. The trees in the meadow form drapes which screen off small glades. Ash pollards grow beside the road.

The field layer is partly of dry meadow character with herbs such as meadow saxifrage, birdsfoot trefoil, ribwort plantain and common rock rose. Humidity in the small, shady glades and under trees and shrubs in the groves, attracts plants such as lily-of-the-valley, ramsons, marsh cinquefoil and the orchids twayblade and broad-leaved helleborine.

Map on p. 111.

59 Upstaigs primeval forest – Forests have always been an important natural resource, heavily exploited by man. Gotland has certainly been no exception. When limeburning and wood distillation for tar production accelerated in the 17th century, vast amounts of fuel and raw material were required. Simultaneously, the sawmills, which had emerged more or less over the entire island, demanded the best quality timber. As a result, the Gotlandic forests were subjected to ruthless exploitation and practically clear-felled during the 17th, 18th and 19th centuries.

Today there is hardly any woodland on Gotland, that has escaped the impetus of human activity. There are, however, a few small woodland areas, which have only been managed on a small scale during the latest century, and have now begun to regain a natural and pristine character.

At Upstaigs, 3 kms WNW of Katthammarsvik, there is an area of about 27 hectacres, which is considered to be one of Gotland's finest examples of long-standing unimproved woodland. The area is a nature reserve.

A small road to the primeval forest leads westwards from just south of Ängmansvik. After about 1½ kms you pass a small bridge over the stream which marks the east margin of the forest. South of the road you will immediately note that there is something special about the forest. The pine trees, which are unusually thick for Gotlandic conditions, bear the mark of old age with their gently curving stems and denudation of twigs up to the small crown of thick and knotty branches, and some bear a smooth, shiny bark. The age of the oldest pines has been estimated at 250-300 years. The spruce in the area are also of old age, although more spruce than pine have died, due to

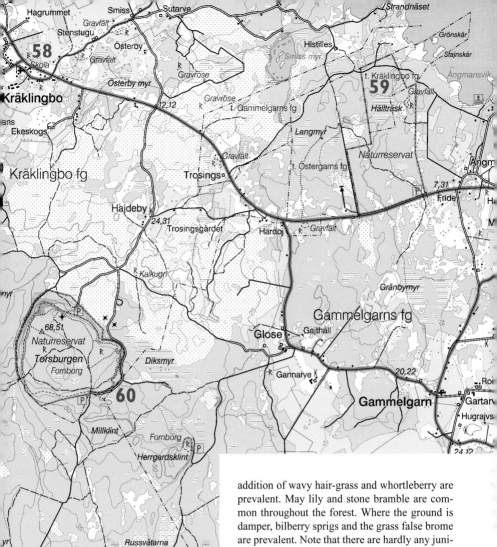

addition of wavy hair-grass and whortleberry are prevalent. May lily and stone bramble are common throughout the forest. Where the ground is damper, bilberry sprigs and the grass false brome are prevalent. Note that there are hardly any juniper bushes in Upstaigs primeval forest; they require dry, sunny ground and do not thrive in this forest, where fly honeysuckle is the common shrub. In early summer, narrow-leaved helleborine abound in the entire forest.

The ancient forest at Upstaigs is unique on Gotland, and probably has few peers in the south of Sweden. There are many reasons for preserving a woodland like this. Several species of moss, lichen and fungi cannot survive in the sunny, windy and dry conditions of a clear-felled area. They need an even supply of light and moisture, as well as the abundance of dead trees which a primeval forest has to offer. Different insects, such as beetles, are reliant on access to dead trees at various stages of decay. As the forest ages, it becomes a vital refuge for plants and animals which are otherwise threatened species. Upstaigs primeval forest is also significant for humans. Visitors are given the opportunity of experiencing a natural, unimproved forest.

parasitical fungi. Several of the dead spruce have fallen down; as they lie on the ground, they add to the feeling of being in a primeval forest.

The forest at Upstaigs grows on a relatively thick layer of soil, which partly consists of sand. The composition of the undergrowth is therefore similar to that of coniferous forests on the mainland. Where the ground is drier, mosses with an

A profusion of narrow-leaved helleborine grow in the ancient forest at Upstaigs.

The area is a nature reserve, where breaking twigs off trees and firelighting are prohibited.
Map on p. 111

60 Torsburgen is one of Gotland's largest inland cliffs and situated in a large woodland in Kräklingbo parish. Both Torsburgen, which towers 68 metres above sea level, and the smaller and lower Herrgådsklint in the south east, are well-preserved remains of hillforts.

Two kms south east of Kräklingbo church, a road leads to Hajdeby and Torsburgen. Where the road forks, the right hand fork leads to a car-park at the foot of the northern precipice of Torsburgen. A path leads up the scree which is full of dislodged boulders, and wooded with spruce. The plateau is accessed through "Tjängvide luke" – one of Torsburgen's many openings. The view, which is partly blocked by the surrounding coniferous forest, is free and extensive from the top of the 15-metre tall viewing tower; from here you can see large expanses of central Gotland. Note that the landscape is dominated by coniferous forest.

In summer 1992, parts of Torsburgen and land north of the hillfort were ravaged by an extensive forest fire, which devastated an almost 10 km² area. In order to preserve parts of the devastated forest, Torsburgen has been placed under the protection of a nature reserve. Many animals, plants and fungi benefit from forest fires, and certain corticolous and xylophagous species live almost exclusively on charred wood. As a result of the 1992 fire, Torsburgen will provide a unique habitat for these fire-reliant and often threatened species for several decades to come.

Scorpion senna still grows on the northern precipice of Torsburgen. Linné found it here on his trip to Gotland in the summer of 1741. This southern European plant of the pea family was then unknown in Sweden. It has later been discovered at several places on Öland and Gotland.

After about 500 metres, the west path, running along the edge of the scree, drops onto a small ledge on the top terrace of the cliff. At the foot of the precipice, there is an almost impenetrable jungle of fly honeysuckle, which is part of the caprifole family, blooming in late spring with pale yellow flowers, which later produce dark red berries.

"Linné's cave" is just south of the ledge. The hole in the roof is thought to have been a pothole, which was destroyed when the cave was formed. The 16-metre deep Burgs lädu lies further north, along with several shallower caves.

Torsburgen has sometimes been described as a "terrestrial Karlsö" (p 125ff). It is of roughly the same size as Lilla Karlsö. The comparison is appropriate when considering that Torsburgen was indeed once an island in the deep seas which emerged after the latest Ice Age. The caves on the northwest flank of Torsburgen are about 60 metres above the present sea level, and were scooped out by the waves of the Baltic Ice Lake about 9 000 years ago.

According to the Gute Tale, the hillfort at Torsburgen was constructed by people who had been banished from the island, due to overpopulation and a resulting lack of food. The natural fort sections were supplemented by vast ramparts built on the lower gradient of the south face. The road down

112

Scorpion senna (left) and marjoram (right) are two plants that can be seen at Torsburgen. Scorpion senna was discovered by Linné in summer 1741.

to Ardre luke winds along the vast east scree. The forest has now been thinned and cleared, in order to enhance the scree and ramparts. As the scree decreases, the ramparts increase in height.

At Ardre luke, the ramparts reach their maximum size, which is 7 metres tall and 24 metres wide. Excavations indicate that the ramparts were erected in two stages. The oldest parts were probably built in the Iron Age, in about 300 A.D. The ramparts were built later in the Viking Age, in about 900 A.D. The top of Torsburgen offers wide, easily negotiated paths. The crown of the scree on the east flank offers a view of the sedge fields in the marsh Diksmyr, where cranes breed in the summer.

The road leading south from Ardre luke is closed to motor vehicles. East of this road, you can see several long, narrow valleys with steep sides. The most outstanding valley, which is 10 metres wide and 600 metres long, can be found about 200 metres south of the car-park. Geologists call these valleys "dry valleys", which are thought to have been quarried from the bedrock by the swift currents of meltwater streams, when the inland ice retreated.

Herrgårdsklint is reached by a 3 km long, narrow, rough road which bears off from the main road at Glose farm, just over 2 kms NW of Gammelgarn Church.

Herrgårdsklint rises some 50 metres above sea level, and is just as impressive as Torsburgen. The forest surrounding Torsburgen and Herrgårdsklint grows largely on sandy, lime-deficient soil, thus resembling a coniferous forest on the mainland.

The vast southern ramparts of Torsburgen hillfort.

At Herrgårdsklint, the spruce are tall and thick, and the field layer supports species such as interrupted clubmoss, bilberry and wavy hair-grass. Fly honeysuckle on the screes at Herrgårdsklint are as profuse as at Torsburgen.

There is also a hillfort at Herrgårdsklint, with well-preserved ramparts on the south face. Remains of house foundations can be seen within the ramparts.

Marjoram (fam. Origanum), which is not particularly common on Gotland, is the prevalent species of the dry-slope flora both of Herrgårdsklint and Torsburgen. The violet buds open into pink flowers at the beginning of July.

Map on p. 111

61 In the woodlands south of Herrgårdsklint there are extensive areas of sparse inland rock pine forests. At several places, the rock is pitted with large, shallow, basin-like depressions, and wherever the rock is uncracked, water is trapped, forming a wetland known as "ephemeral pool". This is the most characteristic feature of Gotland. Most of them are very small, and dry off very quickly in early summer. **Russvätar**, however, is completely dry for just a short period at the height of summer, providing ideal conditions for an unusually lush vegetation, which often forms a compact carpet mainly of low grasses and sedges.

Most of Russvätar is surrounded by inland rock pine forest with a large number of dead trees, and with a rich and typical inland rock flora. The largest community of the Gotlandic subspecies of the Pasque flower grows in a belt south of the ephemeral pools, beginning at the westernmost margin of the wetlands. They differ from the "common" variety (which does not occur on Gotland) by their thicker stalks and lighter, bluer petals. The Gotlandic subspecies normally begins to flower in April/May, and blooms throughout most of May.

Russvätar and the Gotlandic Pasque flower are best reached on foot. Walk northwards along the small forest road, leading from the main road just east of where it crosses the stream Halsgardeån, and passing the east flank of Petsarveklint. When you reach the inland rock area, keep going until the road forks, where you will see the flower.

Map on p. 111

62 Östergarnsberget is a large inland cliff, situated in the middle of the promontory, Östergarnslandet. The cliff is demarcated by steep west, north and east faces, with a gentle incline to the south.

The car-park beside the road to Östergarn Church, on a slope beneath a restored limekiln, opposite the junction to Katthammarsvik, is a good starting point for a walk on Östergarnsberget. The plateau above the limekiln supports typical Gotlandic inland rock vegetation. Stands of pine grow in a "sea" of juniper. Most of the rock is very cracked and slightly undulating. Just east of the road leading up the slope, there is a large stone quarry, which has formed a deep "basin" in the rock. Traces of limestone quarrying can also be seen in the west. The precipice, which slopes steeply down into a coniferous forest, is covered with sharp, angular limestone chips, which have been left behind after stone quarrying from surface pits in bygone days. The only plants to thrive on the stony ground are herb Robert and ciliate melick. Some parts of the rocky precipice support the rare limestone fern, which forms compact light green carpets.

After a walk of about one kilometre along the precipice in a westerly direction, you will arrive at Mattsarveklint, the highest point of Östergarnsberget, 42 metres above sea level. Here, the cliff rises almost perpendicularly 20 metres above its surroundings. From the cliff top you will have a magnificent view of a small-scale, wooded cul-

The largest community of the Gotlandic pasque flower can be found at Russvätar.

tural landscape to the north. In the far distance to the west, Torsburgen rises above the extensive area of coniferous forest. Enormous boulders have tumbled down to the foot of the precipice.

The former Ancylus lake has scooped out several large caves in the cliff face. Some are over 10 metres deep, but their wide mouths give the appearance of an overhang. Sheep graze on the slopes beneath the cliff, and the trampled ground indicates that the overhang and caves are used as shelter from rain and wind. One of the few plants to thrive in the dense shade beneath the cliff is the madwort, whose angled stems are often found beneath overhangs and in caves in the Gotlandic rocky cliffs.

The west, north and east precipices of Östergarnsberget cover a distance of 5 kms. The south road from Östergarn Church meanders around the east precipice, until it reaches Kaupungsklint in the south. Enormous boulders have been dislodged from the cliff, and lie on the slopes in the lush verdure of ash saplings.

Map on p. 115

63 The east coast of Gotland has a low incline and has very few dramatic features that can boast to be on a par with the awesome cliffs along the west coast. **Grogarnsberget** at the far end of the northern coast of the Östergarn promontory is a magnificent exception, and is largely conside-

red to be one of Gotland's most beautiful coastal stretches. The area is a popular destination for a day's outing.

Grogarnsberget is just over 2 kms from Katthammarsvik. The almost 3 km long precipice comes into sight at a great distance. The precipice which at several places is completely covered with enormous heaps of rubble, is concealed by a lush vegetation of trees and shrubs. The rough road across the limestone plateau leads to a car-park east of the cliff.

Pine trees stand on the limestone outcrop without actually forming a forest. The rock is slightly undulating, and higher, drier clints alternate with shallow depressions, which are often wet. The thin soil cover on the outcrop quickly dries up in early summer, and only habitat-specific plants, such as vincetoxicum and ciliate melick, survive the long summer drought. Various types of mosses, lichens and stonecrops surmount the harsh conditions better than any other type of vegetation. Off-track car driving damages the vegetation, leaving thin, unvegetated soil, which is carried away by wind and rain, exposing barren rock.

On the outcrops at Grogarnsberget there are opportunities of seeing some infrequent annual alvar plants. The tiny, light blue breckland speedwell bloom in May. *Arenaria gothica*, a rare sandwort, bloom from May and throughout the whole summer and part of autumn. They can only be

Grogarnsberget, coastal cliff.

found at a few places on Gotland, and at one place in the rest of Sweden (Kinnekulle). Thale cress is another unassuming rarity on Grogarnsberget, blooming in July/August.

There are quite a number of loose limestone boulders on the outcrops north of the car-park. The northbound path along the east edge of the cliff passes low, wide ramparts, built of boulders taken from the outcrops. This fortification provided defence from the south and completed the hillfort formed by the cliff in the north.

Grogarnshuvud, which is the northernmost part of Grogarnsberget, is the highest point above sea level (32 metres) offering a magnificent view. If

Yellowhammer frequent the shrubs at Grogarns-
berget.

you make your way along the east edge you will eventually see the fishing hamlet at Herrvik. Immediately east of where you stand, you will see the offshore islet Östergarnsholm, and to the west you will have large areas of the Östergarn promontory in sight.

Large boulders have been dislodged and slipped down the north precipice of Grogarnsberget, as a result of undermining action by waves. The shrubbery of the talus slopes is the haunt of the barred warbler, and ravens sometimes breed on the actual precipice. Wheatear send out continuous alarm calls by way of a hard "tack" from the almost treeless grounds on Grogarnshuvud. The skylark and yellowhammer are also characteristic birds of the exposed grounds on the clifftop.

From the car-park, continue along the narrow car track, which winds along the foot of the east precipice. The landscape, with its gnarled pine forest on shingle beach ridges, strongly resembles the south of Europe. The road follows the shore southwards to the fishing hamlet at Herrvik.

Map on p. 115.

64 From the fishing hamlet at Herrvik, a road runs eastwards across the spit called **Kuppen**. The coastal biota varies according to the habitat, from open coastline to shrubs and woodland further inland. When the road reaches the shore, it forks, and the northern fork leads to an old restored navigation mark where there is room to turn and park.

Beneath the car-park, dislodged limestone boulders lie on a wide, wave-cut limestone platform. When waves surge in over the platform whirlpools are created, which excavate shallow, basin-shaped depressions in the platform. The water that accumulates in these depressions, known as potholes, is usually filled with toad-tadpoles in early summer. Gutweed also live in the potholes, as they tolerate the high salinity which often develops when the brackish water evaporates.

A layer of sand has accumulated on the inner part of the limestone platform. Here dragon's teeth form a bright yellow carpet in June. Sea milkwort, with their unassuming pale pink petals at the base of the leaves, also thrive here. Landward of the shore platform stands a thick, rather tall-stemmed coastal pine forest. Dead branches of the pines have become a refuge for several very rare species of beetle, some of which have only been found at a few other sites in south east Sweden.

A large community of butterbur grows on a sandbank on the beach, slightly south of the shore platform. Butterbur, which migrated to Gotland during the 20th century, have large heart-shaped leaves and bloom in May.

On the north side of Kuppen, the beach rises to a cliff, which extends to the fishing hamlet at Herrvik. The sea has undermined the cliff, dislodging enormous boulders which then slide down to the water. Some boulders consist of reef limestone, almost entirely composed of stromatoporoids. In the cliff there are also some awesome overhangs and some sections bear indications of sea stack formation. The impact of wind on the coastal environment is illustrated by some pines, whose robust stems huddle close to the ground.

Landward of the cliff, the ground is open. Rabbits can be seen everywhere on the promontory, including here. On the open coastal grassland, vegetation is dominated by ciliate melick and vincetoxicum. Ragwort are also abundant, and are the host of the beautiful cinnabar, which in Sweden is only found in Sörmland and on Gotland. Numerous small Pasque flowers can be found, mainly in sandy soil areas.

Cinnabar.

The shores southeast of Kuppen consist of shingle beach ridges alternating with sandy areas, supporting an abundance of military orchids, which bloom in early summer. Small communities of pyramidal orchids bloom in July.

Map on p. 115.

65 **Sandviken** lies sheltered between Sysneudd in the east and Gryngeudd in the west, on the south coast of the Östergarn promontory. Landward of the eastern end of Sandviken is a sandy beach, whose western section has been placed under the protection of a nature reserve. Although this grand sandy beach has been subjected to intensive bathing activities, the vegetation has largely escaped damage, and typical, often beautiful sandy beach vegetation can be viewed.

Dislodged, enormous boulders at Kuppen.

Sandviken is most easily reached from the road leading from Östergarn Church to the south coast. There are several large car-parks along the road to Sysne.

Low sand dunes form a 20 metre wide zone nearest the beach. They are clad with tall grassy vegetation, including common couch, lyme grass and tall fescue. Blue lettuce grow in the grass; their blue flowers burst into blossom at the end of July. On the dunes, you will also find lesser sea spurrey, with pyramid-shaped young shoots. Sand sedge grows across the whole beach, although it favours either unvegetated patches, or the tops of sand dunes, where surface-layer vegetation is sparse.

Further inland, the sand dunes give way to sandy grassland, supporting small dense tussocks of grey-hair grass and sand fescue, together with low-growing and creeping herbs. Both these grasses have inrolled leaves to impede evaporation, making them well-adapted to the summer dryness of the sand. Yellow rattle, which in places form dense carpets, are a noticeable feature of the grasslands, and bloom in June. Lady's bedstraw follow on, adding a splash of bright yellow in the month of July. The semi-prostrate stalks of the kidney vetch bear flowers in colours ranging from yellow to darkest red. The pinkish flowers of the strongly aromatic mat-forming wild thyme shine in the sun. Flowering maiden pinks add a tint of purple to the sheltered areas by the pine forest.

Just before the sandy beach is succeeded by a low cliff in the west, bluish-purple flowers of the sea pea can be seen on the lee slope of the sand dunes.

In the north, the sandy grassland is succeeded by a sparse coastal pine forest, which supports a species-poor vegetation, almost totally lacking in flowering herbs.

66 At Sandboviken, landward of the headland **Vivesholm**, a tower hide has been erected so that birds can be studied undisturbed.

To reach Vivesholm, take the SW road, leading from the main road just north of the Västerby junction towards NE.

A path leads from a stile over a sheep fence to the tower hide, which offers a view over the shallow bay Sandboviken and the coastal meadows at Räveln in the south east. Bird-life is rich, and interesting breeding birds include about 20 pairs of avocet, and the gadwall.

In spring, flocks of barnacle and greylag geese feed in the coastal meadows, and in autumn flocks of waders use the beaches as staging posts. In early summer, green-winged orchid bloom in the coastal meadows beneath the tower hide.

During the breeding season (from early spring until mid-July) great caution should be exerted, and movement should be restricted to the tower hide and its immediate vicinity. Bird-life is still sensitive in autumn, when geese use the coastal meadows as staging posts.

The coastal meadows at Räveln represent a habitat which has become less frequent along the Gotlandic coast. They have evolved on flat shores with fine-grained sediment, as a result of intensive grazing over long periods of time. When coastal pasturelands are abandoned, which is standard procedure in modern agriculture, changes occur in vegetation and the shore quickly becomes overgrown.

Glancing across the coastal meadows you will notice that low-lying areas are reddish-brown in

Sandviken nature reserve with bathing beach and interesting vegetation.

succulent leaves of the glasswort. Around the salt pan, creeping bent and saltmarsh rush together form a dense, green carpet, and silvery-grey sea wormwood manage to form an upright border – their bitter taste is their protection from grazing.

Many of the plants are coastal-meadow specific. One example is strawberry clover, which is rarely found in any other habitat. After flowering, a swelling forms in the fruit, resembling a minia-ture strawberry. Thrift (ssp. *maritima*), which blooms in early summer, is also part of the charac-teristic coastal meadow flora.

Sagholmen, the headland west of Räveln, is a series of distinct beach ridges of esker gravel, tape-ring out towards the northwest. The dry-slope ve-getation is dominated by wild thyme and lady's bedstraw at the height of summer. Juniper bushes are the only form of high vegetation, and they huddle behind the beach ridges. Strong, saline on-shore winds cause heavy transpiration, and every shoot rising above the surface exposed to the wind dries up and dies.

Purple milk vetch, which is a rare pea plant, found at but a few localities in Sweden, are abun-dant at Varvsholm, landward of Vivesholm, al-though their future existence is under threat, since they demand open, coastal ground, which is quick-ly disappearing at **Varvsholm**, since farmers no longer make use of the pastureland, which has led to overgrowth. It would appear, however, that they have found a new home in the car-park in front of the guest house.

Map on p. 119

67 Mulde nature reserve, about 3 kms south of Klintehamn, can be reached from the first small junction left of the main Fröjel to Klinte Church road. The area was placed under the protection of a nature reserve, when threatened by plans for recreational building. It supports Gotland's most abundant community of white helleborine, which is a south-zone orchid, and the closest neighbour

colour, in contrast to the surrounding green sward. These shallow depressions, called salt pans or pond holes, are formed when groundwater is pushed up to the surface in periods of high-water level. Subsequent evaporation makes the trapped water hypersaline.

Salt pans support a special type of vegetation. Glasswort, annual seablite and creeping bent, along with various goosefoots are plants which are specially adapted to the hypersaline soil in the salt pans; the cell sap of the plants is highly saline enabling them to assimilate the saline water, a characteristic that can be tested by tasting the

Strawberry clover, easily recognised by its swollen fruit, resembling a miniature strawberry.

Sagholmen, a long, narrow headland with distinct beach ridges.

to Gotland is in south east Denmark. Having once been an extreme rarity of Gotland, with just a few known localities at the end of the 19th century, it has now been discovered at some twenty sites. This may be due to keener awareness of the Gotlandic flora, although it is more likely that the species has extended its distribution, as a consequence of a sharp decrease in forest grazing during the 20th century.

A vigorous mixed coniferous forest, rich in herbs and grass, grows on the clifftop. White helleborine bloom in abundance for a fortnight from mid-June. There are also smaller communities of the earlier-blooming narrow-leaved helleborine, and the later-blooming red helleborine.

Purple milk vetch.

White helleborine have creamy white flowers and broad, lanceolate leaves, whereas narrow-leaved helleborine have pure white flowers and longer, narrower leaves. The former are also larger than the latter.

Ivy, which has spread over the entire locality, occasionally forms dense carpets. The mature conifers, in a field layer of bilberry sprigs and stair-step moss, is very similar to the mixed coniferous forests on the mainland. Bloody cranesbill and hepatica, however, bear witness to calcareous soil.

Map on p. 119.

68 Some kilometre ESE of the village of Klinte-hamn, **Klinteberget** towers steeply (25 metres) above its surroundings. A few hundred metres along the road to Hemse, which is partly blasted into the east side of the cliff, a road leads to a car-park on the clifftop. The north side of the cliff, north of the car-park, houses a hillfort. Today there is a meadow there, with benches for those who wish to relax and enjoy the sunset or the panoramic view. The two Karlsö islands can be seen off the south west coast, behind the spire of Klinte Church. From the cliff you have a view of the coastal landscape, stretching some ten kilometres northwards.

Klinteberget is a popular roaming area, and numerous paths, with steps in the steeper sections, lead around the slopes of the cliff. The west side harbours a beech forest. Beech is not native to Gotland, and this stand was planted when Klinteberget was proclaimed common land at the end of the 19th century. Other trees were also planted, the most conspicuous being the larch.

In spring many visitors find their way to the cliff to enjoy the blaze of hepatica. Later, in summer the "botanical celebrities" white and red helleborine bloom on the north slopes. Traces of limestone quarrying from bygone days can be seen south of the car-park on the less inclined south slope. The pine forest growing here is rich in deciduous shrubs, the most common being dogwood.

69 Fonnsänget is situated west of road 142, two kilometres south of Väte Church, where the road is surrounded by shady ground.

Fonnsänget today consists of just over 5 hectacres of well-managed meadowland, although it was once much larger. Over the past few decades, the north end has been left to overgrow.

The thickets north of the meadow consist of dense communities of hawthorn bushes and ash and spruce saplings. The west end of the overgrown part supports typical grove flora, including woodruff, small-leaved elm and wood-meadow grass. The east end is more like a jungle, where the moist ground is dominated by meadowsweet and the leaves of wood cranesbill, which no longer bloom, due to lack of sunlight.

Oak and ash are the prevalent trees in the meadow. Many of the ash bear traces of pollarding, in some cases this has been quite recent. The trees are sparsely spread, and meadow shade is provided by clusters of hazel and other bushes.

Fonnsänget is mainly renowned for its floral splendour in springtime. In May, the dazzling dense carpets of wood anemone can be seen from afar. There is only a modest display of orchids, however, with just a small number of early purple, burnt orchid and twayblade. The open meadow areas are remarkably rich in various tall grasses. Cocksfoot and downy oat-grass are prevalent, although there are dense patches of quaking grass. At the south end of the meadow, mountain melick and wood-meadow grass thrive in the shade of trees and bushes.

Generally speaking, the peak blooming period in the Gotlandic meadows is up to Midsummer. The height of summer does, however, offer a blaze of floral colour. Between Midsummer and haymaking, Fonnsänget produces a magnificent display of dropwort, peach-leaved bellflower and spotted catsear.

In the meadow there are remains of several Iron Age buildings.

White helleborine at Mulde nature reserve.

70 Folhammar, one of Gotland's most beautiful sea stack fields, is situated a few kilometres NE of Ljugarn. South of Folhammar, at a nature reserve, there is a car-park, which is reached by driving north along the small coastal road from the village of Ljugarn, passing the old fishing huts at Vitvär.

The most beautiful sections of the long sea stack field are at the far end of the Folhammar headland, where a number of sea stacks rise to a height of 6 metres, with exciting shapes that fire the imagination. They consist of reef limestone and are part of the Hemse beds, with a high content of fossilised stromatoporoids and crinoids. North of the headland, the rock projecting from the shoreline is of almost pure limestone. Surging waves have sculpted gently curving shapes in the chalky-white limestone, and nearby the waves have also cut out a well-developed overhang in the low cliff.

Landward of the sea stack field, a coniferous forest, which is partly dominated by spruce, grows on calcite-poor, sandy soil.

The area is partly renowned for Gotland's largest community of sea holly, which grows on the beach south of the sea stack field. Sea holly has very spiny leaves and is hardly inviting to be touched, but despite its self-defence it has been ravaged by thoughtless flower-pickers. Although it has been a protected species since the 1930s, this regulation was grossly violated until recent years. Today, however, the sea holly has managed to expand its haunts along the Gotlandic coasts. The shore south of Folhammar also supports sea pea and woad. Near the road, about 100 metres south of the car-park, there is a small fen with a large, dense, light green carpet of marsh fern.

Mallgårds flush fen is a favourite haunt of the russ ponies.

71 At Lojstahajd, the large expanse of forest north of Lojsta, there are considerable numbers of interesting flush fens, which are mainly renowned for their abundance of Alpine bartsia, an extremely rare plant in the south of Sweden.

Although many of the flush fens in the area are most inaccessible, **Mallgårds flush fen**, in the middle of the forest, is very easy to find. About 5 kms SE of Klinte Church, a small 1½ km-long road leads east to a gravel pit, where parking is easy. The fen is immediately south east of the gravel pit. Several typical flush plants, such as short-spurred fragrant orchid, the late-blooming fragrant orchid, marsh helleborine, fly orchid, Alpine bartsia and Alpine butterwort grow in the flush fen.

Mallgårds flush fen was brought under the protection of a nature reserve in 1985. The west margin of the area is demarcated by a barbed wire fence, which also marks the south west boundary of the "russ pony park". Ponies graze in this southwestern paddock from early summer until the "pony show" at the end of July. The flush fen is a favourite haunt of the ponies, and visitors have a good chance of seeing them here, prior to the pony show.

Sea holly on the shore south of Folhammar.

Many people are under the false impression that the ponies have an adverse effect on the flush fens by trampling on the ground and cropping the plants. The rich vegetation, however, actually owes its existence to the presence of the ponies. In bygone days, it was quite natural for horses, cows and sheep to graze in the forest. Now that this type of pasture practice has largely been abandoned, many flush fens risk becoming choked with vegetation.

Map on p. 123.

72 The russ pony park is housed in the extensive coniferous forest at **Lojstahajd**, next to Gotland's highest point, 83.6 metres above sea level. It is just over 5 km² in size, and supports about 80 of Sweden's sole surviving primordial pony, the Gotland russ.

The grazing grounds are divided into three enclosed pastures. The north pasture is used in autumn and early winter. In winter the russ move to the south east pasture, then they spend summer in the south west pasture. At the end of July the herd is gathered into the small fold beside the main road for the annual "pony show", when they are inspected and judged. Prizes are awarded to the ponies with the best pedigree qualities. The show is the highlight of the year at this popular spot for day outings. Since the large enclosures are in a coniferous forest, it is difficult to command a view over the entire area, and the chances of seeing a pony from the road are extremely slim.

Russ ponies have been present on Gotland since the Stone Age, over 3 500 years ago. It is commonly believed that they originate from Eastern Europe.

The russ eventually ran wild, and herds roamed around in the extensive coniferous forests of Gotland right up until the 20th century. The last wild ponies were captured in 1930. When wood-

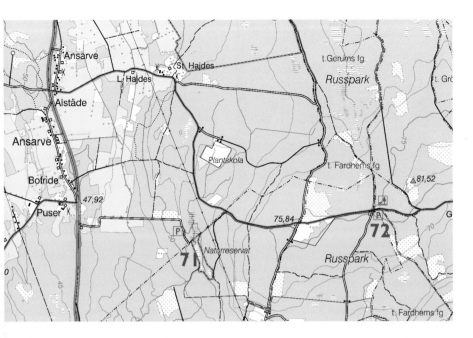

lands were parcelled, i.e. divided up between the farmers, towards the end of the 19th century, tolerance of wild russ plummeted, since they damaged the crops. Simultaneously, more and more farmers changed to large, modern horse-breeds. The russ population decreased drastically during the latter half of the 19th century. By 1930 there were only about 35 wild russ left at Lojsta-hajd, as well as a few domesticated ponies. As early as in 1910, however, some farmers had formed a society, with the aim of preserving the russ, and it is thanks to this initiative that the russ pony park is in existence to this day. There are now about 6 500 russ ponies in Sweden.

Gotland's highest point is just 500 metres east of the park, which means that the park and its surroundings were the first part of Gotland to emerge from the sea about 11 000 years ago. The Baltic Ice Lake was a wide, open sea, giving the wind free scope. The surge of the waves against the islet was thus very strong, resulting in broad, distinct beach ridges, which encircle the highest points just east of the park and north of the road. A "crest beach-ridge" was formed on the top, when gravel and stones were thrust up from all directions.

Since the coniferous forest at Lojstahajd is very extensive and thus relatively undisturbed, faunal-life is relatively rich. This is the haunt of the buzzard, goshawk, Tengmalm's owl, and the black grouse's lek.

Several of the flush fens support a rich and rare flora, including Alpine bartsia and Alpine butter-wort. The grazing and trampling of russ ponies have thwarted overgrowth by shrubs and thickets. In bygone days, forest-grazing cattle performed the same service.

Alpine bartsia grow in several of the flush fens on Lojsta moor.

Woodland brown.

73 The landscape seen from the Lojsta-Etelhem road is quite unique on Gotland. High hills with precipices plunging into long, narrow, bow-shaped lakes are analagous to the rift valley landscape in central Sweden.

A belt of Gotlandic bedrock, running from Fardhem parish in the south west to Etelhem parish in the north east, has an unusually high content of reef limestone, which was once enveloped in stratified limestone. The latter was carried away when the latest inland ice planed the bedrock, leaving high hills of reef limestone.

North of these hills are the lakes Fridträsk, Rammträsk, Hagebyträsk, Broträsk and Sigvaldeträsk, along with some smaller lakes. Several of the lakes are more than 10 metres deep. Rammträsk is the deepest lake, nearly 18 metres deep. (Lakes elsewhere on Gotland are nowhere near as deep – Bästeträsk has a max. depth of 5.5 and Tingstädeträsk 3 metres).

This singular type of landscape – hills of reef limestone with a steep north face plunging into deep lakes – is the result of the erosive activities of the latest inland ice.

(a) Lojsta slott is situated about 2½ kms along the Lojsta-Etelhem road. "Lojsta castle" are actually remains of a fortress, which was erected in the Medieval Period between Rammträsk and Broträsk. On your way to the "castle" you pass a reconstructed Iron Age house.

(b) Lojsta oak tree and parish meadow – South west of Lojsta Church, immediately beside the main road, are the remains of Gotland's former largest and oldest oak tree, with a circumference of almost 8 metres. Although the tree has not borne leaves since 2000, it will act as a habitat for deadwood insects for many more years.

Behind the oak tree is Lojsta parish meadow, which harbours several thick, old oak trees and many ash pollards. Here you will also find majestic crab apple trees and a few spruce. The meadow was formerly much larger than today. The extensive area west of the meadow was earlier managed, but has now been left to overgrow. The protected woodland brown has occasionally been observed in the dense deciduous woodland that has evolved here.

(c) Tonnklint – Immediately north of Lojsta Church a small road leads eastwards to Tonnklint, a small reef limestone hill a few hundred metres east of the church. Tonnklint has been designated an area of specific scientific interest, in order to protect the community of eastern pasque flower and the hybrid between the eastern and small Pasque flowers growing on the hill. In the grove-

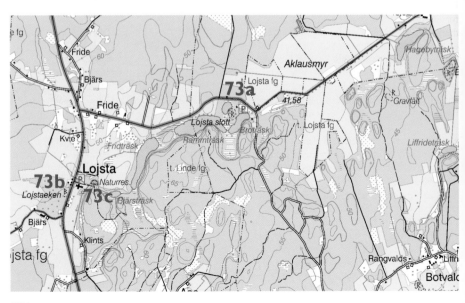

like vegetation around Tonnklint there are plants such as black pea, dog violet and wood melick.
Map on p. 124.

74 The parish meadow at Etelhem is situated a few hundred metres south east of the church, on both sides of road 143. The meadow is medium-sized, and well-managed and dominated by oaks, ash pollards and hazel bushes. The sparsely distributed oaks are relatively thick and solitary. The trees are evenly distributed, forming small glades, but there is also a very large open-canopied area at the western end.

The meadow is not particularly herb-rich, but supports early purple and fragrant orchids. Numerous wood cranesbill and ramsons bloom in the meadow in the first half of June.

75 Halfway between the churches of Garda and Lye, on the south side of the road, is the majestic **Bosarve natural forest**, covering an area of 150x150 metres. Its estimated age is 150-200 years. Although pine can generally reach a much greater age, forests as old as this one are unusual, since coniferous forests on fertile land are often felled at a much lower age. The forest at Bosarve can therefore be seen as an example of a forest-type which was much more common before the intensive deforestation of the 17th century, in order to meet demands for supply of timber to the sawmills, and fuel for limeburning and wood distillation for tar production. Previously, the forests had also been subjected to the impact of livestock grazing.

The aim of bringing the forest under the protection of a nature reserve was to allow it to develop freely under conditions typical for natural forests – a primeval forest. In this type of forest there are plenty of dead and dying trees of various

Black pea.

Lojsta oak, once Gotland's largest oak tree.

ages and sizes, a crucial condition for numerous saprophytic plants and animals, including several lichens, mosses and xyloyphagous invertebrae. The thick trees in a primeval forest are important for cavity-nesting birds and birds of prey.
Map on p 126.

76 Strömmaån, also called Malby å, flows south from its source near Etelhem Church, crossing the main road at Stenstugu, between Lye and Stånga Churches. From Stenstugu and just over 2 kms upstream, the stream displays a remarkably beautiful and winding course. In the south, it merges with Närkån, which branches off to the east and discharges into the bay Lausvik.

A suitable starting point for a walk along the most beautiful section of Strömmaån is from a minor road leading northwest from the main road to Lye, just north of Stenstugu and south of a large farm.

During the great cultivation period of the second half of the 19th century, many naturally winding streams were straightened and dredged to form rectilinear ditches. A several-kilometre stretch of Strömmaån was one of the few watercourses to be spared such encroachment.

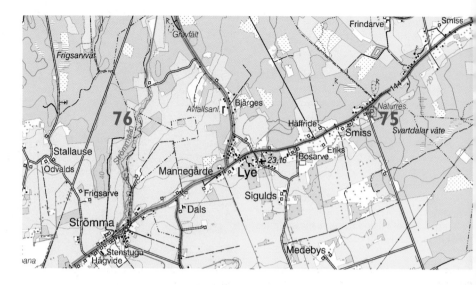

The first two kilometres upstream from Sten-stugu have a gradient of just over 15 metres, and the water also gushes through a 3-5 metre deep canyon. These were ideal conditions for damming the stream for water power. Starting in the 19th century, 22 dams were created along this stretch, each furnished with waterwheels operating mills and saws. The best preserved waterwheel is at Lillrone, otherwise only concrete foundations and decayed stocks bear witness to the heyday of water harnessing.

Vigorous willows form a canopy above the stream, while ash, birch and hazel dominate the slopes. In spring before trees come into leaf, the

Majestic pine trees in Bosarve natural forest.

anemones in full bloom are dazzling, and the ground accessible. In summer, the foliage is compact, and some areas are almost engulfed by tall communities of meadowsweet and nettles, forming a veritable jungle.

The lush vegetation is a habitat attracting numerous birds. The collared turtle dove, a species that has migrated to Sweden over the past 30-40 years, first nested on Gotland in 1965. Today, it is rather common over the entire island.

In winter you may catch a glimpse of the dipper (a small, brownish-black bird with white breast) by the open water. Dipper mainly breed beside brooks and streams in the north of Scandinavia, but migrate in winter to the open watercourses of southern and central Sweden. They plunge into water to feed on aquatic invertebrae, particularly caddis fly larvae. Up to 10 dippers spend the winter here, making the stream one the the island's most important winter habitats for this species.

Map on p. 126

77 Lindeberget, one of Gotland's largest inland cliffs rises about 30 metres above the surrounding agricultural landscape, 5 kms north of Hemse. Visitors venturing to the top, will be rewarded with a panoramic view.

The south slope of the cliff is gentle, whereas the other faces are steep, almost perpendicular precipices. A long valley, (50 metres wide x 100 metres long) has cut into the east precipice, on a level with the northernmost outposts of the village. This is thought to have been cut out by the fast-flowing meltwater from retreating inland ice about 12 000 years ago. The cliff as a whole is probably still in existence thanks to its highly resilient reef limestone composition.

View from Lindeberget.

The crown of Lindeberget is clad in pine forest, while the damper and more nutrient-rich slopes are wooded with spruce. The rare limestone fern grows by the cliff.

On top of several of the precipices, vegetation is very similar to that of the alvar (p.42) in the south of Gotland. The reason is that the ground often lacks soil cover, and is intersected by numerous grykes, causing rapid infiltration of rainwater. Only xeric plants survive these harsh conditions, and ciliate melick is prevalent on the cliffs at Linde.

Ciliate melick is habitat-specific occurring only on limestone outcrops and calcareous gravel on Öland and Gotland. This fact, and its fluffy panicle, distinguishes it from other grasses. Flowering plants on the cliff include viper's bugloss, lady's bedstraw, vincetoxicum and wild thyme.

Prehistoric remains can be found here, as indeed almost anywhere else on the island. Most conspicuous are the two hillforts which are situated in the north and northeast near the edge of the cliff. On the sides where the cliff does not afford protection from attackers, the fort has been completed with stone ramparts which are 4-8 metres wide and up to 2½ metres high.

The best starting point for a visit to Lindeberget is Linde Church. Wooden steps lead up to a path at the top, about 100 metres west of the church. The path runs alongside the precipice in a northerly direction.

Map on p. 127.

78 Sandarve kulle is situated just beside Lindeberget, about 4 kms NW of Hemse. The hill rises 30 metres above the surrounding undulating agricultural district. It is composed of a reef formation of red, resilient reef limestone, known as Etelhem limestone. This rock is highly fossili-

ferous and mainly consists of stromatoporoids, crinoids and corals.

The hill is covered with a sparse, gnarled and beautiful pine forest, with the occasional spruce and deciduous tree. The sparse forest at the south end of the hill affords an unobstructed view of the surroundings. The precipices stretch along the west flank with occasional projections, known as overhangs, and small caves. A small stand of elm grows at the foot of the southwest end of the hill.

A good supply of nutrients and ground water has produced lush grove vegetation on the slopes, with a dense and species-rich shrub layer and a grand flora.

Spring is heralded by a profusion of hepatica and yellow anemone, followed by a number of rarities, including dog violet, proliferous pink and

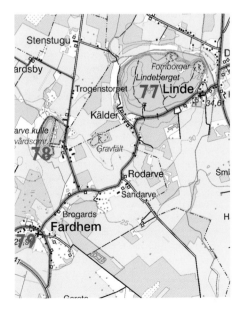

black wild cotoneaster. Rare grasses and sedges include small-leaved elm, wood melick, grey and wood sedge. Between Sandarve kulle and the road to its east lies Storänget – a pastureland with ash and some oak and pine. Both Storänget and Sandarve kulle are grazed by horses in summer.
Map on p. 127

79 The small, but well-managed **parish meadow at Fardhem** is characterized by lush herb-vegetation and numerous thick ash trees, which bear signs of pollarding. Those visiting the meadow in May and June, at the peak of the flowering period, will be met by a magnificent display of orchids and other meadow flowers. Early purple and fragrant orchids are the prevalent species in early summer, while marsh and broad-leaved helleborine abound at the height of summer.

Since the meadow is situated in a depression, the ground is rather damp, and ground vegetation in most of the meadow is characterized by wetland meadow plants such as meadowsweet, marsh thistle and common valerian.

In the west and east, the meadow is flanked by overgrown pollard meadows, succeeded in the south by arable land.

The parish meadow at Fardhem is reached by making your way along the small road leading south, just west of the church and vicarage. You can park beside the church or by the football pitch opposite the road leading to the meadow.
Map on p. 127

80 When you first catch a glimpse of the distant silhouettes of the two islands (tr. Greater and Lesser Charles' Islands) a feeling steals over you that whatever is waiting out there is going to be quite a unique experience. **Stora Karlsö** offers awesome geological shapes, a cultural history to fire the imagination, distinctive vegetation and myriads of birds.

The astonishing numbers of guillemots and razorbills might well prove to be the most enduring memory of your visit to St. Karlsö.

The guillemot, the auk with the pointed bill, is more common than the razorbill. About 7 500 pairs breed on Stora Karlsö, which thus harbours by far the largest colony in the Baltic region.

The guillemot is well adapted to a life in water. The wings are narrow and used for propulsion when it dives for small fish, while its feet serve as rudders. The guillemot can dive to a depth of 50-60 metres, and can remain underwater for a couple of minutes. One of the greatest threats to the guillemot is getting entangled in a fishing net and drowning.

At the onset of early spring, the guillemots return to Stora Karlsö from their winter haunts in the south of the Baltic Sea. In the first half of May the female lays a single, pear-shaped egg directly on a cliff ledge. The male and female take turns to incubate the egg for just over a month, when it is hatched. Prior to, and during hatching the parents entice the chick with a special call. The chick learns to recognise its parents' calls and to distinguish them from the others.

Then, one mild, calm evening in the first half of July, it will be time for the chick to leave the security of the ledge, which is often at a height of 20-40 metres – and the chick, no more than three weeks old, still cannot fly! However futile it may seem, the only option the chick has is to jump.

On a prime "jump evening", when the weather is fair, the water closest to the bird-cliff literally teems with guillemot parents, who unceasingly exhort their progeny to jump. Finally the chick can no longer resist. Taking the plunge, it frantically flaps its short wings in an endeavour to slacken speed. The chicks land in the water – or among the rocks and pebbles on the beach. Very few of those landing on the beach actually die, since their skeleton is still cartilaginous, although some hit the ground so hard that they lay dazed for a couple of minutes. On recovery, the chick quickly waddles to the water, where it is reunited with its male parent, who immediately starts to usher his progeny out to sea.

Many of the chicks which land on the beach are ringed. When ringed guillemots are later recovered, they provide valuable information on their migration routes, winter haunts, survival and cause of death.

Bird life on Stora Karlsö is not all guillemots and razorbills. In the deciduous groves of the island you will see a multitude of small birds, such as the icterine, wood and gardner warblers and the scarlet grosbeak. Even less common species, such as the barred warbler (a regular nester), greenish warbler and red-breasted flycatcher can be seen on the island. The scarlet grosbeak population has increased tremendously since the first breeding attempt in 1949, and today, several pairs breed in the deciduous woodland and in the shrubbery.

The guillemots' nesting cliff and the island as a whole make an exciting chapter on geology. Stora Karlsö is composed of a core of reef limestone. Two large reef formations can still be distinguished to this day – Marmorberget in the west and Röjsu hajd in the east. Softer, stratified limestone envelop the reef body. Since the island mainly consists of the more resilient reef limestone, it has withstood the erosive impetus of the inland ice and seawaves.

Hien at the northwest end of Stora Karlsö. The precipices are often concealed by lush deciduous forests.

When the island emerged from the sea about 11 000 years ago, wave action began work on sculpting the island. Vertical cliffs were chiselled out of the gently sloping flanks. The soil cover left by the ice was more or less completely removed by the waves, leaving vast beach ridges. The Ancylus Lake beach ridges at the upper end of Norderslätt may well be the largest in the country. Further down on Norderslätt, the shingle ridges of the Littorina Sea span the caves Lilla and Stora Förvar.

Other more palpable evidence of the sculpting power of the sea is furnished by several famous sea caves in the precipices on Stora Karlsö. Jung-fruhålet is the largest, with a depth of 20 metres, and Stora Förvar has been gouged out of the cliff east of Norderslätt. Korphålet and Rindhålet, both about 15 metres deep and favoured by guillemots for nesting, are situated in the precipice beneath the lighthouse. The ten-metre deep Kristallgrottan has been scooped out of the precipice at Svart-hällar at the southeast end of the island. This cave has been named after the profusion of calcite crystals in the walls of the cave.

At several places, a beautiful pattern of clefts and ridges has been cut into Stora Karlsö's bed-rock. These are the result of tension partly caused by the enormous weight of the kilometre-thick inland ice. These grooves, or grykes, have been

Guillemot pairs crowd together on the cliff ledges in the breeding season.

Several pairs of scarlet grosbeak (left) and barbed warbler (right) breed on Stora Karlsö.

widened and deepened by carbonic acid in rain-water, which dissolved their limestone walls. Wherever the grykes extend to the cliff face, the surge of the seawaves has scoured and widened them to form small, narrow ravines or caves. Svartsprang is an example of a relatively large cleft cave, which was formed at Hien at the west end of the cliff.

Frost erosion and leaching by rainwater have made the bedrock of Stora Karlsö extremely brittle, and many cliffs have been subjected to landslides. Stornasen in the west cliff was dislodged in 1905, and the landslide comprised several hundred tons of limestone. The most recent landslide, which afflicted Västerberget, was in January 1985.

Alpine hare are common on Stora Karlsö.

Vegetation and cultural history are intimately entwined on Stora Karlsö. In the latter half of the Stone Age, sheltered depressions and precipices on the island lay embedded in a naturally introduced low and windthrown forest of ash, lime, hazel, oak and pine. From this time onwards vegetation and faunal life were affected by the intervention of man and domesticated animals. Much of the cultural history of the island was revealed at the end of the 19th century, when the 4-metre-thick layer of earth, which almost filled the cave Stora Förvar, was excavated, and yielded layer upon layer of remains of Stone Age people who had used the cave as a permanent dwelling from 3000 to 2000 B.C.

The first settlers on Stora Karlsö were mainly hunter-fishers, leaving skeletal remains of numerous birds and mammals, including grey, harp and ringed seals, wolf, gannet, goshawk, eider, mallard, razorbill and guillemot. Remains of deliberately split human bones indicate that Stone Age man might well have been cannibalistic.

Towards the end of the Stone Age, man gradually based his subsistence on animal husbandry, with cattle, goats, pigs and above all, sheep.

The only remains from the Bronze Age (about 1500-400 B.C.) are four cairns with meagre yields. One of them, Röjsu, surmounts the highest point on the island, 51.6 metres above sea level. There are some seventy stone-clad graves in Norderhamn and Suderhamn dated to the Iron Age (400 B.C.-1050 A.D.) Conclusive evidence of permanent settlement in the Bronze and Iron Ages has still not come to light.

Sheep were probably put out to graze on the island almost incessantly between the Stone Age and the end of the 19th century. When the island was partitioned into grazing parcels in the 12th and 13th centuries, grazing was probably intensified on a large scale. Ever since that time, forests have been kept in check by the sheeps' grazing and people's need of firewood, the former being the main reason why the island was so barren and windswept at the turn of the last century – a feature noted earlier by Linné on his visit in summer 1741. The only tree he found on the plateau was an ash, now called Linné's ash, which still rises from the Bronze Age cairn Röjsu.

In 1880, some hunting and nature enthusiasts from the Gotlandic upper class founded the "Karlsö Hunting and Animal Protection Association AB", commonly known as "The Karlsö Club". Their goal was to preserve the guillemot population and the wild game (Alpine hare and razorbill). Ruthless hunting and egg collecting had led to a decimation of the guillemot population, which reached rock bottom in the 1880s, when 20 pairs were recorded. When the Karlsö Club assumed ownership of the island in 1887, sheep grazing was totally banned, partly since the sheep cropped the vegetation clean and partly because they competed with the hares for pasture. Eventually hunting of guillemot and razorbill ceased. In 1970 Stora Karlsö was brought under the legal protection of a Nature Reserve.

Once grazing ceased, trees, shrubs and higher plants began to recapture former territory. The ground, however, is dry and almost bare of soil cover. It will probably take several hundred years before vegetation has regained its original scope. The Karlsö Club aims to accelerate the afforestation of the island, and has planted some species foreign to the island. Among the best survivors are several specimens of walnut, a stand of Northern white cedar on Norderslätt and the shrub St Lucie cherry, which has spread across the entire island. The latter has fruit similar to the bird cherry, which are prized by small birds, which spread the seeds with their excrement.

Stora Karlsö is flora-rich, supporting 560 species of vascular plants, 126 moss species and almost 300 species of lichen. By far the most common is sheep's fescue – a short, densely-tufted, grazing-tolerant grass. The carpets woven by various stonecrops and the purple rounded heads of wild thyme are also striking.

Lesser meadow-rue, which grows up to one metre in height and has distinctive leaves, can be found up on the grassy moor. In spring, the bright yellow flowers of the profuse yellow pheasant's eye shine on the moor. In the autumn the moor is still bright yellow, this time with goldilocks, a plant of a southern range, which is rare in Sweden, but is probably a relict from the warm period. A profusion of the slender St Bruno's lily, with their white starlike flowers grows on the crown of the island. The pride of St Karlsö, however, is the pliant lettuce, a warm-period relict whose stems, tall enough to hide a man, rise from the elm grove at Älmar.

When May merges into June, Stora Karlsö puts on a magnificent display of orchids. Elder-flowered and early purple orchids flourish in the depressions on the plateau. Here and there, the grassy vegetation of the meadow conceals the smaller burnt orchid.

Stora Karlsö is reached by boat from Klintehamn. The boat leaves the harbour at 10 and 11.30 a.m., and is back at 4 and 5.30 p.m. There are bus connections to and from Visby. This service runs from the beginning of May to the end of August. To safeguard the sensitive plant and animal life, visitors are not allowed to wander freely around the island, but must join the guided tours. Bookings for the boat trip, as well as accommodation on the island, can be made by telephone (+46 498 24 05 00) or by e-mail (boka@stora.karlso.com).

It is prohibited to frequent the offshore area within 500 metres from the east, west and south shores of the island, between 15th March and 15th August.

8 | Lilla Karlsö with an area of 1.6 km², is situated about 3 kms off the main island of Gotland. Most of the island consists of an elevated, flat-topped, almost circular plateau, with sheer cliffs or steep precipices plunging down in all directions. Compared to the neighbouring St. Karlsö, the cliffs here are taller and vaster, and the highest point, just over 66 metres above sea level, is almost 15 metres higher. Coastal plains slope gently down from the south and northwest ends of the plateau, while cliffs plummet straight down into the sea or onto a narrow beach from the east and west ends.

Elder-flowered orchids bloom in profusion on Stora Karlsö at the end of May.

The north coast of Lilla Karlsö.

The core of the plateau consists of hard reef limestone, which has managed to resist inland ice erosion, leaving a somewhat hummocky surface. Beach ridges circuiting the highest point of the island bear witness to the fact that the entire island lay beneath the surface of the sea following the latest glaciation; they are thought to have been formed by the Baltic Ice Lake. Traces of the different stages in the development of the present Baltic Sea can also be seen in the numerous caves which have been scooped out at different levels in the cliff faces. Most impressive are Norder Vagnhus and Suder Vagnhus, which are about 20 metres deep and were cut out by the Ancylus Lake.

Sheep grazing was abandoned on Stora Karlsö in 1887, but is still practised on Lilla Karlsö, which has been more or less heavily grazed at least since the Medieval Period. In bygone days, most sheep on Gotland were of the primordial Gotlandic breed with short tails and horned rams and ewes. When in the 1920s, the Swedish Agricultural Board decreed that sheep should not be horned, the Goth breed declined in number, and at the beginning of the 1940s they were on the brink of extinction. Then, when the Swedish Society for Nature Conservation bought Lilla Karlsö in 1954, the island became a refuge for the remaining Goth sheep. Nowadays, about one hundred ewes, along with their lambs and a few rams, graze on the island from March until December.

Sheep grazing has had a strong impact on the landscape. Lilla Karlsö appears to be much more barren and bare than Stora Karlsö, where shrubs and trees have greatly increased their numbers since grazing was abandoned. The Gotlandic landscape was earlier affected by grazing in much the same way as Lilla Karlsö is today. The aim of allowing continued grazing on Lilla Karlsö is to preserve the ancient, unimproved sheep-grazing landscape.

Ground vegetation is heavily grazed with the exception of poisonous plants such as nettles and vincetoxicum, and pungent plants such as wild thyme, marjoram and wormwood, which sheep avoid.

In the screes above Suderslätt there are remains of a former lush deciduous forest. Thick and several-centuries-old elm, oak, ash and whitebeam grow in the shelter of the precipice. These veteran trees are now dying off at an alarming rate, and to prevent the island from becoming completely treeless, saplings are fenced in to protect them from the sheep.

Despite sheep grazing, and provided the summer is not too arid, flowers from many low-growing, grazing-tolerant plants add beautiful splashes of colour to the ground. Orchids, however, are but few – only four species have been found on the island. As on so many other isolated islands, plant and animal life on Lilla Karlsö has been meticulously surveyed. The island is by no means species-poor, when it comes to plants – about 320 different vascular plants have been found, including a few rarities. One of these is the fern hartstongue, which grows in cracks in shady precipices. Hartstongue has only been found in very few places outside Lilla Karlsö.

Wild pliant lettuce, which Linné discovered on Lilla Karlsö when he visited the island in 1741, cannot be found anywhere in Sweden except on Lilla and Stora Karlsö. Closest neighbours are to be found in the deciduous forests of Central Germany. The community on the Karlsö islands is thought to be a relict of the warm period.

A visit to Lilla Karlsö does not afford the same opportunity of studying the guillemots at close hand as on Stora Karlö. The guillemots breed only on Österberget, which is an off-limit sanctuary during the nesting period. Far fewer auks breed on Lilla Karlsö than on Stora Karlsö. The number of guillemots is estimated at about 1 100 pairs. Razorbills are more numerous; about 1 400 pairs breed mainly on Österberget, but there are also a few on Västerberget. There are only about 30 pairs of black guillemots, which are never gregarious. In 1992 the cormorant also began to breed on the island. The population has increased dramatically since then, and there are now over 2 000 pairs.

Although guillemots and razorbills may be the species of greatest interest to the visitor, no one can avoid noticing the fantastic numbers of gulls that frequent Lilla Karlsö. The great black-backed gull is the largest gull, demanding large nesting sites and thus only found scattered along the coasts. About 50 pairs of great black-backed gulls breed on Lilla Karlsö, probably forming the largest colony in the Baltic Sea. Between 100 and 200 pairs of the much smaller lesser black-backed gull breed on the plateau, where the slightest disturbance will unleash an almost deafening sound. The 2 000 breeding pairs of herring gull form the largest gull colony on the island. The herring gull has been favoured by open rubbish dumps and waste material discarded by fishing fleets at sea, leading to a dramatic increase in their numbers.

Hartstongue is a rare fern, which grows on Lilla Karlsö.

The black-headed gull has also found refuge on the island; about 1 000 pairs breed in the small marsh at Suderslätt. The gull population was once checked by control measures such as punching holes in their eggs, or offering them toxic baits. Gulls were thought to swamp out other species by eating their eggs and chicks. It was later noted, however, that the gulls' victims, such as eider and velvet scoter, increased their numbers at about the same rate as the gull colonies. This "persecution" has now ceased.

Since shrub and tree vegetation is so poorly developed on Lilla Karlsö, small-bird life is also meagre. Wheatear and skylark, however, both ground-nesters, are very common over the entire island. Along the shores the rock pipit can often be seen, a bird which is rare on Gotland, but which has a stable and large population of individuals on Lilla Karlsö. The decaying tree stems in the "forest" on the south screes are ideal for cavity-nesting species such as stock dove and starlings. A large number of goosander pairs also utilise the hollow trees as nesting sites. Some raven pairs

Lilla Karlsö is grazed by the horned Goth.

Two of Lilla Karlsö's breeding birds: herring gull (left) and razorbill (right).

breed on the sea cliff ledges, where numerous house martins have cemented cupped nests in holes in the cliff face.

Lilla Karlsö formerly harboured a very dense population of Alpine hare. The hares were an important non-toxic supplementary diet mainly for eagles which found their way to the island in winter. At most, the hares have numbered about 600, but following the harsh winter of 1976-77, the hare population was seriously decimated to just a few individuals, and today these have also disappeared. Apart from fish and birds, there are very few vertebrates on the island. You might see the occasional grass snake basking in the sun on the pebbly beaches. Many of the island's grass snakes are completely black, lacking the customary yellow ring around their necks. Rats and mice are totally absent, although there are at least three species of bat.

In summer there is a daily service to the island. A fishing boat leaves Djupvik harbour at 10 a.m. Bookings can be made by telephone: +46 498 24 11 39. Refreshments are not available on the island, and you are advised to take a packed lunch with you.

Visitors are not allowed to explore the island for themselves, but must join the guided tours. The guides are very knowledgeable and helpful, and you will return from your day trip on Lilla Karlsö filled with many new experiences and fresh knowledge. Youth hostel accommodation is available in one of the buildings on the island.

Disembarkation on the island is prohibited without permission. It is also prohibited to frequent the offshore area within 500 metres of the island between 15th March and 15th August.

82 The coast at Eksta offers a magnificent view and in parts a pristine coastal landscape. Offshore, the huge, sheer cliffs of the two Karlsö islands loom on the horizon. Inland, a windthrown coastal forest provides a backdrop to the greyish-white shingle beach. The stage is set!

The 7 km-long coastal road from Djupvik (also called Djauvik) in the north to Hammarudd in the south passes through **the Eksta coast nature reserve**, which extends along most of this road. Camping and firelighting are prohibited in the nature reserve.

South of Djupvik, the road ascends a low cliff which plunges straight down into the sea. The cliff is lower in the south, and soon merges with a shingle beach. The cliff consists of bluish-grey marlstone, known as Mulde marlstone, the grey tones indicating a high clay content. On the pebbly beach south of the cliff you can see how pieces of the grey, brittle marlstone have been washed ashore and mixed with the lighter, more resilient shingle, which emanates from a bed of purer limestone. Woad and sea rocket grow here, and at the end of July, blue lettuce flowers peep out from among the lyme grass.

The beach south of Kronvalds fishing hamlet is an area of outstanding natural beauty. Here, wave action has banked up distinct beach ridges on the 50-metre-wide shingle beach. Trees and shrubs cannot survive along this exposed coastline, but herbs such as lady's bedstraw, wild thyme and mouse-ear hawkweed form a sparse and creeping vegetation cover.

The coastal forest, which succeeds the shingle beach, is living proof of the impetus of nature at work. Twisted and creeping juniper, pine and spruce form a dense thicket which cowers beneath

View of Lilla Karlsö from Eksta coast.

the westerly winds, the trees seeking shelter behind each other. As the forest spreads inland, it gradually rises to greater heights.

At Hammarudd the coastline deflects towards the south east. When the shingle beach is succeeded by boulder-rich till, you have reached Ugnen bird sanctuary.

Map on p. 135.

83 The bird sanctuary at Ugnen extends from the border of the Eksta coast nature reserve at Hammarudd in the north and about 6 kms southwards along the coast, down to Snoderviken, north of Kvarnåkershamn. The coast is low-lying, and the wide, shallow beach is heavily indented with numerous headlands and bays. Most of the beach is a heavily-grazed coastal meadow, sometimes encompassing land-locked seabays. The beach along this coastline is an ideal habitat for

The motley shelduck breed along most of the shores of Gotland.

many waterfowl and waders, and is probably one of Gotland's bird-densest coastal areas.

When Ugnen's birdlife was surveyed it was found that some 40 species nested within the area. Among these were the shelduck, greylag goose, gadwall, avocet, ruff and dunlin. The dunlin may well be the most interesting species in the area. In order to breed, they are reliant on just the type of low-cropped coastal meadow found within the bird sanctuary. Unfortunately, this grazing regime is being abandoned by farmers, and the dunlin seem to be disappearing at about the same rate.

Ugnen bird sanctuary is also of importance as a stopover for passage birds. In spring many large flocks of barnacle geese feed in the grazed meadows, and in late summer and autumn large, species-rich ducks and waders are frequent passage birds.

To safeguard undisturbed breeding, access to the sanctuary area is strictly prohibited from 15th March to 30th June. However, there are still good opportunities of studying birdlife there. By heading west from road 140 just north of the farm Bopparve, you will reach the littoral road between Langstiteviken and Hammarudd at the northern end. From here, the richest coastal meadows can be viewed. A small junction leads from the road to Kvarnåkershamn to the fishing hamlet Klase, and just south of here, there is a tower hide, from which you will have a good view over the coastal meadows.

Map on p. 135.

84 In **Högby äng**, meadow-managment has been resumed in recent years, having been abandoned for a length of time. A handful of thick, tall and very majestic pines adorn the meadow. Oak, ash, birch and large, mature hazel bushes prevail beneath their crowns.

A newly-built road on the outskirts of a residential area, about 500 metres along the Hemse-Fardhem road, leads to Högby äng.

Map on p. 137.

View from tower hide south of Klase fishing hamlet. Stora Karlsö can be discerned on the horizon.

85 **Hulte kruppar** is the name of one of Gotland's largest managed meadows. Large, open spaces alternate with clusters and rows of oak, ash pollards and hazel bushes.

Hulte Kruppar displays no great luxuriance of orchids, but vegetation is lush, and several different plant habitats with their specific plant communities await the botany enthusiast. Beneath the shady branches of the oak and hazel you will find plants such as herb Paris, sanicle, lesser butterfly orchid and the slender wood-meadow grass. In the glades the ground is drier, supporting other species which are better adapted to this habitat; the most common species are devilsbit scabious, kidney vetch, yellow rattle and imperforate St John's wort.

Since the meadow is very well managed and beautiful, it is well worth visiting even after haymaking, which takes place in July.

86 **Lausvik** is a very wide, shallow bay on the east coast of Gotland. The bay is mainly renowned as a stopover site for passage birds in spring and autumn, including large flocks of swans, ducks and waders; enormous flocks of several hundred, sometimes thousands of certain species have been sighted.

Many of the passage birds come from the Scandinavian Arctic regions and Russia. One of them is bewick's swan, which stops at Lausvik during spring migration, when about 200 individuals can be seen.

Lausvik also supports a rich fauna of breeding birds, including avocet, black-tailed godwit, ruff, yellow wagtail and dunlin. Many sections of the shores at Lausvik are grazed, thus supporting an interesting coastal meadow vegetation.

The southern end of Lausvik is usually the most bird-rich, and the best viewpoint is the beach east of the mouth of the stream Närkån.

Map on p. 138.

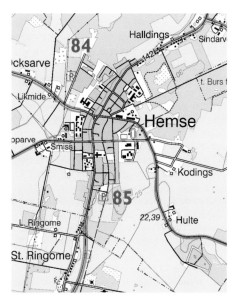

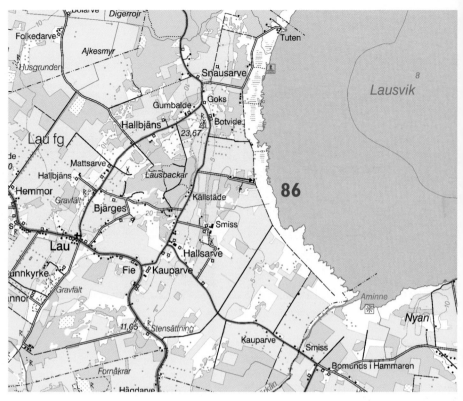

87 **Närsholmen** is an almost 2 km² low-lying peninsula on the east coast of Gotland. This low altitude and the extensive grassy pasturelands impart a remarkably desolate wilderness-like atmosphere to the area. Only occasional juniper bushes and a small pine grove interrupt the low-lying, level horizon of the peninsula.

The southern tip of Närsholmen, on which there now stands a lighthouse, was an islet some hundred years ago, separated from Närsholmen itself by a sound. When the islet rose from the sea, waves of the Baltic Sea, mainly from the south, broke upon its shores. The waves followed the flanks of the islet, and when they reached its northern end, they curved in towards each other. This phenomena is called wave refraction. As a result, the beach ridges, thrust up by the waves, converged at the north end of the islet.

The beautiful pattern of beach ridges is most distinct when viewed while approaching the lighthouse from the north. Another landform created by the ocean waves and currents can be studied in the bay Kroken, at the far end of Närsholmen. Three very long spits, composed entirely of shingle, can be seen offshore.

Apart from an unusual morphology, Närsholmen also supports a fine flora and a rich bird life. About 500 metres north of the lighthouse,

where the road forks, yellow milk-vetch, a pea plant with yellow flowers blooming in June, can be found. Yellow milk-vetch is restricted to dry habitats and is rarely seen outside Öland. Närsholmen is the only site where they grow on Gotland. The dimorphic elder-flowered orchid, producing either red or yellow flowers in May-June, can also be seen on Närsholm, beside the road about 100 metres north of the pine grove.

Out in the pasturelands you are otherwise met by a beautiful but quite commonplace dry meadow

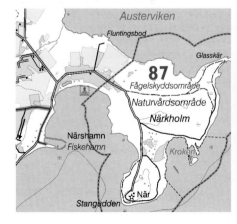

"Juniper savannah" at Närsholm.

flora, including harebell, lady's bedstraw, spiked speedwell and bloody cranesbill. The calcicole bloody cranesbill is far more common in the calcareous Gotlandic soils than in the calcite-poor soils on the mainland.

Austerviken, north of Närsholmen, with its coastal meadows and shallow water, is the favourite haunt of many birds, including a multitude of ducks and waders, such as avocet, ruff and dunlin, which breed here. Austerviken, just like other wide and shallow pasturelands, produces an abundance of nourishment by way of invertebrates and plants, which benefit bird life. The well-stocked larder not only feeds breeding birds, but also numerous waders, ducks and small birds from the North, which stop over to feed and roost during spring and autumn migrations.

Bird life is obviously very sensitive to disturbance, especially in spring and early summer, and access to certain areas is strictly prohibited between 15th March and 15th July. Even at other times of year, for example when flocks of geese feed in the coastal meadows, great caution must be exercised when visiting the area.

Map on p. 138.

88 Nisseviken is one of the few bays on the west coast of Gotland; most bays are on the east coast. Nisseviken is thus a west-coast haven for seabirds preferring the calmness of a bay to the open sea.

This shallow bay is the breeding site of about 25 different species of maritime birds, including

Närsholmen is the only site on Gotland where yellow milk-vetch grow.

waders such as ruff and avocet, as well as seabirds such as mute swan and great crested grebe. These two seabirds have long been common in the shallow eutrophic lakes and inner archipelagoes on the mainland. On Gotland, however, the first breeding pair were not sighted until the end of the 1930s. Since then the populations of great crested grebe and mute swan have risen to about 100 and 200 pairs respectively, breeding both in inland waters and on the coast.

In spring and autumn, Nisseviken is of great importance to the numerous waders and ducks which stop to feed in the bay and the coastal meadow pasturelands. Flocks of curlew, whimbrel, bar-tailed godwit, as well as ruff, dunlin and

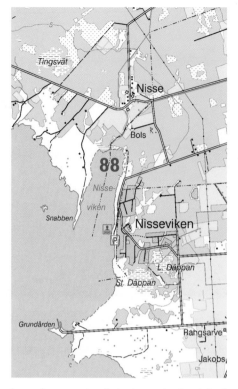

meadowlands. **Pankar prästänge**, just east of Grötlingbo Church, is the heart of one of these deciduous woodlands.

Pankar parish meadow has several large, sunny, open areas, which sharply contrast with the overgrown lands fringing the meadow. Here and there, vigorous, mature oaks rise up, and dense thickets of hazel grow alongside the stone walls.

Meres, fens and high humidity provide the meadow with lush vegetation. The yellow flowers of yellow iris and common meadow rue shine in the fens and meres, and in the glades you will find large self heal, meadow saxifrage, daisies, devilsbit scabious and meadow vetchling. Orchids are represented by the early purple and a few specimens of twayblade, fragrant, lesser butterfly and military orchids. The slender wood meadow-grass and wood melick, as well as herbs such as woodruff, herb bennet and bush vetch grow in the shade of trees and hazel copses.

The surrounding, dense deciduous forest houses a number of ancient monuments, and just south of the managed meadow there are several "giant's graves" (Iron Age house foundations).

Map on p. 141.

90 The east coast of Gotland is heavily indented and richly varied. **Grötlingboudd** is one of the most elongated peninsulas, and to its north is the bay of **Gansviken**.

Despite the lack of groves, the visitor is met by a sheltered natural landscape, thanks to the richness in juniper bushes, some almost as large as trees. Grötlingboudd is slightly convex, and when the road out to its farthest point reaches its crown, views of the low-lying pastureland open up to the south.

barnacle goose, etc. all stop to roost and seek food here. To safeguard bird life you are urged to abstain from entering the coastal meadow areas during breeding and migration seasons.

Map on p. 140.

89 Several of Gotland's deciduous forests can be found at the south end of the island, and have often evolved from abandoned and overgrown

Pankar parish meadow is damp and lush.

Natural features of interest at Grötlingboudd and Gansviken mainly comprise the outstandingly rich bird life in the coastal meadows and the close offshore islets. Water fowl include greylag goose, northern pintail, shoveller and teal. Terns are represented by five species. Apart from the Arctic and common terns, breeding terns include the Caspian, little and Sandwich terns. Waders are attracted to the profusion of coastal meadow pasturelands, and nesting species include the dunlin and avocet. Large colonies of black-headed gull also breed here, which other birds find beneficial. Whenever a predator or bird of prey approaches the colony, the gulls create a terrible din in their attempts to ward off the intruder. Many maritime birds nest in the shelter of the black-headed gull colonies.

Even passage birds are attracted to the lush coastal meadows of the area, as well as the highly nutritious ground water and the remoteness of the offshore islets. Greylag and above all barnacle geese feed here by the thousand, and in Gansviken there are scores of ducks. Various birds of prey winter in the area.

To safeguard mainly the feeding geese and geese shedding their feathers, the farthest end of Grötlingboudd and the offshore islets have been brought under the protection of a nature reserve. Access to the reserve is strictly prohibited from 15th March to 15th July and from 1st October to 15th November. However, in a bird-rich area such as this, greatest caution should be exercised at all times, even beyond the boundaries of the reserve. Avoid the coastal meadows in spring and early summer, and observe flocks of geese at a distance, otherwise they may take to flight in fear, thus

Arctic tern, one of the tern species breeding at Grötlingboudd.

Grey seal are often seen by Näsrevet off the southwest coast of Näsudden.

missing the opportunity to feed and rest, which they so desperately need. There is a car park at the far end of the peninsula, from which a path leads to a hide. From here, you can observe the geese without disturbing them.

Those visiting Grötlingboudd in May or the beginning of June should try to stop at the farm Kauparve, which is about 500 metres after the sharp left-hand bend in the road, which comes just after you reach the shore at Gansviken. There is an enclosed field of birch by the farm, with an abundance of elder-flowered orchids, which thrive in trampled and grazed land. This species is dimorphic, with either cream or red flowers.

Map on p. 141.

91 Näsudden is the only real peninsula on the west coast of Gotland, and offers the visitor an impressive, open pastoral landscape, braided with drystone walls, often bordered with whitebeam, which break up the low, rectilinear horizon.

Näsudden is probably most renowned for its numerous wind power plants and as one of Gotland's most significant staging posts for passage birds in autumn. Many migratory birds fly over land as far as possible, and often hold back for a while before engaging in flight across the sea. Näsudden functions as a funnel, through which passage birds from north and north east converge to a concentrated stream, taking a breather among

the whitebeam, copses and groves at the far end of the peninsula. Many thousands of birds of different species from Gotland and northern Scandinavia may stop off here on one single day in autumn.

The richest faunal life in summer is to be found off the coast at Bodudd, at the south west point of Näsudden on the islets of Flisen, Storgrunn and Lillgrunn, where greylag geese and avocets breed. The islets are also a favourite haunt of seals.

At the height of summer the geese and ducks shed their feathers and grow a fresh set, which means that they lose their ability to fly for a while. The islets off Bodudd are an important refuge for the birds, away from human disturbance.

Näsudden is worth a visit even in late summer. There is a large community of goldilocks just beside the junction to Sigvards, 1 km SW of Näs Church. This species is of a southern range and its presence on Näsudd is thought to emanate from a warmer, drier period, which lasted several millennia following the latest glaciation, when goldilocks, and other warm period relicts were more common and more widespread than today. Nowadays, goldilocks can only be found at a few sites on Öland and Gotland. The plant is about 30 cms tall and its stem is dotted with equally-narrow leaves and topped with an umbel-like cluster of flowers, which adds a splash of yellow to the dry field when they bloom in August-September.

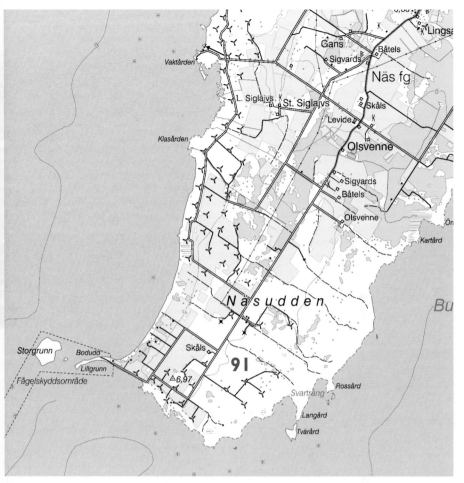

The east coast of Näsudden borders on the bay of Burgsvik, which also harbours a rich bird life, though mainly on the opposite shore, where large flocks of ducks, geese and swans feed in spring and autumn.

Map on p. 143

92 **Fide prästäng** is an easily-accessible, open and enticing parish meadow. It is situated on the west side of the east branch of the main road, 1 km north of Fide Church. Thick-stemmed and often wide-canopied oaks are widely spread around the meadow, and there are also ash pollards.

Nearest the main road there is an open-canopy meadow with an abundance of common meadow plants. Red clover, common rock rose and bloody cranesbill are prevalent, along with common spotted, fragrant, early purple and military orchids. Broad-leaved helleborine, twayblade and lesser butterfly orchids grow in the shadier parts of the meadow. Visitors will also find narrow-leaved helleborine, lily-of-the-valley and the unassuming sanicle.

Goldilocks bloom in late summer at the north end of Näsudden.

Fide parish meadow is bordered by deciduous forests, which were formerly managed.

Map on p. 144.

93 One of Sweden's **largest deciduous forests** grows in an area over 5 kms long, between Fidenäs in the north and Öja Church in the south. It is surrounded and at times interrupted by farmland.

The deciduous woodland has evolved from the overgrowth of meadows and enclosed pastures, and birch is clearly prevalent. Deciduous forests and their thick, at times almost impenetrable shrub-layer of hazel and hawthorn provide a favourable habitat for many species of birds, some of which occur in dense populations.

This habitat is by far the favourite haunt of the Gotlandic tawny owls, and their deep hooting reverberates through the forests on late winter nights. Later, in April, woodpeckers can be heard drumming on dry wood at dawn, claiming territory and seeking a partner. In May and at the beginning of June, the dawn air is filled with song from numerous warblers, thrushes and fly catchers.

In spring and early summer a number of less common birds may be sighted, including the red-breasted flycatcher, hawfinch, scarlet grosbeak and golden oriole. Although golden oriole do not breed on Gotland, they have been seen to stop here several years in succession. The male plumage is bright yellow with black wings, and their song is a flute-like call, which sounds as if it is coming from a tropical rain forest.

A difficult problem for nature conservation has long been that our deciduous forests are gradually being clear-felled and replaced with spruce. Plants and animals reliant on deciduous woodland are now rare, and arguments for preserving the few that remain are strong.

The trush nightingale is common in the deciduous woodland of Fidenäset.

Öja parish meadow.

The deciduous forest between Fidenäs and Öja is often extremely inaccessible, the margins are easily reached from the main roads east and west of the forest, or from the junctions. Björklunda, just over 1 km north of Burgsvik, is a suitable starting point.
Map on p. 144.

94 Öja kyrkänge is a lush and enticing parish meadow, not least due to its numerous and often large hazel bushes, whose curved branches converge to verdant arches. The meadow is situated immediately SW of Öja Church. There is a car park just south of the church.

Tall, beautiful oak, birch and ash trees, as well as an occasional whitebeam rise above the hazel clusters. Sheltered by the hazel and deciduous trees, shade-bearing plants such as herb Paris, lily-of-the-valley, germander speedwell and May lily, as well as the orchids broad-leaved helleborine and twayblade can be found. The shade-bearing and elegant wood meadow-grass also grows here.

The glades interspersed among the hazel groves often display a rich meadow flora with plants such as ribwort plantain, yellow rattle, common rock rose, meadow saxifrage, northern bedstraw and dropwort. The meadows also support a goodly number of fragrant, common spotted and military orchids. At the north east and south west ends, the meadow is flanked by overgrown meadows and pastures.

In May and June the meadow and adjacent dense deciduous forests reverberate with the songs of numerous deciduous forest birds. Warblers, fly catchers, tits and woodpeckers are common. The golden oriole is one of the rarities which visit the meadow.
Map on p. 144.

95 The lake **Mjölhatteträsk** is situated just 2 kms SW of the village of Burgsvik, in a low-lying expanse of barren landscape (alvar p.42), strewn with the prevalent juniper, occasionally interrupted by pine groves or small marshes. The

Common spotted orchid.

Carpets of dragon's teeth in bloom at Killingholm.

coast opens up further west, from **Valar** in the north to Killingholm in the south.

Mjölhatteträsk is large but shallow. Together with Stockviken on the other side of the island, this is the southernmost lake on the island, and is therefore the first lake to be reached by migratory birds, on their arrival in spring. Conversely, it is the last inland-water staging post before the autumnal migration across the Baltic Sea. Large

flocks of swans, geese and ducks can thus be observed during migration periods.

Breeding birds include ducks, terns and waders, such as the avocet. Formerly, the lake supported Gotland's largest colony of great crested grebe, but the dredging of the outlet in the 1950s led to a calamitous drop in the depth of water in the lake.

To the west of the lake, along a path from the road in the north, stands a beautiful birch forest –

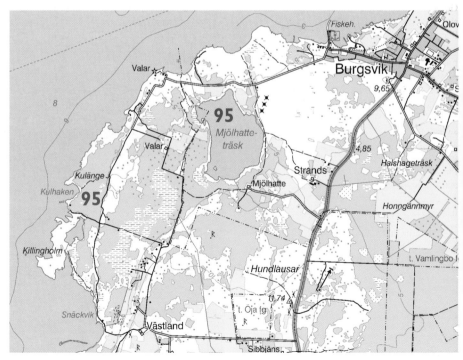

Abrasion by sea waves has created remarkable formations.

open and tall, with lush ground vegetation and with majestic junipers in the shrub-layer, where the ground is sandy, which is favourable to the emergence of a birch forest. Along the south shore there is a lush littoral deciduous forest with a rich bird life, including the scarlet grosbeak and other typical deciduous forest birds. The marsh warbler breeds in the lush thicket of shrubs and herbs. Some years, the golden oriole and the greenish warbler have been sighted. The golden plover breeds on the surrounding alvar. In spring and early summer, occasional specimens of species of a southern or eastern range have strayed up to Gotland. Examples of rarities, which have been sighted in this area, are the black stork and penduline tit.

The coast seaward of Mjölhatteträsk is interesting and beautiful in several ways. The beach is most easily accessed by Valar lighthouse, just off the coast where the gravel road from Burgsvik turns sharp left (almost 1 km from Mjölhatteträsk).

Apart from the occasional oolite limestone, the stones on the shingle beach opposite the lighthouse are mainly of sandstone. Since sandstone is formed by the deposition of sand, layer upon layer, the stones broken up by waves are very flat. Wave action has then abraded the stones, rounding their edges, to form shingle, which often lies on the beach in beautiful patterns. The shingle, combined with whitebeam, which sporadically fringe the backshore, impart an exotic atmosphere over Valar. Along the coast there are several abandoned sand stone quarries, where emergent leafy thickets support a rich bird life, including species such as the marsh warbler and trush nightingale.

Just over 2 kms to the south along the shore, at Killingholm, the sand stone bedrock is exposed, bearing numerous traces of abrasion by sea waves, creating sea caves and other remarkable formations.

The area between the coast and Mjölhatteträsk is occupied by former pastureland with drystone walls and fences. Here, as in many other desolate areas on the island, the vegetation provides such lean pasture that the land can no longer match the tremendous present-day economic demands made on livestock breeding. Large grazing areas have thus been abandoned, and the open cultural landscape is becoming overgrown. Some comfort can be gained from the thought that these dry, nutrient-poor lands need a long time to become overgrown, in contrast to the many abandoned hay meadows and pasturelands on more fertile soil.

In the coastal meadows 1 km SW of Valar lighthouse, there is a lush community of elder-flowered orchids. Apart from the red and cream-coloured

Marsh warbler.

Tower hide at Stockviken.

flowers, there are various intermediary varieties.
Map on p. 146.

96 **The meadow beside the farm Lasses,**
near the Burgsvik-Faludden road, is richly varied
and beautiful. Glades at the east end give the meadow a light and open character, while the west
end is shadier. Hazel groves alternate with rows
of mature oak, birch, occasional whitebeam and
hazel bushes.

The meadow is herb-rich and lush. Orchids
include the lesser and greater butterfly orchids and
broad-leaved helleborine. There is also an abundance of the fragile eyebright – a species which
almost vanished from Sweden with the introduction of managed meadows. Rich communities can
now only be found on Gotland.

The meadow at Lasses bears traces of prehistoric
Celtic fields, which are units of squares, divided
by lynchets and with a slightly depressed surface.

On the other side of the road, just south of Lasses, there is another meadow which is well worth
a visit, if you happen to be in the area. It is very
open and consists almost entirely of large meadowlands, with scattered, beautiful, solitary birch trees
of awesome size.
Map on p. 148

97 **Faludden and Stockviken** are situated on
the south east coast, 5 kms SE of Burgsvik. This
is considered to be Gotland's most bird-rich coast-
land. Out on the peninsula Faludden, the landscape is low-lying and almost everywhere pastureland seems to spread out, regularly partitioned by
drystone walls. Some typical Gotlandic farms, and
an occasional pine grove form oases in the open
grassland.

Stockviken is a bay just south of Faludden, on
the border between the littoral open wetland meadows, and the inland shady, sheltering deciduous
forests. From the road north of Stockviken, a path
leads down to a tower hide by the northeast shore
of Inre Stockviken. From here you have a fine
view of the lake and the coastal meadows beyond.

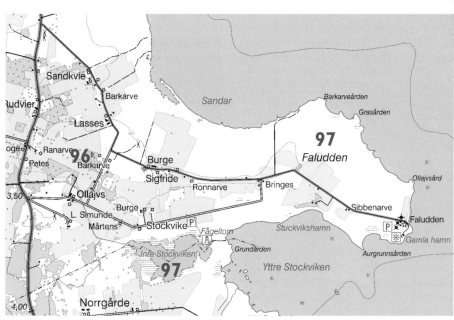

Inre Stockviken, one of Gotland's bird-richest lakes.

As late as at the end of the 19th century, Inre Stockviken was a seabay, which was later blocked off by a 300-metre long isthmus, following isostatic rise, transforming the seabay into a landlocked sea. Stockviken is, however, connected to Yttre Stockviken and the sea beyond, by its outlet, the furrow known as Grundgången.

The abundance of birds is most striking in Inre Stockviken and in the fringing coastal meadows, which often have a mosaic formation of wet furrows and pools, which is most favourable to bird life. Every type of Swedish surface-feeding duck, including the gadwall, teal, pintail, garganey, shoveller and wigeon breed in Inre Stockviken. Little grebe, Sweden's smallest grebe, have also been sighted here for several years in the breeding season.

The coastal meadows support a very dense wader population, and the nesting species include dunlin, ruff, black-tailed godwit, curlew and avocet. Another wader, which breeds in the proximity of Faludden, is the golden plover. This species is normally found in desolate alvar areas (p 42), and this is the place to stop if you wish to hear its mournful, fluty whistling. The favourite haunt of the golden plover is at Austerrum, the kilometre-wide alvar territory which extends along the coastline north of Faludden. The open land at Austerrum is the result of many years of heavy grazing by enormous flocks of sheep. This grazing

Well-grazed and bird-rich coastal meadows at the far end of Faludden.

149

Breeding waders at Stockviken: black-tailed godwit (top left), ringed plover (top right), redshank (centre left), lapwing (centre right) and ruff (bottom).

regime has gradually been abandoned, however, mainly due to the high costs of fencing, and juniper, pine and spruce have invaded the area.

Since Faludden projects way out into the sea, the area has become a natural staging post for numerous passage birds. The most renowned are probably the enormous flocks of barnacle geese, which stop over to feed in the grasslands during their spring migration to the Arctic Ocean. Flocks of several thousand individuals have been sighted. Greylag, brent geese, whooper and bewick's swans, as well as ducks, waders and various small birds also stop to feed here. Both in spring and autumn rare birds from southern and eastern Europe regularly stray up to this area. Birds of prey, such as rough-legged buzzard, golden eagle and white-tailed eagle also winter here.

In spring and early summer, Stockviken displays interesting flora. Green-winged orchid, moonwort and adderstongue grow in the coastal meadow between the tower hide and the road. Adderstongue are small ferns and typical coastal meadow plants.

98 Holmhällar is the name of the headland which forms Gotland's southeastern outpost, where one of the island's most remarkable sea stack fields attracts many visitors.

If you make your way to the beach along the path from the guest house Holmhällar pensionat, you will soon encounter the undulating and open, grassy landscape which occupies most of the Holmhällar area. This topography was formed by wave action, which banked up beach ridges when the headland first emerged from the sea. The sea stack field is further out on the beach and extends more than a kilometre along the gently curved outlines of the shore.

The sea stacks stand in a narrow belt from the waterline and in towards the precipice which demarcates the interior of the headland. They often stand crowded together, some of them tall and towering, others low and rounded. One reason for the singular shape of these stacks is that they consist of a very special type of reef limestone, known as crinoidal limestone, or more popularly (but incorrectly) marble. This limestone is almost entirely composed of crinoidal stalks and stromatoporoids. The profusion of these fossils will be enhanced if you pour some water onto the sea stack.

Looking towards the north east you will see another headland, Hammarshagehällar, where the beach is also strewn with sea stacks, but unfortunately much of the natural beauty of this area has been destroyed by gravel pits which have left ugly scars in the landscape.

The kilometre-long sandy beach of Skvalpvik lies between Holmhällar and Hammarshagehällar. Here you can observe how nutrient-poor and dry sand is successively invaded by highly resilient plants such as blue lettuce, and grasses such as lime grass and marram. Blue lettuce was first dis-

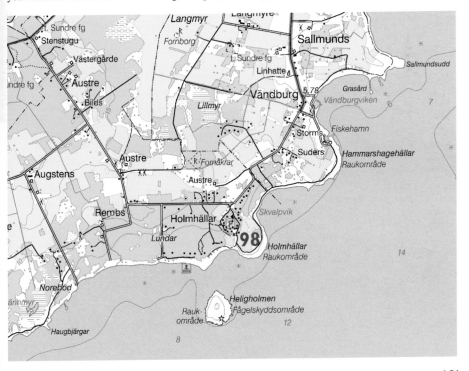

Sea stacks at Holmhällar.

covered on Gotland in 1928, since when it has spread, and today it can be found on most Gotlandic sandy beaches. At Skvalpvik a special type of wild pansy grows – a species which is common on the mainland, but rare on Gotland.

Kilometre-long sandy beaches form the coastline west of Holmhällar. Together with the beach at Skvalpvik, they are largely considered to be the best bathing beaches in the south of Gotland. Here and there along the sandy beaches, the wind has formed small sand dunes. The sandy beach-specific sea pea blooms at the end of June, and its reddish-purple flowers can be enjoyed throughout the rest of the summer. Musk orchid and sea holly, both protected species, can also be found here.

Heligholmen is an islet with sea stacks, caves and a rich bird life, lying at a distance from the shore at Holmhällar. Large colonies of various gulls and terns breed on its shores and on the treeless, low-lying and grassy inland. This islet has been brought under the protection of a bird sanctuary to safeguard the breeding and feeding birds. Access is prohibited from 15th March to 30th June.
Map on p. 151.

99 **Muskmyr** is a sedge fen, fringed with a chain of small areas of open water. It is situated NE of Sundre Church, beside the main road. A path leads from the car park to the edge of the fen.

When driving to Muskmyr along the main road in a southerly direction, the landscape suddenly opens up about a kilometre north of Sundre Church. You have arrived at Gotland's largest "al-var" (p 42), known as the Alvar of Sundre, which extends about 3 kms south east of Sundre Church right down to the coast.

A walk northwards along the west shore of Muskmyr in spring and early summer will lead you to the magnificent display of flowers in the coastal meadows at the north end of the fen, which supports German asphodel, an array of orchids including marsh helleborine, and fly, fragrant, Pugley's marsh, early marsh, flecked marsh and cream early marsh orchids. Common fumana, known in Sweden as "Gotland rock rose", grow on the alvar surrounding the fen.

Bird life at Muskmyr is most interesting in autumn (September-October), when several species of birds of prey pass and visit the fen on their southbound passage. Since this is the only larger waterhole in the alvar area, Muskmyr is of significance to all faunal life.

The outlet of Muskmyr is rather special. A stream flows northwards, but just after passing beneath the main road, the water suddenly disappears into a sink-hole in the bedrock, which was formed when carbonic acid in rainwater dissolved the limestone walls of a crack, thus enlarging it. The water is then conducted along the joints of the limestone bedrock.

Caterpillars of the rare pine processionary can be found in the alvar east of Muskmyr. They rest clustered together on branches and tree stems by day, and are active at night, when they set off on "hikes" in single file.
Map on p. 153

100 Hoburgen, the southernmost point of Gotland, is the crowning glory of a long stretch of high, rounded cliffed coast, called **Husrygg**. This part of Gotland offers magnificent and richly varied natural features, including views across a widespread, undulating alvar landscape (p 42), fields and farms with shady deciduous trees – all against the backdrop of the Baltic Sea.

Although the Hoburg area harbours both an interesting flora and a rich bird life, the most striking features are nevertheless the landforms and geology. The youngest bedrock on Gotland is the very resilient limestone forming the cliffs at Hoburgen. They are known as "Hoburg marble", are reddish-brown and consist almost entirely of crinoidal fossils of creatures which lived among the reefs here about 400 million years ago.

Husrygg, the low-lying coastline north of Hoburgen, mainly consists of marly limestone. As this is softer than reef limestone, it has been

View from tower hide at Muskmyr.

At the end of the road – Hoburgen at the southernmost tip of Gotland.

abraded to rounded shapes by seawaves. Sandstone, known as Burgsvik sandstone, can be found at the foot of Husrygg, nearest the sea. Scattered small stone quarries bear witness to the former, now virtually abandoned, sandstone quarrying activities.

At Hallbjäns, 2 kms north of Hoburgen, you can see a "visor". This is a piece of reef limestone,

Hoburgsgubben.

which projects from the bedrock of Husrygg. Just north of this, a road leads up to a valley cut out by inland ice.

Hoburgsgubben, the famous "old gaffer from Hoburg", a signposted seastack at Hoburgen, and the large sea caves in the same cliff, were once cut out by the waves of the Ancylus Lake. The level bedrock surfaces, the underwater ledges, which extend out to sea undergo constant abrasion by today's seawaves. The same goes for the circular depressions in the ledge, known as potholes.

When the land here emerged from the sea, the soil was washed away, leaving just a very thin soil cover. Since there is also very little precipitation at the southernmost end of Gotland, and since sheep have grazed here since prehistoric times, an extreme alvar vegetation has evolved. The uplands are dominated by ciliate melick, a grass which from July onwards is easily recognizable by its glimmering bottle-brush-shaped spikes. Ciliate melick is totally adapted to life on stony, dry ground. Other common xeric plants are viper's bugloss, wild thyme, vincetoxicum, whitebeam and juniper.

From the end of April and several weeks afterwards, an abundance of yellow pheasant's eye bloom on Husrygg. This is predominantly a southeast European steppe plant, which in Sweden can only be found on Öland and Gotland. The flowers are large and bright yellow like buttercups. Further north, on the alvar at Nackshajd there is also a large community of the common fumana (Sw: Gotland's rock rose) also a rarity. Husrygg is under the protection of a nature reserve.

As Gotland's southernmost outpost, the Hoburg area is a popular staging post for passage birds, both in spring and autumn. On an early morning in April-May the shrublands between Hoburg cliff and Rivet, the southernmost headland, literally teem with small birds, which have arrived in the night and at dawn. Apart from myriads of largely commonplace Nordic species, rarities are sighted every year. These have included white-billed diver, king eider, peregrine falcon, red-footed falcon, hoopoe, turtle dove, golden oriole and greenish warbler. During the most intensive migratory periods, birds are ringed in this area. The open lands are also popular hunting grounds for both migratory and wintering birds of prey.

Map on p. 153.

Yellow pheasant's eye bloom in profusion at Husrygg in May.

A red-breasted flycatcher has been caught and ringed. Numerous passage birds are ringed at Hoburgen in spring and autumn.

Angling

The 700 km-long coast of Gotland offers rich opportunites for rewarding angling. Coastal fishing is free, allowing you to lay out nets, or fish with hand tackle from the shore (except in some nature reserves). Fishing in lakes and rivers, on the other hand, requires prior permission from the owner of the fishing rights. A fishing permit is necessary in Tingstäde träsk and Paviken.

Gotlandic sea trout fishing has become increasingly popular in recent years. Sea trout can be caught from October, although the best season is during spring, from February to May. Sea trout can be caught around the entire island, often by wading (beware of undercurrents when wading near the underwater ledges!) The minimum size for sea trout is 50 cms. Salmon and trout fishing is prohibited in all Gotlandic watercourses during the spawning season from 1st October to 31st December, when all fishing is also prohibited in the Baltic Sea within the protected zones around the estuaries of the following streams: Arån, Vällesån, Vaste å, Ihre å, Lummelundaån, Själsöån, Kopparsviksbäcken, Varbosån, Robbjänsån, Snoder å, Tutenån, Svajdeå/Lavasån, Bane å, Gartarveån, Hugreifsån, Halsegårdaån, Gothemsån, Vike å, Vägumeån, Bångån and Hultungsån.

Salt-water fishing for salmon has been taken up by an increasing number of anglers over recent years. The fish are caught from trolling boats. The minimum size for salmon is 60 cms.

Pike is caught all year round, mainly off the east coast of the island. The minimum size for pike is 40 cms. Perch is caught at the same locations, and coarse perch is also caught in lakes.

Cod can be caught all year round from land, e.g. from Digerhuvud on Fårö. The most favourable time for cod fishing, however, is in winter. The minimum size at present is 35 cms, but since fish of this size have hardly managed to spawn at all, fish less than 40 cms should not be taken.

At the end of May/beginning of June, garpike move in to spawn on the sea-weed beds along the Gotlandic coast.

From the beginning of August and roughly until Christmas, and in April-May, rod-fishing for Baltic herring from the underwater ledges and piers can be rewarding. Autumn is also the right season to catch flatfish (minimum size 21 cms). Flatfish are protected from 15th February to 15th May off the east coast of Gotland. Every province in Sweden has chosen an 'official provincial fish', and turbot has been designated the official provincial fish of Gotland. It is bottom-fished, and the best season is in May and June. The minimum size is 30 cms.

Ide angling is popular in March-April, when the ide swim up the larger streams to spawn. The most renowned watercourses for ide angling are Gothemån, Närkån and Snoderån.

Information on fishing on Gotland is available at Tourist Offices and the County Administrative Board.

156

Right of public access and common sense in the countryside

The right of public access means that you may roam freely in the countryside, and that you may pick berries and mushrooms without prior permission. This custom, which is only partially statutory, is virtually unique to Sweden. The second chapter of the Government constitution states that everybody shall have open access to the countryside in accordance with the stipulations in the Law of Right of Public Access. This right, is, however, subject to a series of restrictions, by virtue of the environmental code, whose regulations make provisions to protect plants and animals, and prohibit littering. Each national park and nature reserve has its own regulations restricting the right of public access within its boundaries. Picking plants, lighting fires and camping, for example, are all prohibited in nature reserves. It is prohibited to gouge out fossils from the stacks and rocks at the Gotlandic sea stack reserves.

If we are to retain this right of public access, we must safeguard and respect the life of the countryside, by adhering to the following rules:

Do not forget to seek prior permission from the landowner, if you wish to camp for more than 24 hours, or to park your caravan.

We are allowed to:
- walk or ski across private land (exception: gardens, plantations or other sensitive ground)
- cross private water
- bathe on beaches that are not part of private gardens
- pick berries, mushrooms and flowers which are not listed species
- camp on private land for 24 hours without prior permission (but not close to dwellings or on sensitive ground)

We are not allowed to:
- damage land, trees or shrubs or crops
- travel across gardens without permission
- travel across crops or sensitive land
- moor a boat at a jetty or bathe on a beach which form part of a garden
- leave litter
- allow dogs to go unleashed except under strict control, so as to avoid causing distress to wildlife
- light a fire, if there is a fire-risk
- damage fences or forget to close a gate
- drive a vehicle off-road (exception: vehicles for agriculture and forestry)
- camp for more than 24 hours or too close to dwellings without the land-owner's permission; this also applies to caravans, which may only be parked at the roadside
- pick or uproot listed plants

Flora and fauna – Protected species

It is strictly prohibited to pick, uproot, or in any other way remove or harm wild living species of the following plants on Gotland. It is also prohibited to remove or damage seed or other parts of the species:

Vascular plants

Orchids, all species of the *Orchidaceae* and *Cypripediaceae* families.
Adderstongue spearwort, *Ranunculus ophioglossifolius*
Belgian gagea, *Gagea villosa*
Branched moonwort, *Botrychium matricariifolium*
Bur medick, *Medicago minima*
Common centaury, *Centaurium erythraea* var. *erythraea*
Common ragwort, *Senecia jacobaea* ssp. *gotlandicus*
Crocus-leaved goatsbeard, *Tragopogon crocifolius*
Eastern pasque flower, *Anemone patens*
Eyebright, *Euphrasia stricta* var. *suecica*
Gotlandic corydalis, *Corydalis gotlandica*
Gotlandic pasque flower, *Anemone pulsatilla* ssp. *gotlandica*
Grey mouse ear, *Cerastium brachypetalum*
Hairy milk vetch, *Oxytropis pilosa*
Hairy rock cress (sim.), *Arabis planisiliqua*

Green-winged orchid. All orchids are protected species.

Hartstongue, *Asplenium scolopendrium*
Helichrysum, *Helichrysum arenarium*
Irish eyebright, *Euphrasia salisburgensis* var. *schoenicola*
Leathery moonwort, *Botrychium multifidum*
Lesser hawkbit, *Leontodon saxatilis*
Lesser snapdragon, *Misopates orontium*
Madwort, *Ranunculus acris* ssp. *friesianus*
Meadow clary, *Salvia pratensis*
Mistletoe, *Viscum album*
Mountain ash (sim.), *Sorbus teodori*
Mountain zigzag clover, *Trifolium alpestre*
Northern dragonhead, *Dracocephalum ruyschiana*
Pliant lettuce, *Mulgedium quercina*
Purple milk vetch, *Astragalus danicus*
Ray's knotgrass, *Polygonum oxyspermum*
Red hemp nettle, *Galeopsis angustifolia*
Rustyback, *Asplenium ceterach*
Schistophyllum bifurcum
Scorpion senna, *Hippocrepis emerus*
Sea holly, *Eryngium maritimum*
Sea kale, *Crambe maritima*
Sharp-leaved fluellen, *Kickxia elatine*
Shepherd's needle, *Scandix pecten-veneris*
Simple moonwort, *Botrychium simplex*
Soft shield fern, *Polystichum aculeatum*
St Bernard's lily, *Anthericum liliago*
Stinking chamomile, *Anthemis cotula*
Swordleaf inula, *Inula ensifolia*
Thale cress, *Sisymbrium supinum*
Thyme broomrape, *Orobanche alba*
Tuberous pea, *Lathyrus tuberosus*
Tubular water dropwort, *Oenanthe fistulosa*
White horehound, *Marrubium vulgare*
White mullein, *Verbascum lychnitis*
Yellow pheasant's eye, *Adonis vernalis*
Yellow salsify, *Tragopogon dubius*

Gotlandic corydalis.

Mosses

Roger's bristle moss, *Orthotrichum rogeri*
Green-shield moss, *Buxbaumia viridis* (Exemption: collections of covering specimens are permitted if they are of significance to the monitoring of the species, if there is no other satisfactory alternative, and the continued survival of the population in question is not imperiled. The responsible collector must submit a report to the County Administrative Board by 31st January each year, stating which species have been collected the previous year, how many specimens have been collected, where they were taken, and the purpose of the collection. Detailed information on new localities, as well as information on which collection the specimens have been conserved in, should be submitted to the Art Data Bank at the Swedish University of Agricultural Sciences at Uppsala. The collected material shall be accessible to research work).

Hairy milk vetch.

159

It is prohibited to uproot wild living specimens of the following species. It is also prohibited to pick or in any other way collect specimens of these species for any commercial purpose, including offering them for sale:

Hepatica, *Anemone hepatica*
Cowslip, *Primula veris*
Club moss families, all species of the *Lycopodiaceae* family

It is prohibited to kill, harm, capture or in any other way collect wild living specimens, or to remove or damage the eggs, roe, larvae or nests of the following faunal species:

Reptiles

Grass snake, *Natrix natrix ssp. gotlandica*
Smooth snake, *Coronella austriaca*
Adder, *Vipera berus* (exemption: it is permitted to capture and remove wild living specimens found in private gardens. If it is not possible to capture the creature and no other suitable solution is at hand, it may be killed).
Glow-worm, *Anguis fragilis*
Common lizard, *Lacerta vivipara* (exemption: eggs, roe, larvae and tadpoles from wild living specimens may be collected in limited numbers and preserved for studies of their development, but not for commercial purposes. The creatures must be returned to the place they were taken from as soon as possible. The prohibition does not apply to those specimens temporarily captured for study. The creatures may not, however, be removed from the site and shall be returned to the spot where they were captured as soon as possible).

Amphibians

Green toad, *Bufo virides*
Smooth newt, *Triturus vulgaris*

Smooth snake.

Common toad, *Bufo bufo* (exemption: eggs, roe, larvae and tadpoles from wild living specimens may be collected in limited numbers and preserved for studies of their development, but not for commercial purposes. The creatures must be returned to the place they were taken from as soon as possible. The prohibition does not apply to those specimens temporarily captured for study. The creatures may not, however, be removed from the site and shall be returned to the spot where they were captured as soon as possible).
Moor frog, *Rana arvalis* (exemption: eggs, roe, larvae and tadpoles from wild living specimens may be collected in limited numbers and preserved for studies of their development, but not for commercial purposes. The creatures must be returned to the place they were taken from as soon as possible. The prohibition does not apply to those specimens temporarily captured for study. The creatures may not, however, be removed from the site and shall be returned to the spot where they were captured as soon as possible).

Invertebrates

Apollo butterfly, *Parnassius apollo*
Great diving beetle, *Dytiscus latissimus*
Cucujus cinnaberinu
Woodland brown, *Lopinga achine*
Stag beetle, *Lucanus cervus*
Hawker dragonfly, *Ophiogomphus cecilia*
Dagger wasp, *Scolia hirta*
Large blue, *Maculinea arion*
Dragonfly, *Leucorrhina albifrons*
Marsh fritillary, *Euphydryas aurinia*

Apollo butterfly.

Amenities

Gotland's Museum of Natural History is part of the County Museum of Gotland and is housed at Strandgatan 14 in Visby, along with the other department of the County Museum, the Historical Museum. The exhibitions in the Natural History Department describe the geology and wildlife of Gotland. Information is available on nature trips and events, and literature on outdoor Gotland can also be purchased at the museum.

Self guiding nature trails have been laid out in the following nature reserves: Grausne flush fen (site 19), Kallgatburg (site 30), Brucebo (37), Allekvia forest meadow (44) and Muskmyr (99). Guide sheets can be found in a box at the starting point of the trails of the first three sites. They can also be downloaded from the County Administrative Board's website: www.i.lst.se

Tower hides have been erected at Träskmyr (site 21), Storsund (50), Paviken (51), Vivesholm (66), Ugnen bird sanctuary (83), Stockviken (97) and Muskmyr (99).

Allekvia meadow, starting point of a nature trail. Most nature reserves have a self-guiding nature trail.

Associations

The Botanical Society of Gotland is an association for anyone interested in the Gotlandic flora. The association publishes a club magazine, called *Rindi*, (4 issues/year) and arranges excursions and lectures. The association is also in charge of a project which will result in a new landscape flora. Enquiries: Jörgen Petersson, Humlegårdsvägen 18, 621 46 Visby, tel. +46 498 21 45 59.

The Entomological Society of Gotland is an association for anyone interested in insects and other invertebrae. The association publishes a club magazine, *Körkmacken,* (3 issues/year). Enquiries: Mats Björck, Majstre, Sundre, 620 10 Burgsvik, tel. +46 498 49 74 22.

The Swedish Local Heritage Movement/Gotland Section has a meadow committee which encourages and aids the management of forest meadows. The association publishes an annual book, *Från Gutabygd,* which includes articles on the wildlife of Gotland. Enquiries: Gotlands hembygdsförbund, Södertorg 12, 621 57 Visby, tel. +46 498 21 88 45.

The Gotlandic Ornithological Society is an association for anyone interested in bird life on Gotland. The association publishes a club magazine, *Bläcku* (4 issues/year) and arranges excursions and lectures. Enquiries: Bimbi Ollberg, Trädgårdsgatan 199, 621 54 Visby, tel. +46 498 21 95 44. The association also has an answering machine (+46 498 21 04 42), providing information on current bird observations and outings.

The Association for Shooting and Hunting is the regional County Game Preservation Association. The Association can give information on hunting and game preservation. Enquiries: Gotlands Skarpskytte- och Jägaregille, Lövsta, 620 23 Romakloster, tel. +46 498 21 13 43 or 27 99 16.

Gotland's Travel and Tourism Council arranges guided tours in the summer, often incorporating areas of natural beauty. The Tourism Council can also give information on current events. Enquiries: Gotlands turistförening, Hamngatan 4, Box 1403, 621 25 Visby, tel. +46 498 20 17 00, fax +46 498 20 17 17, e-mail info@gotlandinfo.com, website www.gotland.com

The Swedish Society for Nature Conservation on Gotland is a local section of the national association. The Gotland section works with current issues concerning the natural legacy and environment on the island, arranges excursions and meetings. The association publishes a club magazine, *Natur på Gotland* (2 issues/year). Enquiries: Anders Lekander, Pl 4854, 621 41 Visby, tel. +46 498 21 95 44. Website: www.gotland.snf.se.

Photo credits

Photographers

Stellan Hedgren: p. 9, 15 top, 15 bottom, 16 top, 16 bottom, 17, 18, 19, 20, 22, 23, 25 top, 25 bottom, 26 top, 28 top, 28 bottom, 30 top, 30 bottom, 33 top, 34, 35 bottom, 36, 37, 38 left, 38 tight, 40 top, 40 bottom, 41, 44 bottom, 45, 46 left, 47, 49, 50, 53 bottom, 67, 71 left, 71 right, 73 bottom, 75, 76, 77 top, 77 bottom, 78, 79, 80 bottom, 82 bottom, 85 left, 86, 87 top, 90 bottom, 95 top left, 96 top, 96 bottom, 98 top, 98 bottom, 100, 102, 103 bottom, 104, 106, 107 left, 107 right, 109 top, 109 bottom, 113 top left 113 top right, 114, 116 bottom, 118, 119, 120 bottom, 121, 122 top, 122 bottom, 123, 124, 125 top, 125 bottom, 129 top, 129 bottom, 130 top right, 130 bottom, 131, 132, 133 top, 133 bottom, 134 top left, 137, 139 bottom, 143, 147 bottom, 148, 149 bottom, 150 bottom, 153, 154 top, 154 bottom, 155 top, 157, 158, 159 top, 159 bottom and 160.

Raymond Hejdström: 94.

Jens-Henrik Kloth: p. 11, 12, 27, 31, 43, 44 top, 62, 64, 66, 69, 70, 72, 73 top, 74, 82 top, 83, 87 bottom, 90 top, 91, 94 top, 95 bottom, 97, 103 top, 108, 110, 112, 113 117 bottom, 120 top, 126, 127, 139 top, 140, 145 bottom, 146, 147 top, 149 top, 152 and 162.

Magnus Martinsson: p. 10, 26 bottom, 32, 48, 53 top, 61 bottom, 80 top, 85 right, 88, 99, 101, 105, 116 top, 117 top, 134 top right, 150 centre left, 150 centre right and 155 bottom.

Jörgen Pettersson: p. 59, 94 bottom, 130 top left, 144 and 161.

Per Smitterberg: p. 24, 29, 35 top, 39, 51 top, 51 bottom, 52, 61 top, 89, 95 top right, 136 top, 136 bottom, 141, 142, 145 top, 150 top left and 150 top right.

Göran Ström: p. 7.

Index

Species

167

Pliant lettuce *Lactuca quercina* 131, 133, 159
Pochard *Aythya ferina* 67, 89, 104
Prickly saltwort *Salsola kali* 25, 59
Prionus coriarius 63
Proliferous pink *Kohlrauschia prolifera* 96, 127
Pugsley's marsh orchid *Dactylorhiza traunsteineri* 33, 48, 73, 92, 95, 152
Purple loosestrife *Lythrum salicaria* 108
Purple milk vetch *Astragalus danicus* 120, 159
Purple moor-grass *Molinia caerulea* 33, 98
Pygmy shrew *Sorex araneus* 49
Pyramidal orchid *Anacamptis pyramidalis* 48, 90, 91, 117

Quaking grass *Briza media* 121

Rabbit *Oryctolagus cuniculus* 49, 118
Ragwort *Senecio jacobaea* 117
Ramsons *Allium ursinum* 40, 90, 95, 99, 110, 125
Raven *Corvus corax* 21, 133
Razorbill *Alca torda* 20, 21, 51, 130, 131, 133, 134
Red clover *Trifolium pratense* 143
Red fescue *Festuca rubra* 27
Red helleborine *Cephalanthera rubra* 48, 60, 74, 103, 120
Red hemp nettle *Galeopsis angustifolia* 159
Red-berried elder *Sambucus racemosa* 98
Red-breasted flycatcher *Ficedula parva* 61, 128, 130, 144
Red-footed falcon *Falco vespertinus* 52, 155
Redshank *Tringa totanus* 109, 150
Reed canary-grass *Phalaris arundinacea* 102
Reed foxtail *Alopecurus arundinaceus* 29
Reed warbler *Acrocephalus scirpaceus* 67
Reflexed stonecrop *Sedum rupestre* 44, 96
Reindeer moss *Cladina* sp. 45
Ribwort plantain *Plantago lanceolata* 110, 145
Ringed plover *Charadrius hiaticula* 150
Ringed seal *Phoca hispida* 21, 49, 130
River warbler *Locustella fluviatilis* 101
Roach *Rutilus rutilus* 31
Rock pipit *Anthus spinoletta* 133
Rock whitebeam *Sorbus rupicola* 94, 98

Roger's bristle moss *Orthotricum rogeri* 159
Roller *Coracias garrulus* 51
Rough small-reed *Calamagrostis varia* 41, 98
Rough-legged buzzard *Buteo lagopus* 151
Rowan *Sorbus aucuparia* 96
Rudd *Scardinius erythrophthalmus* 31
Rue-leaved saxifrage *Saxifrage tridactylites* 44, 96
Ruff *Philomachus pugnax* 67, 100, 136, 139, 149, 150
Ruffe *Acerina cernua* 31
Russ, Gotland pony *Equus caballus* 49, 122, 123
Rustyback *Ceterach officinarum* 159

Salmon *Salmo salar* 156
Saltmarsh grasses *Puccinellia* 27
Saltmarsh rush Juncus gerardii 27
Sand fescue *Festuca polesica* 118
Sand sedge *Carex arenaria* 60, 118
Sanderling *Calidris alba* 52
Sandwich tern *Sterna sandvicensis* 141
Sandwort *Arenaria gothica* 66, 115
Sanicle *Sanicula europaea* 137, 143
Scarlet grosbeak *Carpodacus erythrinus* 69, 130,144,147
Scaup *Aythya marila* 52
Scentless mayweed *Macricaria perforata* 24
Schistophyllum bifurca 159
Scorpion senna *Coronilla emerus* 112, 113, 159
Sea arrow-grass *Triglochin maritima* 27
Sea aster *Aster tripolium* 28
Sea campion *Silene maritima* 72
Sea club-rush *Scirpus maritimus* 28
Sea holly *Eryngium maritimum* 60, 122, 152, 159
Sea kale *Crambe maritima* 60
Sea mayweed *Matricaria maritim* 28
Sea milkwort *Glaux maritima* 27, 117
Sea pea *Lathyrus maritimus* 60, 118, 121, 152
Sea plantain *Plantago maritima* 27
Sea rocket *Cakile maritima* 25, 59, 74, 134
Sea sandwort *Honckenya peploides* 25, 60, 118
Sea trout *Salmo trutta trutta* 30, 75, 91, 156
Sea wormwood *Artemisia maritima* 27, 119

Sermountain *Laserpitium latifolium* 98
Serrated wrack *Fucus serratus* 18
Sharp-leaved fluellen *Kickxya elatine* 159
Sheep *Ovis aries* 49
Sheep's fescue *Festuca ovina* 26, 63, 69, 131
Sheepsbit scabious *Jasione montana* 63, 96
Shelduck *Tadorna tadorna* 109, 136
Shepherd's needle *Scandix pecten-veneris* 159
Shoreweed *Litorella uniflora* 30, 45
Short-spurred fragrant orchid *Gymnadenia odoratissima* 33, 48, 77, 86, 88, 97, 98, 122
Shoveller *Anas clypeata* 141, 149
Simple moonwort *Botrychium simplex* 159
Skylark *Alauda arvensis* 116, 133
Slender sedge *Carex lasiocarpa* 79
Slender spike-rush *Eleocharis uniglumis* 28
Small cow wheat *Melampyrum silvaticum* 42
Small pasque flower *Anemone pratensis* 96, 117, 125
Small-leaved elm *Ulmus carpinifolia* 38, 89, 99, 100, 106
Small-leaved lime *Tilia cordata* 100
Smooth newt *Triturus vulgaris* 53, 160
Smooth snake *Coronella austriaca* 53, 160
Snails *Gastropoda* 6, 7, 14, 66, 80
Soft shield fern *Polystichum aculeatum* 159
Soft-leaved sedge *Carex montana* 107
Soft-shell clam *Mya arenaria* 17
Southern marsh orchid *Dactylorhiza incarnata* 35, 47, 48, 69, 76, 80, 152
Spiked speedwell *Veronica spicata* 44, 80, 83, 96, 139
Spotted catsear *Hypochoeris maculata* 100, 121
Spotted crake *Porzana porzana* 68, 79, 105
Spotted flycatcher *Muscicapa striata* 61
Sprat *Sprattus sprattus* 19
Spring pea *Lathyrus vernus* 40, 77, 107
Squid *Loligo vulgaris* 6, 14
Squirrel *Sciuridae sciurinae* 49
St Bernard's lily *Anthericum liliago* 159

171

Field Guide – a gazetteer

1. Gotska Sandön – a sandy national park
2. Ullahau – colossal sand dune
3. Langhammarshammar – tall sea stacks and creeping junipers
4. Digerhuvud – Sweden's largest sea stack field
5. Gamla hamn – sea stack area and beach ridge coast
6. Alnäsaträsk – a bird-rich lake
7. Mölnorträsk – bird-rich lake
8. The road to Norra gattet – barren Fårö landscape
9. Klintängarna and Limmorträsk – bird-rich area, clifftop meadows, beautiful woodland, drained lake
10. Ryssudden – magnificent beach ridge landscape
11. Burgbackar, Hässleänget and Bästeträsk – inland beach ridges, deciduous forest and Gotland's largest lake.
12. Hallshuk – magnificent marine cliff with wide-range views
13. Grodde Nature Reserve – shingle coast of natural beauty
14. The Nature Reserve Vitärtskällan – spring with rich flush fen vegetation
15. Sigsarvestrand – beautiful beach and cliffed coast
16. Irevik – beautiful coastal scenery, meandering river
17. Stigmyr – old pine tree forest on inland rock, fringing a sedge fen
18. Jungfruklint – Gotland's tallest sea stack, calcareous tufa formation
19. Grausne Flush Fen – nature trail through flush fen and forest
20. Ekebysänget – oak-dominated meadow
21. Träskmyr – large undrained sedge fen
22. Fardumeträsk – bird-rich lake
23. Fardume marlstone quarry – former stone quarry with rich fossil fauna
24. Lergrav and Husken – sea stack area
25. Kyllaj – sea stack area and outcrops of pure limestone
26. St Olofsholm – a large reef-limestone promontory with offshore sea stacks
27. Hammarsänget – large plant-rich meadow
28. Othems korsänge – highly varied meadow
29. Hejnum hällar and Filehajdar – widespread areas of flat limestone outcrop
30. Kallgatburg – nature trail through flush fen and stand of yew
31. Bälsalvret – large area of ephemeral swamps
32. Laxare äng – orchid-rich meadow
33. Bogeklinten – sea stack field beside an inland cliff
34. Lummelunda kyrkänge – beautiful forest meadow
35. Dam by the former Landträsk marsh – bird-rich irrigation dam
36. Lummelunds Bruk (Works and Mills) – dripstone cave and thickly wooded park
37. Brucebo nature reserve – nature trail through varied Gotlandic wildlife
38. Bro parish meadow – pine-dominant meadow
39. Biota in and around Visby
40. Ölbäcks flat limestone outcrop – plant-rich flat limestone outcrop area
41. Slättflis – Langs hage – unusual type of flat limestone outcrop
42. Flush fen at Klinte in Follingbo – flush fen vegetation with short-spurred fragrant orchid
43. Högklint – viewpoint, roamer-friendly cliffed coastline
44. Allekvia änge – varied forest meadow
45. Mangsarveänget – a plant-rich forest meadow
46. Alvena lindaräng – forest meadow with Gotland's largest stand of lime trees
47. Lina myr – bird-rich former marsh
48. Gothemån – tall herbal vegetation in Gotland's longest watercourse
49. Gothemhammar – beautiful coast with beach ridges
50. Storsund – bird-rich lake with tower hide

51. Paviken – bird-rich former seabay
52. Maldesänget – an open-canopy forest meadow
53. Mästerbyänget – large, orchid-rich forest meadow
54. Halla klosteränge – large deciduous woodland
55. Möllebosån in Viklau – meandering stream in pastureland
56. Liste ängar – coastal meadow, orchid-rich former meadow, thick-stemmed coniferous forest
57. Anga prästänge – forest meadow with great burnet and Swedish eyebright
58. Kräklingbo prästänge – small, beautiful wooded meadow
59. Upstaigs primeval forest – area of ancient forest
60. Torsburgen and Herrgårdsklint – inland cliffs with viewpoints, caves and hillforts
61. Russvätar – limestone outcrops with large ephemeral pools and the Gotlandic Pasque flower
62. Östergarnsberget – inland cliff with cave formations and a magnificent view
63. Grogarnsberget – tall coastal cliff, inland rock and beautiful view
64. Kuppen – beautiful, varying coastal features
65. Sandviken nature reserve – bathing beach with typical sandy beach vegetation
66. Vivesholm and Varvsholm – plant and bird-rich coastal meadow
67. Mulde nature reserve – white helleborine in lush coniferous forest
68. Klinteberget – inland cliff with panoramic view, beech forest
69. Fonnsänget – varied, floralistically rich forest meadow
70. Folhammar – sea stack field and interesting beach flora
71. Mallgårds flush fen – flush fen with grazing ponies (russ)
72. Russ pony park at Lojstahajd – large enclosed pasture with Gotlandic "russ ponies"
73. Lojsta area – deep lakes in singular landscape
74. Etelhem parish meadow – beautiful, well-managed meadow
75. Bosarve natural forest – small area with tall pine forest
76. Strömmaån – meandering stream with lush vegetation
77. Lindeberget – inland cliff with view, alvar vegetation and hillforts
78. Sandarve kulle – reef limestone hill with grove flora and beautiful view
79. Fardhems prästänge – small herb-rich parish meadow
80. Stora Karlsö – bird cliffs, small-bird-rich deciduous woodlands, alvar vegetation, orchids and caves
81. Lilla Karlsö – bird cliff, barren sheep-grazing landscape and caves
82. Eksta coast nature reserve – stretch of coast of great natural beauty
83. Ugnen bird sanctuary – wide, shallow beach area with rich bird life
84. Högby äng – forest meadow with mature pine trees
85. Hulte Kruppar – large forest meadow rich in variety
86. Lausvik – stopover for passage birds
87. Närsholmen – low-lying peninsula with beach ridges and rich bird life
88. Nisseviken – bird-rich bay
89. Pankar parish meadow – lush and open meadow
90. Grötlingboudd and Gansviken – bird-rich coastal area
91. Näsudden – open pastoral landscape, passage-bird site
92. Fide prästäng – beautiful, plant-rich meadow
93. Deciduous forest between Fidenäs and Öja – large, bird-rich deciduous woodland
94. Öja kyrkänge – lush, bird-rich parish meadow
95. Mjölhatteträsk and Valar – birding site, alvar and beautiful coastline
96. Änge at Lasses – herb-rich meadow with good eyebright
97. Faludden and Stockviken – bird-rich lake and seabay, extensive pasturelands
98. Holmhällar – headland with sea stack field and adjoining sandy beaches
99. Muskmyr – sedge fen, orchids and migrant birds of prey
100. Hoburgen and Husrygg – interesting geology, yellow pheasant's eye and migrant birds

Other Publications published by Gotlands Fornsals förlag

A Cultural and Historical Walk around Visby Town Wall
World Heritage Site
Waldemar Falck
Acquaint yourself with the town wall surrounding Visby by walking around the wall in the company of this book. The history of the wall and its construction, its gateways and towers are presented in a highly readable style. The photographs and drawings help you to get your bearings along the wall. Enjoy the experience of reading about this cultural treasure – the only preserved town wall in the Nordic countries. The author of the book, Waldemar Falck, PhD, is a renowned authority on Visby.

Hardback. Richly illustrated. 95 pages.

Guide to Visby
Britt Svensson, Thore Nilsson, Maria Domeij
Visby – Hanseatic Town and part of World Heritage – is described in this book. The informative text, the numerous recently-taken photos and the illustrations that capture the imagination, all combine to become your conversant guide during your exploration of the town of ruins and roses.

Hardback. Richly illustrated. 184 pages.

Hanseatic Sites, Routes and Monuments
Gun Westholm
A traveller's guide to the past and present. A guide book, initiated by the Council of Europe Cultural Routes programme. It includes the history of the Hanseatic League, a list of the most important museums, maps of the Hansa's most important production areas. Descriptions of 220 towns in 13 countries, parts of this commercial organisation. Out of these towns 54 have been chosen as highly recommended for cultural tourism.

Paperback. Richly illustrated. 144 pages.

Medieval Manner of Dress
Documents, Images and Surviving Examples of Northern Europe,
Emphasizing Gotland in the Baltic Sea
Else Marie Gutarp
Priests, monks, burghers and peasants – how did they dress in the Nordic countries during the Middle Ages? What materials and colors were used? Which changes of fashion occurred? Knowledge of the medieval manner of dress must be drawn from visual and written records – art, provincial statutes and court findings, supplemented by the all too few examples of surviving textile material. The book also contains diagrammed cutting patterns for several simple medieval garments.

Hardback. Richly illustrated. 109 pages.

Sunstones and Catskulls – Guide to the Fossils and Geology of Gotland

Sara Eliason

Gotland harbours an enormous wealth of fossils derived from a tropical coral reef environment at a time when this part of the world was situated close to the Equator. The book covers the geology of the island, the life of the organisms now found in fossilised form and recommended sites for fossil-hunting.

Hardback. Richly illustrated. 166 pages.

Treasures – Gotland

Who could have imagined that such well-concealed riches would once again glitter in the light of day many centuries later? Gotland has aptly been called the world's largest treasury. From the Viking Age alone, over 700 hoards have been discovered. In proportion to its area, the island has the greatest abundance of treasure hoards in the world. This book covers the study and interpretation of some of these hoards, focusing on design, myths and legends, human nature and destiny.

Paperback. Richly illustrated. 43 pages.